PENGUIN CLASSICS

THE FOREST OF THIEVES AND THE MAGIC GARDEN

PHYLLIS GRANOFF received a Ph.D from Harvard University in Sanskrit and Indian Studies and Fine Arts in 1973. She teaches Sanskrit and Indian Religions at McMaster University in Hamilton, Ontario. Her first book, *Philosophy and Argument in Late Vedanta: Sri Harsa's Khandanakhandakhadya*, was first published by D. Reidel in 1978. She has written extensively on Jain literature, particularly Jain religious biographies. In 1992 she published *Speaking with Monks: Religious Biography in India and China*, co-authored with her husband Koichi Shinohara (Mosaic Press). She has also translated a collection of short stories by Bibhutibhushan Bandhopadhyaya (*A Strange Attachment*, Mosaic Press, 1982) from Bengali to English. She currently edits the *Journal of Indian Philosophy* and continues to work on traditional and modern Indian literature.

The Forest of Thieves and the Magic Garden

An Anthology of Medieval Jain Stories

Selected, translated and with an Introduction by
PHYLLIS GRANOFF

PENGUIN BOOKS

PENGUIN BOOKS

Published by the Penguin Group
Penguin Books Ltd, 80 Strand, London WC2R 0RL, England
Penguin Group (USA) Inc., 375 Hudson Street, New York, New York 10014, USA
Penguin Group (Canada), 90 Eglinton Avenue East, Suite 700, Toronto, Ontario, Canada M4P 2Y3
(a division of Pearson Penguin Canada Inc.)
Penguin Ireland, 25 St Stephen's Green, Dublin 2, Ireland (a division of Penguin Books Ltd)
Penguin Group (Australia), 250 Camberwell Road, Camberwell,
Victoria 3124, Australia (a division of Pearson Australia Group Pty Ltd)
Penguin Books India Pvt Ltd, 11 Community Centre,
Panchsheel Park, New Delhi – 110 017, India
Penguin Group (NZ), cnr Airborne and Rosedale Roads, Albany,
Auckland 1310, New Zealand (a division of Pearson New Zealand Ltd)
Penguin Books (South Africa) (Pty) Ltd, 24 Sturdee Avenue,
Rosebank, Johannesburg 2196, South Africa

Penguin Books Ltd, Registered Offices: 80 Strand, London WC2R 0RL, England

www.penguin.com

First published by Penguin Books India 1998
Published in Penguin Classics 2006

006

Printed and bound in Great Britain by Clays Ltd, Elcograf S.p.A.

ISBN 978-0-140-45523-6

www.greenpenguin.co.uk

In honour of my mother Dorothy Granoff
and
in memory of my mother-in-law Masako Shinohara

CONTENTS

TRANSLATOR'S NOTE

My chief purpose in translating selections from this rich literature was to bring it to the attention of a new audience, those who knew little or nothing of it before. This led me to several choices in the translations. Firstly, I wanted the result to read as naturally as possible and therefore did not aim for a literal translation. At the same time, I hoped that I might preserve something of the flavor of the original, where those two aims were not entirely incompatible. I occasionally, supplied information in the story that an educated reader of the time might well have been expected to know. For example, when the story said that someone accepted the vows of a householder, I listed the vows individually although they were not listed in the story itself. Occasionally I even supplied a line of context, where a story formed part of a larger unit and the translation began in the middle, so to speak. In other stories I tried to help the reader by providing background information about characters in the story and their relationship to each other. Thus in the section about Rāma and Lakṣmaṇa, which contains a summary of the *Rāmāyaṇa* plot, I added some identifying marks for the various characters mentioned, explaining who they were and in some cases what they had done. In some instances I did not translate technical terms as technical terms, fearing that the subtleties would be lost on a general reader. For example, I simply glossed the type of knowledge that a demi-god has as 'supernatural knowledge', rather than supplying a technical term. In other cases, in an effort not to encumber my translations with too many foreign terms, I omitted the names of heavens and different realms of gods and simply translated the basic fact that so-and-so was reborn as a god. I also did not try to standardize terms, but relied more on the flow of the prose.

Where stories contained both verse and prose, I initially tried to retain some of the distinctiveness of the style by indenting what was verse in the original, hoping to indicate in that way that the original combined both poetry and prose. In the final editing, much of this was edited out. In all cases, I gave prose translations of the verses. I laboured to unpack the puns and plays on words that are so important to the traditional Indian poet and writer of prose. Translators over the years have done many different things with these plays on words, which are so easily made in Sanskrit and its closely related vernacular languages and so utterly impossible in English. Some translators choose to render one meaning in the translated text and put the second in footnotes, explaining how the original yields both meanings. I did not want to burden these stories with footnotes, and so I tried to put both meanings into the translation. What is lost, of course, is the playfulness and challenge that these puns bring to a text. These are only some of the choices I eventually made; I hope that the gains in readability will make up for any loss in exactitude.

INTRODUCTION

'Blessed One, how can I make my way safely through the forest that is the cycle of rebirths? And once I cross the forest, where will I be?' The monk replied, 'Listen. There are two forests; one is the forest that exists outside us, in nature, and the other is the forest that is within us, the tangle of our thoughts and desires. Let me use the forest that exists in nature as a parable to teach you of that other, equally treacherous forest. Imagine there was a merchant, who wanted to go from one city to another. He announces to all and sundry, "I seek someone to accompany me to the city such and such; I will make sure that no harm befalls him on the journey, as long as he follows my advice." When they hear this announcment many merchants hasten to join him. Before they depart, the merchant describes to them the conditions of the road that they must travel. "My friends, my travelling companions!" he begins. "There are two paths to choose from; one is straight, but the other is somewhat tortuous. Believe it or not, it is easier to follow the crooked path; eventually it leads one onto the straight way and to the city we seek. The straight path is harder to travel. Although it leads to the goal more quickly, it is dangerous and arduous. For as soon as one enters the straight path there lie in wait for him terrifying creatures, lions and tigers, that obstruct his way to the city he seeks. They pursue him until he reaches the city that is the object of his desires. They kill the person who steps off the path even for a moment, but they cannot harm the one who keeps to the right road . . . ."

'Here is the explanation for the parable. The merchant is the Noble Jina, honored by gods and anti-gods, the crest jewel of the universe. His proclamation is his teaching of the Jain doctrine, through various techniques, telling stories that attract the listener to the Jain doctrine and turn the listener away from false doctrines; telling stories that cause the listener to feel disgust for worldly existence and delight in the religious life. The travellers are the souls who set out for the city of Liberation, making their way across the forest of transmigratory existence. The forest is the entire cycle of rebirths, which includes births in hell, as animals, humans and gods. The straight path is the way of the renunciate; the path that is slightly crooked is the way of the lay practitioner. In the end it leads onto the path of renunciation . . . The city that is the object of the traveller's desires is the city of peace, of final release, which is devoid of the torments of birth, old age, death, disease, grief and the like. The tigers and lions are the destructive passions such as lust, pride, greed, delusion, and anger, all of which are obstructions to the attainment of Liberation.'

(From the *Samarāiccakahā* of Haribhadra, pp. 391-4)

The stories and their themes

The stories in this collection will take you deep into a tangled forest, the haunt of wild beasts, savage tribes and merciless robbers. As we see in the quote, the forest is one of the Jain metaphors for the life we all lead. The dangers of the forest, here described as wild animals and in other accounts as violent thieves, are the passions that lie in wait for the unsuspecting traveller. They attack the traveller and rob him of the power to know things as they truly are and to lead a virtuous life. We all wander in this forest of transmigratory existence without direction, lost in the thick growth, unable to find our way out. For each of us, the forest is the sum total of all of our existences, for as the parable makes clear the Jains, like the Buddhists and Hindus, believe that we go from birth to birth in a beginningless cycle. The parable also teaches us that there is a way out of the terrifying forest that can lead us to a city of peace and bliss. To find that way we must heed the call of the Jina's words. The way out of the forest is in fact twofold; the most direct way is to renounce the world, leaving behind all relationships, attachments and possessions, to become monks and nuns. For those who are unable to take this path, there is the way of the householder, who is taught how to live in accordance with the basic principles of Jain ethics, to guard against doing violence to living beings, to be honest and never to steal, and to be moderate in the accumulation of material possessions and faithful in marriage. As the parable teaches us, the ideal is that the lay life properly lived should ultimately lead to a life of renunciation.

The correct way of renunciation and the correct rules for

behavior were said to have been taught by a series of Jinas or 'Conquerors', most recently by Mahāvīra, who was an older contemporary of the Buddha. Although Jainism is a renunciatory religion, we see in the parable, and we shall see even more vividly in the stories translated in this collection, that there is much that lay men and women can do to further their own religious quest, strengthen the Jain community and ensure the preservation of Jainism.

Early in their history the Jains split into two main groups, the Digambaras or 'sky clad', whose monks go naked, and the Śvetāmbaras or 'white robed', whose monks wear robes of simple white cloth. While there are many points of difference between the sects, Śvetāmbaras and Digambaras shared their love of stories, which they often used to teach ethical concepts and even to illustrate abstruse points of doctrine. Much of the richness of medieval Indian storytelling has come down to us because Jains so carefully preserved these stories. An account is told of a Jain monk who so loved to hear stories that he would go out in disguise to hear a Brahmin storyteller recite his tales. A pious Jain layman took pity on the monk and hired the Brahmin to come and recite his stories for him, so that he would no longer have to go to the trouble of donning a disguise.

Many of the stories Jains told are clearly recognizable as simple folk tales, while others are complicated and sophisticated narratives containing numerous characters who go through rebirth after rebirth in an intricate set of relationships. Some of these rebirth narratives seem uniquely Jain, while others have parallels elsewhere, often in Buddhist story literature. The Jains also told their own versions of the great Hindu epics, the *Mahābhārata* and the *Rāmāyaṇa*. They made changes, some subtle and some not so subtle, to the familiar stories to make them conform more strictly to the standards of Jain morality and to make them more suitable as didactic tools with which they might teach Jain doctrine.

The Jains also wrote about the lives of the Jinas and the

famous monks in the different monastic lineages. They recounted the glorious deeds of wealthy lay patrons, whose donations sustained the monks and nuns and built the magnificent temples, many of which are still in worship today. Medieval history writing in some parts of India, as it has come down to us, is virtually synonymous with the chronicles kept by Jain monks. Jain monks also collected stories told of important pilgrimage sites. Indeed there is almost no subject or theme about which the Jains did not tell stories. They told their stories in Sanskrit, the language of the elite and learned in ancient and medieval India, as well as in various vernaculars. They told them in poetry, in ornate prose and in simple colloquial language.

The sheer abundance and variety of medieval Jain story literature made the choice of stories my first challenge. I soon realized the futility of trying to make my selection 'representative'; even a 'representative' sample of Jain stories, I suspect, would fill a good-sized bookshelf. This left me with the inviting possibility of choosing my favorites. I soon abandoned that strategy, since some of my favorite stories turned out to be too long, too complicated or too allusive and therefore, I feared, too elusive for the general reader. I decided at last to translate stories that reflected a general theme or set of themes: monks and the women and children, the friends and relatives, whom they leave behind. I eventually indulged myself by adding a few stories here and there that pushed the boundaries I had set just a little farther than might be expected. These additional stories, I hoped, would enrich the reader's experience by providing a slightly different perspective on a given theme, often with a measure of humor.

There are some excellent accounts in English of Jain religious beliefs; Padmanabh Jaini (*The Jaina Path of Purification*, University of California Press, 1979) and Paul Dundas (*The Jains*, Routledge, 1992) have written lucid and engaging discussions of Jain belief and practice. Instead of providing here a short summary of Jain doctrine, which could not possibly do justice to its complex subject, I would like to let the stories I have selected speak for themselves. The Jainism they describe is richly textured. While the stories acknowledge that renunciation of all family and social ties is important for religious development, we see that they also make room for a wide range of meritorious activities that have little to do with monastic asceticism. Tending a temple garden, indeed financing the building of a temple and going on a pilgrimage, are also significant religious acts in the world of these stories. In keeping with the general principle that all acts have appropriate consequences, these good deeds lead to abundant rewards. And so we see that in addition to the goal of Ultimate Release from transmigratory existence, which monks in the prescriptive texts are enjoined to seek, these stories make room for religious goals such as rebirth in heaven or even simply a life of wealth and status, goals that are also open to lay men and women. In addition, in these medieval stories even the career of a monk is more nuanced and potentially varied than what we might expect if we read only the prescriptive texts of the tradition. In these stories monks who renounce the world may still have an important role to play in society, settling disputes, consecrating religious images and temples, curing disease and even advising kings. The women that monks are told scrupulously to avoid in the texts that list rules for the behavior of monks, may here turn out to be more knowledgeable in Jain doctrine than the monks themselves. In addition, the very act of renunciation itself is often not so clear-cut in these stories; in the cycle of rebirths the ties that bind mother and son, husband and wife may prove to be very tenacious indeed, as abandoned wives and mothers return in new births to torment the men who left them. In this and other ways the stories make us see some of the painful emotional consequences of the decision to renounce, particularly for those who are left behind.

These stories make graphically real many of the basic Jain doctrines that are also expounded in prescriptive texts. While there are many texts that tell Jains that they must not take the life of any living being, in these stories we see described in vivid language what happens to someone who commits such an evil act: the man who sacrificed a goat is himself reborn as an animal to be sacrificed! Stories can also venture into areas that other genres of text, rules for monks or even philosophical treatises, did not treat as fully; thus we see that some of our stories are explorations into the very nature of human nature. Again, where a philosophical text may state that the soul is by nature pure, stories in their leisurely pace may dramatize how evil takes over an innocent person and causes him or her to do wrong. But it is time to turn to the stories themselves.

The collection begins with a story about the monk Ārdrakumāra. This is a story about the difficulties of renunciation, for both the monk and the loved ones he abandons. It is a moving account of a young man who has renounced the world, but is eventually persuaded to break his vows and marry. He does not forget that he was once a monk, however, and sees the birth of his son as his chance to release himself from the bonds of his domestic life. Rationalizing that his wife will no longer be alone, he decides to leave his family and take to the life of the homeless wandering ascetic. The monk and his wife had been man and wife in a previous life, perhaps making their bond even harder to sunder in this life. This story explores both a husband's pain of abandoning a wife and the poignant efforts of the wife and child to keep the family intact.

In the story of Vajrasvāmin's childhood we again meet a young man who desires to become a monk, but marries reluctantly, only to abandon his pregnant wife. She gives birth to an unusual child who longs to follow his father's footsteps and renounce the world, but must somehow convince his mother to let him go. This is a sensitive portrayal of the ties of love that bind a mother and a child. Although its ultimate conclusion is that the youngster did right in rejecting his mother, despite the pain he has caused her, the story suggests that renunciation could be a complicated emotional ordeal with its own moral ambiguities that needed to be acknowledged and resolved.

The story of Vajrasvāmin, to a certain extent, invites us to sympathize with the plight of the mother who must give up her child. In other stories we are taught that as powerful as they are, even ties like those that bind mother and child are not entirely benign. In the story of the monk Sukośala, a king renounces the world to become a monk, and his wife turns her grief into anger and hostility. She desperately attempts to keep her son from becoming a monk, but like Vajrasvāmin, this child too longs to follow in his father's footsteps and he renounces the world. The mother dies and is reborn as a tigress; consumed by her anger, she devours the monk who had once been her son. In this story we encounter again an important theme in Jain literature: ties of affection, emotional relationships of love and hatred, extend beyond a single birth into potentially infinite rebirths. Past connections determine present relationships; there is an order to our connections with others that is determined by these past emotional ties. At the same time there is an unpredictability to our lives as social beings, for what repeats itself is the emotional bond, the bare fact of connectedness and not necessarily the exact relationship itself. The mother who gave birth to the son has become his killer in this story; in other stories a wife will become a sister or a mother; a wife's lover may become her son, and a father may become the goat killed for his own funeral offering. These are the themes of other stories in this collection, the story of Maheśvaradatta and the story of the twins Kuberadatta and Kuberadattā. The realization that social ties are terrifyingly unpredictable as well as tenacious may, indeed, be the critical moment at which a person decides to leave them all behind and renounce the world.

Stories are sometimes the only genre of liteature that provides answers to this fundamental and to us very natural question: why did men and women leave behind their loved ones and renounce the world to become monks and nuns? The stories are sometimes explicit in raising this question; at other times we must read between the lines. Some men are like Vajrasvāmin, simply inclined to renunciation. Others have a significant moment of conversion; for Ārdrakumāra the sight of the Jina image sparked his remembrance of his past births. In the stories of Maheśvaradatta and Kuberadatta the moment of insight is more shocking.I have also included two stories which have a lighter touch in their answer to the question of what makes a person renounce the world: these are the stories of the sweetmeat eater and Sanatkumāra.

With the story of Celanā we continue to explore the pain and anger of abandonment. In this story we again see past ties between people continuing into another rebirth.Here, the wife left behind when her husband became a monk, dies and becomes a demi-goddess who torments the naked monk in a particularly embarrassing way. The story also celebrates the cleverness and devotion of a female lay devotee who comes to the monk's aid. We shall see that in many of these stories the exemplary piety of some women is as prominent a theme as is their irascibility or infidelity.

Many of these stories also emphasize a masculine community in contrast to the feminine world of the mothers, wives and children left behind; indeed, in several of the stories the abandoned male children eventually become part of that greater male community. Sons follow fathers to become monks, friends join friends to become monks. Relationships between men often continue into the monastic life. The stories of Bhadrabāhu and Jīvadeva, two stories from a medieval biography collection, are very different from the didactic stories I have just discussed. Both stories tell of two brothers who are religious rivals. They also give us further insight into some of the activities of monks who have left their families behind and yet remain active in the social affairs of the religious community. Renouncing the world in these stories does not necessarily imply a total withdrawal from society and its concerns, nor need it signal a total break from family tensions.

In the story of Amarasiṃha (Amarasīha in Prakrit) we clearly see the power of the renunciate to work within the society from which he has technically withdrawn. Here a monk enters into a debate between two people about the efficacy and desirability of performing blood sacrifices. The Jains, who often summarized their religious teaching as the practice of total non-violence, vigorously opposed the Hindu cult of animal sacrifice. In this story the Jain monk stops the practice of blood sacrifice, puts an end to a plague and proves to everyone the greatness of the Jain religion. We also see in this story that the main character Amarasīha remains a layman, but leads an exemplary life and is rewarded with abundant wealth and power.

The story of Abhayasiṃha (Abhayasīha) opens with a dialogue between a historical figure, king Kumārapāla of Gujarat, and the Jain monk Hemacandra. Many of the stories in this collection are inserted into a larger frame story in their original setting.The frame story in which the story of Abhayasiṃha is set describes the conversion of King Kumārapāla to Jainism by the monk Hemacandra. With this story, which celebrates non-violence, we gain further insight into how Jain stories sought to inculcate the virtue of non-violence, instilling in their listeners a horror of taking life. In a typically Jain fashion, meat eating is made synonymous with cannibalism, something that would surely have struck all listeners as repugnant. In a similar use of an extreme violation of a taboo, all sex in other stories will be equated with incest. While the first-time reader may have trouble making these leaps, as you wander deeper into the forest of thieves you will see that the animal killed for a ritual feast may indeed have been your father (Maheśvaradatta), and the woman you desire may well have been your sister or mother (Kuberdattā). In the story of Abhayasiṃha we meet with several other now familiar themes; we see ties of motherly affection extending into a next rebirth and lay piety and honesty amply rewarded.

The stories of Amarasīha and Abhayasīha, along with those of Ārāmaśobhā, Devadhara and Devadiṇṇa included in this collection, not only tell us about monks and how they interact with the world they have left behind; they also offer us a glimpse of the possibilities for living a rewarding life without renouncing the world, and describe that world in somewhat more positive terms. The secular world may well be a battleground between forces of good and evil, but it is possible to choose good, and thereby triumph. In these stories the renouncing of all action, such as is enjoined for a monk in the prescriptive texts, is not the only path. For example, in the story of Ārāmaśobhā a young girl is rewarded for her pious act of tending a garden attached to a Jain temple by having a magical garden that follows her around wherever she goes. At times her life seems to be lived in its idyllic shadow. Although these stories may seem at first glance to stray from the theme of monks and those they leave behind, I included them because I felt that they can deepen our understanding of the world that monks renounce .These stories depict the secular world as a place of pleasure and an arena for doing good, more like Ārāmaśobhā's garden than a frightening and dangerous forest of thieves. Nonetheless, stories such as these will often explicitly remind the listener that a life of such worldly pleasures is not the ultimate ideal of Jainism. Thus we see that many stories of lay piety conclude with a summary statement that their heroes and heroines eventually renounced the world to become monks and nuns.

Most of the stories in this collection paint a darker picture of human relationships and social life, and many of these negative stories are decidedly misogynistic. Durgilā is one such story, where the woman is treacherous and unfaithful. Sundarī, by contrast, is a model of wifely fidelity, although the final message of the story is still that one must renounce all ties to loved ones. Sundarī refuses to leave her husband's side even though he is dead. This is both a story of wifely honor and a cautionary tale about the inevitability of death and the delusory power of love. The story of Lakṣmaṇa's death from a Jain version of the *Rāmāyaṇa* makes a similar point; attachment to a beloved brother here becomes a form of madness that must be cured. The cure leads to a total rejection of attachments, that is, renunciation of the world. These stories are portraits of emotions in excess, but the conclusion we are asked to draw is that the emotion itself is at fault, and not just its degree or intensity. These vivid descriptions of love's power to delude are meant to instruct us further to view all of our ties of affection as dangerous entrapments.

The story of Siddhi and Buddhi clearly bears the stamp of a folk tale and belongs with the less flattering portrayals of women that we see in the story of Durgilā. The Siddhi and Buddhi story was most often told as part of a cycle of stories in which a man and his wives argue over the man's determination to renounce the world. The wives narrate this story as a warning: wanting too much, you may well come to a bad end. Several other stories I have translated belong to this cycle: the stories of Maheśvaradatta and Kuberadatta are told by the aspiring monk, while the story of Durgilā is told by one of the wives. Through these stories we are actively drawn into the debate between a man and his wives: whether he should or should not renounce the world. As the arguments sway from one side to the next, we are made to see that there could well be different perspectives on what constituted the good life, depending on the vantage point of the perceiver.

In contrast to women like Durgilā, the heroines of several other stories translated here are exemplary women. These stories help us flesh out the hazy, often sketchy, portraits of women that emerge from the stories which centre around the men who leave women and become monks. The exemplary women in these stories are often richly drawn and complex characters. It is instructive, I think, to reread the accounts of the women left behind after reading some of these tales of exceptional women. Through these stories we see that the Jain tradition could value women and their religious accomplishments. For example, Siṃhikā is the faithful wife whose chastity is such that it has magic power and can save her husband, who is dying of an incurable disease. The story of Siṃhikā also introduces us to several themes that recur in many Jain stories of pious women. The first has already been noted, namely, the miraculous power of their piety and chastity. In this story we also see the chaste Siṃhikā wrongfully accused of infidelity by her husband, who cruelly rejects her. This may well be a Jain reworking of the famous theme of the *Rāmāyaṇa*, in which the king Rāma rejects his pregnant queen after he has rescued her from her abductor, because he fears that his subjects will doubt her fidelity. This sub-theme lends a particular poignancy to many of the stories of pious Jain women.

Women may even outshine men in these stories in their devotion to the Jain cause. Thus in the story of Rudradatta's beloved, a pious Jain wife eventually convinces her husband, a worshipper of Śiva, of the greatness of Jainism, while in the story of Padmalatā, a pious Jain woman eventually wins over her Buddhist father-in-law and husband. Jain women in these stories are beautiful, desirable, intelligent and resourceful, and they use their gifts to insure the triumph of their religion. In the story of Revatī (Revaī), the Jain lay woman is singled out for praise even at the expense of a Jain monk.This story also gives us a glimpse into Jain-Jain conflicts beyond the major sectarian divisions. Revatī knows the Jain doctrine and remains firm in her faith, while the monk succumbs to heretical doubts on certain points. Women may even become goddesses, often achieving this status through the intensity of their suffering and unnatural deaths. Two stories here, the story of Ambikā and the story of Āryanandila, introduce us to two of the more popular Jain goddesses.

The story of Nala and Damayaṃtī is one of the most complex stories that I have translated here, and is an excellent example of a story of a pious woman. It is a Jain version of the famous story in the Hindu epic, the *Mahābhārata*. In this story Damayaṃtī has become the model Jain heroine. Abandoned by her husband, she manages to save herself and others through her chastity. We see in this story, too, how the power of love is such that Nala is unable to abandon Damayaṃtī in a final act of renunciation to become a monk. At many points this story invites us to view Damayaṃtī as the stronger of the two, more firmly committed to the religious life. Nala is not the only monk who succumbs to such weakness; the story of Ārdrakumāra, with which this collection begins, also tells of a monk who desires his former wife, now a nun. The account of Madanakīrti included here goes a step further and even depicts a fallen monk; it is a sectarian story, told by one group to show the alleged vices of its rivals.

In closing this brief review of some of the themes in these stories, I would mention three other stories: accounts of Mohadeva and Lobhadeva and the long account of virtues and vices that closes this collection. The stories of Mohadeva and Lobhadeva, like the story of Durgilā, describe the perfidy of friends and lovers, and so are meant as cautionary tales warning a person against trusting human relationships and seeing any permanent value in them. Jain stories use many strategies to teach us that we must renounce attachments to friends and families; the story of Rāma and Lakṣmaṇa, for example, shows us that attachment itself is a form of madness; the story of Lobhadeva frightens us in another way, by showing how a good person comes to a miserable end by trusting a friend. This story seems to be saying that there is no such thing as friendship, and we would be wise to guard ourselves against those we would consider 'friends'. The story thus raises some fundamental questions about human nature: Is human nature simply evil, so that from the start we must conclude that there is no such thing as a good person, a good friend? Must all friends be bad? If people are not by nature evil, then what makes a bad person act as he or she does? The answers, I think, are revealed by the metaphor which I chose as the title of this collection. Stories like that of Lobhadeva are studies of the thieves, the passions that lie in wait for us as we stumble through the forest. We are not intrinsically bad, but we are all subject to the control of the passions that rob us of our innate goodness. And since that is so, as Lobhadeva's treachery shows us, friendship is a very dangerous and risky business. I included a very brief story on deceiving a deceitful friend, which suggests that there are at least some temporary remedies a person has at his disposal to help deal with a deceitful friend. Nonetheless, through the humour the message is still clear: friends are not to be trusted.

The account of virtues and vices that closes the collection comes from a text that is perhaps the most sustained Jain narrative that grapples with the profound question: what exactly is human nature? The text is written as a complicated autobiography, a journey of the soul through different rebirths, and has drawn freely on an earlier work, the Prakrit original in which the stories of Lobhadeva and Mohadeva were told. The message is clear: these thieves are not us; passions and vices are extrinsic to our basic nature, although we must guard against them. And because they are not part of our real nature, it is possible for us to leave them behind and come safely through the forest in which they hide, ready to ambush us at the slightest provocation.

It is perhaps easier to describe the individual thieves than it is to describe the tangled forest, but I hope that the diversity of descriptions these stories together provide will be a start. I have deliberately tried to complicate the picture by translating stories of evil and exemplary women; accounts of monks who leave the world, renouncing all ties to family and friends, and other accounts in which renunciates still remain active in the world, settling disputes, overseeing the building of temples, curing diseases, and above all teaching people about the true nature of the cycle of rebirths and the need for Ultimate Release. I have further complicated things, I hope, by including stories that do not paint secular life in totally negative terms but make a place for a rich and rewarding existence as a lay devotee. Ārāmaśobhā, the girl with the magic garden, or Revatī, the woman who knows more than the Jain monk, are not simply women to be left behind. They are engaging and intelligent individuals, and the world they inhabit can seem meaningful and fulfilling. Indeed, the forest of thieves can at times seem more like a magic garden than a terrifying jungle. Of all types of religious literature, religious stories are perhaps best suited to convey such ambiguities, securing for them a place of special importance in the study of religion.

A note on the texts

These stories, all by Jain monks, come from a variety of texts, some written in Sanskrit and some written in Prakrit. They date roughly from the seventh to the fifteenth century C.E. The texts were written in different styles and represent different genres in the extensive corpus of Jain literature. Most of the texts I selected belong to the Śvetāmbara sect, which was strongest in northwest India. Only a few belong to the Digambara sect, which was centered further south. Some of the texts are collections of didactic tales, which often include stories of different length, some of which may be very short. The *Bṛhatkathākośa, Mūlaśuddhiprakaraṇa* and *Kathākośa* belong to this genre of writing. The stories in such collections are diverse and it is difficult, if not impossible, to identify a common theme. For this reason I would hesitate to consider the *Kuvalayamālā* as simply a didactic story collection, although many of the stories that it tells also appear in the standard anthologies of this type. The *Kuvalayamālā* sets its didactic stories within a larger frame story, somewhat in the style of a medieval romance, and the sequential rebirth narratives provide an overall structure that is missing in the didactic collections. Didactic stories also were transmitted through the rich commentaries added to explicate various texts, canonical and extra-canonical. One story in this collection of translations comes from a late commentary to the *Nandīsutta*.

In their retelling of both the great Sanskrit epics, the *Mahābhārata* and the *Rāmāyaṇa*, Jains authors could either tell the revised epic as a whole or privilege certain stories from it. My translation of the story of Nala and Damayaṃtī actually comes from the *Kumārapālapratibodha*, where the story is told as a warning against the evils of gambling. My examples of medieval biography writing are taken from the *Pariśiṣṭaparvan* and *Prabandhakośa*, texts which are actually very different in style. The *Prabandakośa* is written in a racy colloquial Sanskrit, while the *Pariśiṣṭaparvan* is written in the more refined style of Sanskrit court poetry. Both of these texts also contain sections that could well be considered examples of medieval Jain history writing. By contrast, the *Kumārapālapratibodha* (The Awakening of King Kumārapāla) has only a short section on contemporary history; it is really a didactic story collection. The *Upamitibhavaprapañcakathā*, a selection from which concludes this book, is a unique text. Its author describes the text as an autobiography. As the selection included here makes clear, it is an autobiography of a soul over numerous rebirths; it is also an allegory. I have also included stories from two different pilgrimage texts. The *Vividhatīrthakalpa* is a collection of short entries on different pilgrimage places. Some of the entries are in verse and some are in prose; some are in Sanskrit and some in Prakrit. The author, a fourteenth-century Śvetāmbara monk, tells us that he visited many of the places and collected the stories from various sources. The *Śātruñjayakalpavṛtti* is a commentary on a short verse text in praise of one of the most famous Jain holy sites, Mount Śatruñjaya, in the present state of Gujarat. The commentary, mostly in Sanskrit, glosses the verse text and amplifies it with stories.

The boundaries between one type of text and another are often difficult to define precisely. The account of King Kumārapāla's conversion, for example, includes stories familiar from many of the didactic collections. The spiritual autobiography, the *Upamitibhavaprapañcakathā*, owes much to the delightful stories in the *Kuvalayamālā*. Many of the individual stories I have translated here exist in many different versions and no doubt have their own complex histories; some are clearly much older than the texts from which I have taken them. We know little about the process of transmission of Jain stories, although we do know that stories were often a favoured vehicle for preaching. A story is told of a monk who comes to a village and is denied access to the monastic library by rival monks; needing material for his sermon, he simply writes his own collection of didactic stories! We know that other story collections were written down by monks for wealthy lay patrons. Often these collections gather together stories that seem to have constituted a shared cultural resource; so many of the stories appear again and again in different texts. But there are also exceptions, which seem to be original creations. Some stories clearly bear the stamp of oral transmission, and one story, 'The Sweetmeat Eater', even includes instructions to the storyteller to improvise and add his own verses at certain places in the story. Other texts are carefully crafted, refined literary works that demonstrate a familiarity with Sanskrit courtly aesthetics. If this sheer variety of texts and stories makes it difficult to generalize, it also stands as the most sure and reliable witness to the strength and vitality of medieval Jain story literature.

Texts and their dates

Avacūri to the *Nandīsutta,* ed. Ācārya Vikramasūri and Śrībhāskaravijaya, Śreṣṭhi Devacanda Lālabhāi Jaina Pustakoddhamra, No. 107, Sūrat, 1969.

Bṛhatkathākośa of Hariṣeṇa (931-932 C.E.), edited A.N. Upadhye, Bombay: Singhi Jain Series, Vol. 17, 1943.

Dharmābhyudayamahākāvya of Udayaprabhasūri (1233 C.E), edited Muni Chaturavijayaji, Bombay: Singhi Jain Series, Vol.4, 1949.

Kathākosā of Prabhācandra (10th c. C.E.), edited A.N. Upadhye, Manikachandra D. Jaina Granthamala No. 55, Varanasi: Bharatiya Jnana Pitha, 1974.

Kumārapālapratibodha of Somaprabhasūri (1195 C.E.), edited Jina Vijaya Muni, Baroda: Gaekwad's Oriental Series, 1920.

Kuvalayamālākathā of Ratnaprabhasūri (13th c. C.E.), edited A.N. Upadhye, Bombay: Singhi Jain Series, 46, 1970.

Mūlaśuddhiprakaraṇa with commentary of Devacandrasūri (1089-1090 C.E), edited Amritlal Mohanlal Bhojak, Ahmedabad: Prakrit Text Society, 1971.

Padmapurāṇa of Raviṣeṇa (678 C.E.), edited Pannalal Jain, Kashi: Bharatiya Jnana Pitha, 1958.

Pariśiṣṭaparvan of Hemacandra (12th c. C.E.), edited Hermann Jacobi, Calcutta: Asiatic Society of Bengal, 1932.

Prabandhakośa of Rājaśekharasūri (1349 C.E.), edited Jina Vijaya Muni, Santiniketan: Singhi Jain Series, Vol. 6, 1935

Śatruñjayakalpa of Dharmaghosa (15th c. C.E.), edited Labhasagaragani, Ahmedabad: Agamodhara Granthamala No. 41, 1969.

Upamitibhavaprapañcakathā of Siddharṣi (906 C.E), edited Hermann Jacobi, Calcutta: Asiatic Society of Bengal, 1899.

Vividhatīrthakalpa of Jinaprabhasūri, (1333 C.E.), edited Jina Vijaya Muni, Santiniketan: Singhi Jain Series, Vol. 10, 1934.

Some of these translations appeared elsewhere:

The stories of Bhadrabāhu and Varāha, Āryanandila, Jīvadeva, Madanakīrti, Ambikā, Devadhara, Devadiṇṇa are taken from *The Clever Adultress and Other Stories: A Treasury of Jain Literature*, edited by Phyllis Granoff, Oakville, Ontario: Mosaic Press, 1990.

The stories of Maheśavaradatta and Kuberadatta and Kuberadattā are taken from 'Life as Ritual Process: Remembrance of Past Births in Jain Religious Narratives' by Phyllis Granoff, in *Other Selves: Autobiography and Biography in Cross-Cultural Perspective*, edited by Phyllis Granoff and Koichi Shinohara, Oakville, Ontario: Mosaic Press, 1994.

The story of Sanatkumāra is included in an article on cures and karma entitled 'Self, Soul and Body in Religious Experience' that will appear in a special issue of *Numen*, edited by Albert Baumgarten.

I thank David Shulman, Wendy Doniger, Paul Dundas and Luitgard and Jayandra Soni for their help and encouragement as I struggled to write this book.

1

ĀRDRAKUMĀRA

There is in the middle of the continent of Jambuddīpa a beautiful country filled with hundreds of wondrous things and bustling with happy people. This country, called Magahā, has been made pure by the touch of the footsteps of the Jina, who led the religious life that was so difficult to lead, and by his direct disciples. It is rich in crops and money. Now in this country may be found the city Rāyagiha, the abode of all the excellent qualities that a city can possess, a lovely ornament for the forehead of the Lady Earth. The city Rāyagiha is known far and wide in all the ten directions.

It is like the garden of the gods, its lofty palaces like the garden's huge trees; it is like a king's triumphal gate, if you know how to make a good pun, for the gate has heavy bolts, while the city has many buildings, both expressed by the same words; it is like Mount Meru, for both are places where propitious things may happen; it is like the peak of

Mount Kailāsa, where Śiva lives, for in the city dwell rich men, and Śiva and the rich are both called by the same word, 'lord'; it is like the land of the gods, filled with temples, homes of the gods; it is like the sky, which has constellations while it is adorned with paintings; it is like a big family, for a large family is filled with many relatives while the city is filled with many dwellings, if you can unravel these puns! What more can I say?

It is splendid in its regular layout of grand roadways, crossroads and forks, where three roads or even four might meet; it is beautiful with its shops and drinking stands, gardens, lakes, tanks and wells. King Seṇiya, a lion who had torn apart his enemies, who are like so many elephants, rules over that city, which is like the city of the gods. And in that city there is no fear from anyone who might do it harm.

And here are yet more puns: the king is like the far-off land of Mahāvideha, which has the mountain peak Vijaya, 'Victory', for the king has many victories; he is like lake Mānasa, for the lake is always frequented by royal swans, while the king is ever served by other kings who wait on him; he is like Viṣṇu who carries the discus, while the king supports the right faith; he is like the rising sun, whose orb is red, for around him are a circle of loyal attendants; he is like the god Brahmā, who sits on a lotus, while he is the abode of the Goddess of Fortune; he is like the moon, for both gladden the eyes of everyone who beholds them.

The king has two wives, both soft-spoken and pretty, endowed with knowledge and humility, right belief, courage and virtue. The king loves both these wives, Sunandā and Cellanā, and they in turn are proud of their husband's love. They are both pious Jain ladies, upholders of the Jain lay vows: they vow never to harm any living creature, always to tell the truth, never to steal, always to be faithful to their husband and not to accumulate too many possessions. They also practice restraint, limiting the places they go so as not to harm living creatures, agreeing not to use certain items and forever giving up vices like gambling.

Now Sunandā has a son, who in the greatness of his intelligence is the equal of Bṛhaspati, the preceptor of the gods. He is the foremost of the five hundred ministers of the king and is capable of bearing the burden of the great kingdom all by himself. His name is Abhayakumāra. And all of the members of the royal family spend their days enjoying the various pleasures of the senses, acquiring wealth by lawful means, devotedly serving the glorious community of monks and worshipping the glorious Jina, Mahāvīra.

Far away from this land of Magahā, in the midst of the ocean, is a country called Addayadesa, and in that country there is a grand city named Addayaura. King Addaya rules there; many great vassal kings bow down at his feet, setting them asparkle with the rays that bounce from the jewels of their crowns. His queen, named Addayā, surpasses the lovely women of the gods in her many virtues and great beauty. She has a son named Prince Addaya, who is like an excellent necklace; the necklace has a most wonderful thread, while the son has most excellent qualities, both expressed in the same words. He offers relief to those who are suffering and is the abode of all propitious virtues; he brings comfort to the hearts of many men and women; indeed, his intentions are always honorable and because he is so pure in mind, he has no vice whatsoever. Now this son leads a most pleasurable life as a result of the merits he has accumulated in past births.

Every day King Seṇiya and King Addaya, out of respect for the friendship established by their ancestors, send each other valuable gifts as a token of their mutual affection. One day an envoy came from Seṇiya. He was admitted into the presence of the king by the doorkeeper, who announced, 'Lord! An envoy sent by King Seṇiya waits at your door!' At that King Addaya, his hair standing on end for joy, replied, 'Show him in at once!' Without further ado the doorkeeper ushered the envoy into the king's court. The envoy bowed respectfully and sat down on the seat provided for him. He was honored with the usual gifts of betel and other things. King Addaya asked him, 'Tell us, how is King Seṇiya and his family?' The envoy replied, 'My lord, they are well.' Then the envoy presented his gifts of fine cloth, blankets, leaves of the nimba plant and salt to the king. When the king saw these things, he said, 'King Seṇiya is my best friend; surely I have no other friend like him.' When Prince Addaya heard his father's words that were so filled with affection, he asked,' Father! Who is this King Seṇiya?' The king replied, 'Son! He is the ruler of the land of Magahā, and a king whose rule extends far and wide. Our family has long had this relationship of great affection with those of King Seṇiya's lineage. And it is his envoy who has come to us bearing these gifts.' Prince Addaya turned to the envoy and asked, 'Does your master have a son who is worthy of him?' When he heard these words the envoy was delighted and replied,

'Indeed, he has a fine son, who is endowed with the four types of intelligence, natural cleverness and the others. This son is the master of five hundred ministers, a hero, honest, handsome, of pleasing words, and ever ready to speak. He is clever and grateful to those who help him; he has mastered many texts and sciences and is skilled in the many arts. This young man is endowed with wisdom, humility and a sense of modesty; he is possessed of virtuous conduct and compassion and gives liberally to those in need. He is extremely good-looking and of fine build; he follows the will of his subjects, is steadfast and adorned with auspicious marks. He is unwavering in his faith in Jainism and is ever vigilant in pursuing the duties of a lay Jain. He is like a bee, ever hovering around the lotus feet of the lord of Jinas, Mahāvīra. He is devoted to the excellent monks and is ever eager to do what is necessary for those who share his religious faith, for his subjects, and for those who bow down to him in respect or need. What more can I say? This son of King Seṇiya is honored even by the gods, who think him to be a man of great virtue. And the name of this most excellent prince is Abhaya. It is because of Abhaya's great prowess that Seṇiya is able to pursue his life of pleasures without any worries. O Prince! Everyone in the world has heard of Abhaya; how can you not have heard of him?'

When he heard these words, Prince Addaya cried out in joy, 'Father, if you allow it, then I would like to become friends with Abhaya.' The king replied, 'Son! It is only fitting that we perpetuate the mutual affection between our families that has existed throughout the generations. For they say:

> The affection of a good person is like an elderly man. Both start slowly and hesitantly; the one walks carefully behind you leaning on a bamboo stick, while the other is passed on down the family, never lessening (and here is a pun that you must catch, on the words "bamboo" and "family"!) Neither falters, and while the old man grows older, the affection of an honest man grows deeper.
> Fortunate indeed are those good men whose affection is constant and daily grows, to be passed on to their sons like some long accumulated debt.'

At this, Prince Addaya said to the envoy, 'When my father gives you leave to go, please come and see me.' The envoy agreed. King Addaya's men escorted the envoy to a lofty mansion where he was to stay. King Addaya presented the envoy with gifts of gemstones, pearls, coral and the finest silks. The next day the king again honored the envoy with presents of clothes and jewellery and dispatched some of his chief retainers, likewise laden with rich gifts, to accompany the envoy on his journey home. After this royal send-off, the envoy hastened as promised to the dwelling of the prince. He explained to the prince that the king had formally dismissed him. The prince, too, presented the envoy with gifts of large pearls and glittering gemstones, among other things, and said, 'You must give Prince Abhaya this message from me. Tell him, 'Prince Addaya desires to form a friendship with you.'' With these words Prince Addaya dismissed the envoy.

The envoy returned to Rāyagiha, travelling without a stop and encountering no obstacles. The doorkeeper announced the return of the envoy to King Seṇiya; he ushered him into the presence of the king. Having bowed respectfully to his sovereign, the envoy sat down. The retainers of King Addaya,who had accompanied the envoy home, presented King Seṇiya with the gifts that they had brought. They also gave Prince Abhaya the gifts that Prince Addaya had sent. When King Seṇiya and the others who were present beheld those gifts, they were greatly astonished and exclaimed, 'How marvellous are these gifts!' The envoy then repeated to Prince Abhaya what Prince Addaya had said. Now Prince Abhaya knew well the words of the Jina and he was pure in mind, and so he thought:

'In most cases affection arises between living beings who are similar in virtue and vice; furthermore, when people have the same nature, their friendship bears the greatest fruit.

Therefore I must find some means to awaken him to the truth of the Jain religion and thus show to him the greatest act of friendship conceivable. For it is said,

> He is truly a friend who awakens another from the drunken sleep of delusion, here in this house called worldly existence, that is ablaze with the flames of heedlessness.

Now it is just possible that when he sees an image of the Jina he will recall his past births. I will use this occasion of exchanging gifts as the pretext for presenting him with an image of the Blessed One.'

Thinking this, he made ready an image of the Blessed First Jina, fashioned from every jewel that exists, calm and beautiful in appearance. He concealed that image in a small container that he put into a larger box. He also gathered together the articles necessary to worship the image, such as an incense burner and bells. He put locks on the box and then sealed it officially with his own seal. When King Seṇiya was ready to dismiss the retainers of King Addaya, he presented them with jewellery and money and fine silks; Abhaya also gave them the box and further instructed them, 'You must tell Prince Addaya from me, 'Do not open this box until you are all alone. Then, you may break the seal and open it and look inside. But you must not show it to anyone." Having agreed to do exactly as they had been told, the men departed. They reached home after travelling without a stop. They did all that was to be done, precisely as they had done before, and then went to the dwelling quarters of the prince. They related to him all that they had been told. At that, the prince retired to his inner chambers. As soon as he opened the box he saw the image, which illuminated the ten quarters with its rays of light. Prince Addaya exclaimed, 'How wonderful! Here is something I have never seen before in my life! Do I wear it on my head or on my ears? Or perhaps I should hang it around my neck? Maybe it's for my arms, or my hands, or my feet? I've no idea what this thing could be!'

But suddenly he couldn't help feeling that maybe he had seen it before. And as he wondered and reflected carefully where that might have been, the prince swooned and dropped to the ground. He came to without any assistance from anyone else and stood up. A second later he remembered his past births and began to think, 'Three births ago I was a farmer named Sāmāia in the village of Vasantapura, which is located in the country of Magahā. I had a wife named

Bandumaī. One day I heard the Jain religion from the teacher Suṭṭhiāyāria. I was struck with terror at the dangers of worldly existence. My wife and I both renounced the world. I became a monk. I studied the doctrine and the rituals and wandered from place to place with other monks, who were similarly motivated by a fear of worldly existence. In the course of my wanderings I came to a certain city. My former wife, now in the company of some nuns, also chanced to come to that very city in the course of her wanderings.

'When I saw her, I remembered the delight I used to have in making love to her and I felt the stirrings of desire for her again. I told this to the monk who was with me. He, in turn, told it to the leader of the nuns, who told Bandhumaī. Bandhumaī proclaimed, "Strange indeed are the workings of karma! See how even a learned monk can harbor such evil thoughts! Blessed One! Even if I go away from this place, he will never stop wanting me; he will never leave me alone. It is better for me to renounce all food and die by starvation. For it is said,

> It is better to enter a blazing fire than to break one's vow of chastity; it is better to die never having done a wrong deed, than to live a life of dissolute behaviour."

'Making this firm resolve, she renounced all food and with the proper religious instruction died a pious death from fasting. When I heard everything that had happened, I was gripped by a terrible realization of the worthlessness of worldly existence and thought to myself, "This noble lady killed herself out of fear of breaking her vows. But surely I have already broken those same vows. I must also renounce all food." And without saying a word to my teachers I renounced food. I died and was reborn in heaven. In time I fell from heaven and was reborn here. Can it be that, after renouncing everything to become a monk under an excellent teacher, I have been born here in this uncivilized land because of the desire J harbored in my heart? I must revere above everyone that person who has awakened me, despite the fact that I have been born in a land without culture and true religion.

'For sure, Prince Abhaya and no one else is my teacher, my brother, my friend, my father. For he has rescued me, about to fall into hell, through his own cleverness.

'If I had not formed a friendship with that noble one, then, bereft of the practice of the proper religion, I would have wandered endlessly in the cycle of rebirths.

'Why should I suffer any longer? Let me go at once to that land where there are educated and cultured people and where the true religion exists. I must become a monk, for that alone will release me from all my suffering.'

And with these thoughts he got up and asked his servants for flowers and the other items he needed to worship the image. When he had completed his worship, he went to see the king. 'Father!' he said, 'I have formed a close friendship with Prince Abhaya. If you, my father, agree, I shall go to Prince Abhaya; surely, when we see each other face to face, we will love each other even more.' The king replied, 'Son! Our relationship to King Seṇiya and Prince Abhaya is different; it is more formal. Under no circumstances are you to go there.' But the king saw that when he forbade his son from going, the prince took no delight in his usual enjoyments. The king feared that the prince would go without his permission, and so he assigned five hundred of his retainers to guard the prince. In private he told them, 'If the prince goes, it is on your heads.' They replied, 'The king's words are our command,' and they began to follow the prince everywhere. Meanwhile, the prince decided, 'I will somehow trick them and go.' One day he informed them, 'I wish to practice my horseback riding.' 'Whatever the prince commands,' they replied, and they brought him the best horse from the stables. They went out to the riding grounds and they put the prince on a horse. The first day the prince rode only a short distance, but with each day he went further and further, until he disappeared altogether from their sight. He would wait a bit and then come back, just when it was the peak of the heat at noon. The bodyguards would wait in the shade for him. In this way he lulled them into trusting him and made his getaway. He had taken into confidence a few people and had told them to fill a ship at the ocean's shore with jewels; he first placed the image of the Jina on the boat and then got in himself.

In this way he came to the civilized world. The first thing that he did when he got there was to send the image to Abhaya. He then prepared to become a monk: he sponsored great festivities in the temples of the Jinas; he gave the jewels to his loyal retainers and to the poor and needy; he donned the garb of a monk and ceremonially pulled out his hair; but when he was about to proclaim publicly his monastic vows of total renunciation he suddenly heard the voice of a goddess in the sky, 'Hear now, great one! Do not become a monk. You still have some karma that you need to enjoy. After you have enjoyed that karma you may become a monk.' But Prince Addaya liked to think of himself as a hero and so he shouted back, 'What can karma do to me?' With that he renounced the world and became a monk. He set off on his life of wandering and in time came to the city Vasantaura. There he stood in a posture of meditation in a temple just outside the city.

In the meantime, Bandhumaī, who had been his wife in a previous life, fell from heaven and was born into a merchant family in that very city; she was born as Sirimaī, the daughter of Dhaṇavaī, the wife of the chief merchant Devadatta. One day she was playing with her girlfriends in that very temple; they were playing the game 'choose a husband'. Her friends all shouted, 'Choose a husband! Choose a husband!' The other girls all chose one of their group, but Sirimaī said, 'I choose this ascetic.' As soon as she had made her choice, a goddess proclaimed, 'Well done. This young girl has chosen well,' and with roaring thunder she showered the girl with a rain of jewels. Frightened by the roar of the thunder, Sirimaī fell down at the ascetic's feet. The ascetic, thinking that this pleasurable event would disturb him in his religious practice, hastened to move on.

Now when the king heard that a rain of jewels had fallen, he went to the temple along with the townspeople. The king began to gather the jewels that had rained down. The goddess stopped him by causing a display of such things as terrifying snakes, their hoods raised in fury. She said, 'I made this rain of jewels in approval of the choice this young girl made for her husband.' And so it was that the merchant, the girl's father, gathered the jewels and put them in a safe place. The young girl, too, went back into the city.

Now suitors began to come, wishing to marry Sirimaī. She asked her father, 'Father, what do these men want?' The merchant answered, 'Daughter! They come to ask for your hand in marriage.' She hastened to say, 'Father, it is against all rules of conduct to give a daughter away twice. For it is said,

> 'There are three things in this world that are for once and for all: the words of a king, the words of a monk and the giving away of a daughter.

'And I have been given by you to the one whose wealth you accepted. What's more, even the goddess approved my choice. How could I choose another?' The merchant replied, 'Daughter! How shall we even know who he is?' The daughter said, 'Father! When I was terrified by the sound of the thunder and fell at his feet, I saw a distinctive mark on his right foot. You will know him by that mark.' At this the merchant said, 'In that case, daughter, give alms to all the mendicants. Perhaps he might come here with the others to receive alms.' And fate so ordained it that after twelve years had passed, that monk lost his way and ended up back in that very city. Sirimaī recognized him and began to speak to him.

'O my lord! O repository of all fine qualities! O my heart's joy! Having abandoned me in my loneliness and sorrow, where have you been all these years? From the very moment that you were chosen by me as my husband, there has been no room in my heart for anyone else! Now I know that I have accumulated much merit, for you are here at last. O beloved! Take pity on me by grasping my hand in marriage!'

When he heard these words, the merchant came to see what was going on. He summoned the king. They told the monk, 'O Noble One! This woman has said again and again that she does not want anyone but you, not even in her wildest dreams. She insists, 'I vow that either that noble one will touch my body with his soft hands or a blazing fire will consume it.' So please agree now to marry her.'

Because he still had karma that he had to enjoy ; because he remembered the words of the goddess, and because they so importuned him, for all those reasons, the monk married that girl. As they took pleasure in each other a son was born to them. When the child was a bit older, the husband tried to take leave of his wife. He said to her, 'I am going to become a monk. Now you have company.' In an effort to make her child understand what was happening, she took up a bobbin and a piece of thread that was lying around and began to spin. Her son asked, 'Mother, why are you about to do something that only poor women do?' She replied, 'This is also what women who have no husbands should do.' The child said, 'Mother, why do you say this, when Father is right here?' She replied, 'Your father seems determined to leave.' Her son said, 'Where will he go? I will tie him up so that he cannot go anywhere.' And with those childish words he grabbed the bobbin that had fallen from her hand and wound the string around his father's feet again and again. When he was finished with his task he said, 'Mother! Do not worry. I have tied Father up. He won't go anywhere now.'

The father thought, 'Aha! My child's love for me is strong indeed. I will remain for just as many years as the number of times that he has wrapped the thread around my feet.' And when he counted he saw that the child had encircled his feet twelve times. He remained there for twelve years. When that time period had come to an end, in the last watch of the night, he woke up and remembering all that had happened to him, he began to lament:

'What good am I? Look at what I have done! Though I was a barbarian, I became a monk, renouncing everything, and then failed to heed my vows and threw myself into the dung heap of carnal pleasures. Though the goddess tried to prevent me, I insisted on climbing to the peak of the mountain of vows. O woe is me, see how I have fallen into the dank well of worldly existence. In my previous birth I broke my vows just by harbouring desire in my mind, and for that sin I was born in a barbarian land. Ah, I do not know now what rebirth I will have to endure for what I have done this time. Alas, alack, this time I have sinned, knowing full well what it was that I was doing. Surely for this I will have to wander from birth to birth in this endless cycle of rebirths. For it is said,

> They are to be pitied in this world, who do not get to hear the words of the Jina. But even more pitiable are those who know the words of the Jina but do not act on them.

'But what use is it to cry so over something that is already done? Now I must truly live a life of restraint and austerity, with utmost sincerity. For it is said,

> Those to whom austerities, restraints, forbearance and chastity are dear, make it first to the world of the gods, even though they may have been born later.'

And so the very next morning he bade farewell to his beloved wife and donned the garb of a monk. And then as a lion goes forth from a mountain cave, he went forth from that house and took the road to Rāyagiha. On the way he ran into the five hundred retainers, who had once been assigned by his father to protect him. They were now living as thieves in the forest. He recognized them right away. And when they saw him at once they fell at his feet. The holy one asked them, 'Why have you undertaken to earn your livelihood in this despicable manner?' They replied, 'Master! After you tricked us and fled we searched everywhere for you; we got this far but found no sign of you anywhere. Having been unsuccessful in our search, how could we show our faces to the king? In shame and fear we could not go back to the king. And having no other way to survive, we earn our living in this way.' Then the Blessed One said, 'Noble men! You should put your efforts into leading a religious life! For it is said,

> Having attained a human birth, a person sunk in the ocean of transmigratory existence should exert himself to lead a religious life, which is the noble course that leads to the fulfilment of all desires.

'And you must never for a moment relax your vigilance. For it is said,

> That people are not endowed with wealth; that they are not free of misery; that they are plagued by illness and disease; that they are not perfectly handsome in form, adorned with every desirable quality; that they do not get to heaven nor attain the bliss of Final Release, in which there is not the slightest trace of fear, the cause of all of these things is simple: it is nothing but wicked lack of vigilance, which is like a

> swift sword that cuts to shreds the garland of all good fortune.

'Therefore you must give up this life of sin and exert yourselves in leading a religious life.'

When they heard these words, the thieves all folded their hands in reverence and replied, 'Blessed One! If you find us worthy, then ordain us all as monks.' The holy one replied, 'Become monks!' And they answered, 'We will do so,' and followed him out of the forest. Now when the Blessed sage Addaya had reached the outskirts of the city Rāyagiha, Gosālaga heard that the self-enlightened sage Addaya had come to worship the Blessed Mahāvīra and he challenged him to a debate. He was defeated by Addaya with clever retorts. You may learn of the details of their debate from the Sūyagaḍānga. I do not give them here for fear of making my text too long.

Sage Addaya went on his way and when he had almost reached Rāyagiha he came upon the hermitage of some ascetics known as Hathitāvasas, "Elephant Ascetics". They would kill a single elephant and live on its flesh for many days. They said, 'What good is it to kill many small living creatures like seeds and other things? It is much better to kill a single elephant.' Now they had brought one large elephant from the forest and had it tied up in their hermitage. It was held fast with heavy metal fetters and tied down by strong iron chains. When that great sage arrived on the scene, the elephant was suddenly possessed of excellent discernment. He saw the Blessed One, who was worthy of being honored by many, surrounded by the five hundred noble princes. And as soon as the elephant saw them he thought to himself, 'I would also like to bow down to the Blessed One.' As soon as that thought entered his mind, all of his chains dropped off, through the great power of that Holy One. Freed from his shackles, the elephant proceeded to bow down to the Blessed One. A cry arose from the crowd who saw what was happening, 'Alas, alas, the great sage will be killed by this elephant!' But the elephant bent down and touched his forehead to the lotus feet of the Holy One; fixing its gaze on the Holy One the elephant retreated into the forest. The Elephant Ascetics were crazed with jealousy when they saw the power of the Holy One. They rushed to challenge him to debate. They were silenced by that Blessed One, with his intellect practiced in the doctrine of multiple viewpoints. They were awakened by his discourse on the right religion and went to the assembly of the Blessed Tīrthankara Mahāvīra. There they all became Jain monks.

It was not long before King Seṇiya heard about the many wondrous powers of that Holy One, how he had released the elephant and performed so many miraculous feats. His eyes wide open in astonishment, King Seṇiya hastened to see the Holy One along with Prince Abhaya and other members of his court. Filled with faith, he circumambulated the Holy One three times and bowed to him in respect. This is what he said:

'Praise to you, who have abandoned the life of the householder! O abode of all the excellent virtues of the practice of restraints! Praise to you, who are a wild lion who destroys the mighty elephants, those ascetics of other religions, who are puffed up with pride at their own supposed virtues!'

The Holy One blessed the king, wishing that the king one day would come to realize fully the true religion. Here is what he said:

'O lord among men! May you one day possess that true religion which makes way for every good fortune and destroys all evil; it is a torrent of water to wash away all the mud of sin and gives rise to the true happiness that comes from Liberation.'

The king, assured of the monk's comfort, then sat down on a spot of ground that was free of living creatures. He said, 'Blessed One! It is truly a great miracle that the elephant was released from its tight bonds through your power.' To this the Blessed One replied with a verse,

> 'O King! Far easier it seems to me was it to free a mad elephant in the forest from its bonds, than it was to free myself from the bonds of the threads that were wound around me.'

The king asked, 'Blessed One! What do you mean?' And so the Holy One told the king what had happened to him. 'O Great King! Once, bonds that were made of mere pieces of simple thread were wound around me by my son; in truth, they were bonds of love and I cast them off with the greatest difficulty. They seemed to me far more difficult to break than the bonds that can hold an elephant down. That is what I meant by the verse that I recited for you.'

When they heard this many people were awakened. King Seṇiya and Prince Abhaya were also greatly pleased. They bowed down to the Holy One and returned to their palace. The Holy One worshipped the Blessed Mahāvīra and then resumed his life of severe penance and solitary wandering. He attained the highest knowledge and reached the state of highest bliss, the state of Final Liberation.

(from the *Mūlaśuddhiprakaraṇa* of Pradyumnasūri, pp. 6-12)

2

THE CHILDHOOD OF VAJRASVĀMIN

Next in the monastic lineage of Suhastin was the monk Vajrasvāmin, who transmitted the teaching and strengthened the religious community. His story now begins.

Here on this very continent of Jambūdvipa lies the country called Avanti, the ornament of the western sector of the land Bharata. It was like heaven in its splendour and wealth. In that country was a settlement called Tambuvana, that was like the abode of all material fortune, bringing joy even to the gods. In Tambuvana lived a Jain layman, the son of a merchant, who was like a son of the Goddess of Wealth herself. His name was Dhanagiri, "Mountain of Wealth", and indeed his heaps of wealth resembled so many mountains.

Although Dhanagiri was young and vigorous and strikingly handsome, no stirrings of desire ever entered his mind. An attitude of complete calm stood guard like a doorkeeper over his heart. Though many a text on the proper conduct of life declares, "Money comes from the practice of religion", in his case, his practice of religion stemmed from his wealth, which he gave liberally to appropriate recipients. Knowing that becoming a monk and abstaining from all sexual activity leads to Heaven and Final Release, he did not want to marry. He steadfastly devoted himself to the doctrine of the Arhats. Whenever his parents, intent on finding him a wife, approached some family to ask for their daughter's hand in the joyful celebration of marriage with their son, Dhanagiri would go to that family and declare to them outright, 'I intend to become a monk. Surely I would be wrong not to tell you this.' At this the daughter of the wealthy merchant Dhanapāla, insisted, 'I must be given to Dhangiri. He must be my husband.' And so the wealthy merchant Dhanapāla gave his daughter to the man she had herself chosen, to this Dhanagiri, despite the fact that he wanted to become a monk. Sunandā's brother Āryaśamita had already become a monk at the feet of the teacher Siṃhagiri.

One day Sunandā was in her fertile period and had taken her ritual bath. Despite his resolve to remain celibate, Dhanagiri made love to her, for a person is destined to live out the results of his karma. A particular god, who had once heard Gautamasvāmin recite the text known as the *Puṇḍarikādhyāyana* on sacred Mount Aṣṭāpada, descended into Sunandā's womb. When Dhanagiri, pure in mind, realized that Sunandā was pregnant, he said to her, 'Now you are not alone. This child that you carry will be your companion. It is time for me to leave you and become a monk. I married you against my will. I care for nothing but becoming a monk. I wish you all the best from now on.' With these words Dhanagiri left her, as a merchant hastens to leave behind him the customs house. He went to the monk Siṃhagiri, under whose guidance he became an ascetic. Enduring the trials and tribulations that beset a monk, hunger and thirst, cold and heat, insect bites and the like, he practiced austerities that were difficult to perform, indifferent to the comfort of his own body. Endowed with the proper qualities of a good disciple, with steadfastness, honesty and humility, he drank deeply the draught of the teaching from his guru, as if from a deep well.

At the end of nine months, as a pond gives rise to a lotus, Sunandā gave birth to a son, who brought joy to everyone. The women who cared for Sunandā in her lying-in chamber and stayed awake all night watching over mother and child, told the baby, 'If only your father had not been so eager to become a monk, there would have been a fine party to celebrate your birth! A home is not a proper home without its master, no matter how many women there are in it. The sky, even though it may be studded with stars, does not shine without the moon.' The child, though just a baby, could understand things, for he had very few obstructing karmas that might block his comprehension. He listened intently to what the women were saying and absorbed it all. He thought to himself, 'My father has become a monk.' No sooner did he think this, than he remembered his past births. Recalling his past births, that baby knew as well that worldly existence is worthless, and though just a baby, drinking his mother's milk, he wished to follow the path his father had taken. He thought to himself, 'How can I make my mother so fed up with me that she will let me go?' And this is the way he chose. Even when his mother held him he would cry, night and day, without a stop. Nothing his mother did could make him stop crying; he would never stop, not even when she sang sweet melodies to him; not even when she showed him toys; not even when she made a hammock for him out of the sari she was wearing and rocked him back and forth; not even when she spoke coaxingly to him; not even when she made him dance on her lap; not even when she made funny noises popping the air she held in her puffed-out cheeks; not even when she kissed his head. Through all of this he just kept right on crying.

The baby cried like this for a good six months. Even Sunandā began to get fed up with this child of hers. Now one day Siṃhagiri happened to come to Tambuvana, surrounded by some of his disciples, including Dhanagiri and Āryaśamita. When their guru Siṃhagiri had settled into the place where he was to stay, Dhanagiri and Āryaśamita bowed reverently to him and asked, 'Blessed One! We have relatives here in this town. If you allow us, we will go and pay our respects to them.' As they were making this request of him, the greatly learned Siṃhagiri saw a favourable omen. He said to them, 'There is great gain to be made here and you two ascetics will surely do it. Obedient to my orders, you must accept whatever it is that you are given, whether it is a living being or something inanimate.'

The two great ascetics then set out for the home of Sunandā. When they got to her door, some of the women of her household told Sunandā that they had come. All of those women said, 'O Sunandā! Give that son of yours to Dhanagiri. Let us see what he will do with him.' After all the women had told her this, Sunandā, without joy, took the baby who still nursed at her breasts, for by now she had truly had all she could stand. She went to the door and said to Dhanagiri, 'I have cared for this baby till now as if he were my very own self, but he has driven me to my wits end. All he does is cry, day and night. Even though you have renounced the world and become a monk, you must take this child. Do not abandon him as you once abandoned me.'

Dhanagiri, skilled with words, smiled and replied to her, 'O lovely lady! I will do as you ask, but later you will regret this. Do not give up your child; or if you are determined to give him up, then do so in the presence of witnesses. You cannot have him back later on.' And so Sunandā, despondent, summoned some people to act as witnesses.

She gave her son to Dhanagiri and he accepted the child. The child stopped crying as soon as Dhanagiri wrapped him in the piece of cloth he used to hold his begging bowl, as if there had been some secret promise between the two that this is the way things would be. The two ascetics then left Sunandā's house. They took the child with them as their teacher had ordered them and returned to their teacher.

When Simhagiri saw Dhanagiri coming, his arms sagging with the weight of that jewel of a child, he called out, 'You seem to be having a hard time carrying the alms that you bring for me. Give it to me, O gentleman! Give your arms a rest.' When he heard those words, the monk Dhanagiri carefully took the child, who was as handsome as a child of the gods, and who was the abode of Good fortune, and handed him to his teacher. The best of teachers took the child in his own arms; the baby was aglow with light that streamed from him, as the sun glows with its rays. At that instant the very earth on which the master Siṃhagiri was sitting sank into the ground under the great weight of the child; it bent low just as a person might lower his cupped hands to gather water in them. Siṃhagiri, his hands unsteady from the weight of the child, was filled with astonishment. He said, 'This is really a thunderbolt, a vajra; it only looks like a child. I cannot hold him any longer. This child will become a famous, meritorious monk, who will pass on the teaching and preserve our religious community. You must watch over him carefully, for jewels are known to attract trouble.'

The teacher Siṃhagiri gave the baby to the nuns to look after. They named him Vajra, 'The Thunderbolt', since he was as heavy as a thunderbolt. The nuns handed him over to the family of lay devotees who provided them with lodging and other necessities, saying, 'You must look after this child with the same care as you look after yourselves.' The women of the house, skilled in caring for children, lavished on this child even more love than they gave their own children and watched over him diligently. That child, a veritable treasure house of auspicious qualities, went from the lap of one woman to the lap of another, like a swan fluttering from one lotus to the next. The women talked to him in baby talk and were wild with joy as he talked back to them. Those lucky women took care of the child, vying with each other for the privilege of bathing or feeding him. Even though he was just a baby, Vajra behaved more like an old man. He restrained himself and never once did anything childish that might cause them distress. Wise Vajra ate only those purest foods allowed Jain monks and only what he needed to stay alive. From remembering his past births he had also gained the knowledge of what was right and what was wrong to do, and he knew the proper rules for monks. Even though he was a baby, whenever he needed to urinate, he would make a clear sign to whomever was carrying him. He was equally affectionate to all of the other children in the home, as if he were their twin brother. Every day he made the noble ladies laugh, playing at gathering up the things a person might need if he were going to study and become learned.

One day Sunandā saw how handsome and well-behaved Vajra was. She asked the Jain family for him back, saying, 'He is my son.' They told her, 'We know nothing about this child being your son or your being his mother. We know only that the monks gave him to us to take care of for them.' They would not give the child to Sunandā and so she would watch him from a distance, as if he did not belong to her. She finally convinced them to let her help look after the child in their home and so, like a nursemaid, she lovingly cared for him, even giving him milk to drink from her breasts.

There was a place in the prosperous district of Acalapur, between the famous rivers called Kanyā and Pūrṇā where a number of ascetics were living. One of these ascetics knew how to make magical unguents to apply to the feet. He would smear the paste on his feet and put on special sandals, and then he could walk on water as if on land. In this way he would go back and forth to the city, along the water, astonishing everyone who saw him. That ascetic would also make particular fun of those who were devoted to the Jain monks, chiding them, 'I bet there is no one of your religious belief who has the kind of power I have!' The teacher Āryaśamita, Vajra's maternal uncle, chanced to come to that place in the course of his monastic wanderings. He was a great ascetic and had acquired certain powers through the practice of yoga. The Jains all explained to that best of teachers how the local ascetics were making fun of their faith. When he heard this, Āryaśamita did not need to think very hard to find a solution. He told his followers, 'This miserable ascetic does not have any particular power that comes from performing austerities. He is just using some kind of trick to deceive you. Just as a magician can amaze his audience by stunts like making flowers bloom when they shouldn't be blooming, this ascetic is using some magic on you. That he can walk on water is not the result of any special ascetic practices he has performed. The goal that you seek can only be achieved through the proper teaching; you must not be fooled by this trick into believing in these ascetics. If you do not believe me, then invite that ascetic to your house. Wash his feet and his sandals.' The Jain lay devotees then found some excuse or other to invite the ascetic to one of the Jain homes. He went there, surrounded by a crowd of people. The Jain layman and his family pretended to be faithful followers of the ascetic. The head of the house greeted him at the door with these words, 'Blessed One! Let me wash your lotus feet. Those who wash your feet indeed wash themselves clean of all sins. You must grant me your favour and allow me to do this, for noble-minded men never reject the faithful service of their devotees.' And so the Jain layman forced the unwilling ascetic to allow him to wash his feet and sandals with warm water.

And as he washed and washed them, not a trace of the unguent remained on them, much as affection does not long remain in the heart of a scoundrel. That best of Jains then served the ascetic a sumptuous meal; there are times when one must honor even those who hold false beliefs to accomplish what is necessary. The ascetic was troubled that his Jain host had wiped off the unguent; he was so worried that it would lead to his humiliation that he could not even enjoy the taste of the food.

The ascetic finished eating and went back to the river's bank. A crowd gathered, eager to see him perform feats like parting the waters. That fool, thinking that some of the unguent still remained on his feet, rashly tried to walk out onto the water as he had done before. Glub, glub, like a pot thrown into the river, that young ascetic sank below the water's surface right at the river's edge. Even those who had been firm followers of the wrong belief were now distressed and thought, 'We have been deceived by that trickster for too long.'

As the crowd began to jeer and shout, the teacher Āryaśamita, chief of those who know the Jain doctrine, arrived on the scene. Desirous of strengthening his own religious group, the teacher threw into the middle of the river some powder over which he had recited a spell. That best of teachers, foremost of the noble-minded, then called out to the river, 'Come, my child, so that I may cross to your other bank.' At that, the two banks of the river came together and the teacher and his followers crossed to the other bank. The ascetics and their followers, seeing the miracle that the teacher had performed, were struck with fear. All of the ascetics cast off their wrong beliefs, and all together they became Jain monks under the guidance of the teacher Āryaśamita. Because they came from a place called Brahmadvīpa, the scriptures tell us that they were called by the name "Brahmadvīpa Monks".

In time, living in the same Jain family, Vajra turned three

years old and Dhanagiri and the other monks returned. When Sunandā heard that the monks had come back, she was delighted, for she thought to herself, 'Dhanagiri will come and I will get my son back.' Sunandā asked those great ascetics for her son, but they would not give him to her. They said to her, 'We did not ask for your son; you gave him to us of your own free will. Who would ever want to take back the food he had vomited up? A person no longer has any rights over something he has given away, anymore than he retains the rights to something he has sold. Do not ask for your son back; you gave him away and he now belongs to another.'

As Sunandā and the monks argued in this way, people gathered. They all said, 'Let the king decide which of you is right.' And so Sunandā and all the townspeople went to the court of the king. The monks and all the Jain lay community went there, too. Sunandā sat at the left of the king, while the Jains sat at his right; the other people sat down in their appropriate places. When he heard what the two contending parties had to say, the king passed this judgement, 'You both shall call out to the child. He shall belong to the party to whom he goes.' Both of the contending parties agreed. They asked, 'Who should call the child first?' The townspeople, who were quick to take the side of a woman in any dispute, said, 'The child has been brought up by the monks and has a longstanding bond of affection with them. He will never disobey them. Let the mother call him first. The woman's is the harder task; surely she is to be pitied. This is the only way the thing can be done.' And so Sunandā showed the child all kinds of toys and delicious things to eat. She said, 'Look at these elephants! And here are horses, and soldiers and chariots, too! I have brought all of these things for you to play with. Take them, child! And here are sweetmeats and cakes, grapes and sugar candies. You can have anything you want. Take them, my child! With my whole body I bow down to you and pray, may you have long life, may you always be happy, may you bring happiness to me, Sunandā! You are my god, you are my son, you are my very life. Revive me, my child, by your embrace. Do not embarrass me, son, in front of all of these people. My heart will split in two, like a plump cooked dumpling! Come, child, with your charming steps like the gait of a swan! Come into my lap. Can't you do just this in return for the many months I bore you in my womb?' But despite all the toys, the food and the coaxing words, the son of Sunandā did not budge.

Even though wise Vajra knew well that a person can never repay the debt that he owes his mother, he still thought to himself, 'If I turn my back on the monks out of pity for my mother, then I shall be doomed to wander in the cycle of rebirths for a terribly long time. And my mother is surely one of those fortunate souls with little remaining karma. She will eventually renounce the world and become a nun. I must not worry about the momentary pain that I will cause her now.' This was what Vajra, with his ability to know the future, thought. His resolve as firm as a diamond, he remained where he was and did not move an inch, as motionless as if he were a statue.

The king said, 'Sunandā, step aside. The child did not come, although you called him, as if he did not even know that you are his mother.' It was Dhanagiri's turn, and the king let him proceed. The monk showed the child the broom that monks use to sweep their path as they go, and he spoke these carefully chosen words, 'If you are determined to became a monk, if you know the truth, then faultless one, take this broom, which is like the banner of right faith.' Instantly, Vajra stretched out his hand, as a young elephant might extend its trunk, and he ran over to Dhanagiri, his anklets jingling. That pure-minded one then climbed onto his father's lap and picked up the broom, as if it were a lotus to play with. The broom, raised high by Vajra in his two lotus-like hands, looked like a fly-whisk held high in honor of the Glory of the Jain community. Vajra smiled and his teeth glittered like tiny white jasmine buds. He never for a moment let his glance waver from the monk's dust broom.

Sunandā wilted, like a lotus pond at night when the lotus blossoms close. Resting her chin in her hand, she thought to herself, 'First my brother became a monk and then my husband too became a monk. Now my son is going to become a monk. I too should renounce the world. I have no brother and no husband; now I have no son, either. It is far better for me to renounce the world than to continue to live as a householder.' Having come to this conclusion all on her own, Sunandā then returned home. The monks too went back to their dwelling, taking Vajra with them. When the monks realized that in his determination to become a monk the little Vajra refused to nurse anymore, even at his young age, they ordained him and then gave him back to the nuns. Sunandā totally lost interest in the pleasures of worldly life, on account of the ripening of her good karma. She became a nun and was ordained by a leading monk in the same lineage. Vajra read on his own and listened to his teacher expound the eleven *pūrva* texts; brilliant, the Blessed Vajra studied the doctrine, possessed as he was of the ability to learn the whole from just one word. Vajra lived with the nuns until he was eight years old, at which time the great ascetics, filled with joy, took him with them to their lodgings.

(from the *Pariśiṣṭaparvan* of Hemacandra, Ch. 12)

3

The Monk Sukośala

King Kīrtidhara had become a monk. He wandered from place to place, performing extreme asceticism, as solid in his forbearance as the earth itself, his only bodily covering the dirt that clung to him; he was devoid of pride, noble in thought. His body was emaciated from fasting; he was steadfast in his resolve. His head was bare; it shone with a special lustre that had been imparted to it by the ritual of plucking out his hair that he had performed when he renounced the world. His long arms hung down and his gaze was fixed directly in front of him. He walked naturally with a gait like that of a noble elephant in rut. He was unmoved by anything, calm and collected, humble and devoid of all desires. He carried out the rules for a monk as they were set down; his mind was pure in its compassion; he was devoid of the stain of affection and suffused with the glory of the monastic life. As he wandered among the houses he came to the house in which he had formerly lived. That sage, having fasted for a long time, now entered his former home in search of alms. Sahadevī, who had been his wife, was looking out the window just then and when she saw him her face turned red with rage. Her lips pressed tightly together, that wicked woman commanded the doorkeepers, 'Chase away this monk who cares nothing for the sanctity of the family, before the innocent, tender young prince, beloved of all, naturally soft-hearted, sees him. And if I ever see any other naked ascetics here in this house, then I shall punish you all, O doorkeepers, mark my words! For that one, without a trace of compassion, abandoned his own son, who was just a baby. Ever since that moment I have lost all patience with the likes of him. People like him despise the glory of kingship, which is the preserve of heroes. They cause even vigorous men to become disgusted with the activities of this world.' The doorkeepers, sticks in hand, chased the monk away, obedient to the cruel words that came from her mouth.

All the ascetics were then banished from the city, in an effort to ensure that the prince in his palace would never even hear the word 'religion'. Now his wet nurse, Vasantalatā, heard how that heroic monk was cut by the chisel of cruel words; she saw, too, how he was chased away, and was filled with grief. She recognized the monk as her former master King Kīrtidhara, and ever loyal to him, she began to cry loudly and uncontrollably. The prince Sukośala rushed to her when he heard her crying. Trying to comfort her, he asked, 'Mother, tell me, who has wronged you? My mother only gave me birth, but in truth my body is what it is now because of the milk you gave it. You are more important to me even than my own mother. Now tell me who, eager to enter the jaws of death, has insulted you? Even if it was my own mother who hurt you, I will punish her. You can be sure that I will treat harshly anyone else who has caused you this pain.'

And so it was that the nursemaid, Vasantalatā, with difficulty stopped the flood of tears from her eyes and explained to the prince what had happened. 'Your father installed you on the throne, and fearful of the many pitfalls of transmigratory existence, which is like a cage that traps living beings, he betook himself to the forest to practice asceticism. Today he came to your house in search of alms and he was violently turned back by the doorkeepers, who were acting on your mother's instructions. When I saw him being rudely expelled I was unable to contain my grief, and that is why, my child, I cried like this. Who would dare to insult me, when you hold me in such high regard? Now I have told you why I cry. When I think of all that your father did for me, a blazing fire of sorrow consumes my body. Surely, I only live this life of misery now that your father has gone, because I do not have the good fortune to die; my body seems as indestructible as if it were made of iron. Because your mother is afraid that if you see a naked Jain monk, you will want to renounce the world, all ascetics have been barred from entering the city. You see, it is the tradition of your family that the king installs his son on the throne and retires to the forest to become a monk. Surely, now you understand why the ministers have decided that you can never leave this house. Even when you are allowed to walk the streets outside, you are actually still within the palace, led about by the clever ministers.'

Now when Sukośala heard all that she said, he quickly descended from the upper storey of the palace. He threw aside all the marks of kingship, like the royal umbrella. Radiant nonetheless, he proceeded to leave on foot; his feet were soft and lovely like lotuses. He asked everyone, 'Have you seen a most excellent monk come this way?' In his eagerness he found his father. The servants, who had followed him out of the palace carrying the insignia of royalty, were caught off guard; they were confused and did not know what to do. Three times the prince circumambulated the monk, who was seated on a stone surface that was free of living creatures. His eyes were filled with tears and his thoughts were pure. He raised his hands and folded his palms in reverence. Filled with affection, he bowed down to the monk. His hands folded, he stood before the monk in all humility, as if he were ashamed that the monk had been chased away from his house. And then he spoke, 'Until now I have slept the deep sleep of delusion. But now you have awakened me, just as the thundering roar of clouds might awaken a man who slept in a house consumed by a blazing fire. Grant me your favour, O Lord! Consecrate me as a monk under your tutelage. Rescue me from the terrors and miseries of transmigratory existence.'

No sooner had Sukośala, his head bowed low, finished speaking these words, than the royal retainers arrived on the scene. His despondent wife Queen Vicitramālā had come too, though the way had been particularly difficult for her, since she was in an advanced stage of pregnancy. She was accompanied by many women from the harem. Hushed sounds of crying, like the buzzing of bees, came from the women, who realized that Sukośala was about to become a monk.

Sukośala, free of any desire for worldly things, spoke. 'It may well come to pass that the child Vicitramālā is carrying is a boy. I give to him my kingdom.' And then, cutting the bonds of desire, burning up the snares of affection, breaking asunder the chain that is the family, throwing aside the kingdom as if it were no more than a worthless blade of grass, Sukośala cast off all his jewellery, along with all his inner and outer attachments. He sat calmly in the lotus posture and pulled out the hair on his head. Sukośala received the vows of the monk from his preceptor, and then, calm at heart, he set off with his father. He wandered the good Earth, as if making offerings to her of lotuses at every step, with the rosy rays that came from his feet. Everywhere people looked at him in amazement. Sahadevī died harbouring evil thoughts; that wicked woman, who did not believe in the right religion, was reborn as an animal.

Sukośala and his father wandered from place to place, stopping when the sun went down. The rainy season came upon them, darkening the expanse of the sky. It looked as if hosts of black clouds had been painted onto the surface of the sky, while here and there a string of cranes crossed the sky, like so many water lilies scattered in worship. Plump kadamba buds, resounding with the hum of bees, seemed to sing a paean of praise to the rainy season, that was now king. The entire world seemed covered by chunks of black collyrium, as big as lofty mountains. The sun and moon seemed to have fled, frightened by the roar of thunder. As the rain poured down in torrents it was as if the sky itself was melting, while the earth, delighted, donned a new blouse of green grass. The surface of the earth, once bumpy, not level, was entirely smoothed over by the rush of water that flowed over it so quickly. In the same way the difference between good and bad, high and low, is erased in the mind of a wicked person. On the ground the torrents of water roared, while in the sky the clouds thundered; it was as if both of them were in hot pursuit of their enemy, summer. The mountains, covered with new sprouts and adorned by waterfalls, could themselves be mistaken for clouds that fell from the sky, too heavy now with water to float any longer. Bright red beetles glittered along the ground, like chunks of the sun reduced to powder and fallen to the earth. Flashes of lightning rushed from one corner of the sky to the next, like so many eyes of the sky, racing to see which places were filled with water and which needed some more. The heavens were adorned by a multicoloured rainbow, like a beautiful ceremonial arch of unusual height. The rivers, now muddy, overflowed their banks; with their waters swirling in frightening whirlpools, they rushed blindly forward, like women following their own desires. Terrified by the roar of thunder, some women, their eyes darting hither and thither like the eyes of frightened does, could only throw their arms around the pillars in their room, for their husbands were still abroad in the frightful storm. These women, whose husbands were travelling, cast their eyes into the distance, as the roar of thunder crashed through their hearts and agitated their minds.

Noble Jain monks, ever compassionate, sought out a proper place, free from living creatures, to wait out the four months of the rainy season. Jain lay people restricted their comings and goings, so as to minimize the harm they might do living beings; to the best of their abilities they practiced various restraints, ever intent on serving the community of monks.

When the rainy season had arrived with all its might, the two Jain monks, father and son, observing all the rules set down for monks, came upon a cemetery on a mountain, that was difficult to reach and terrifying even to those creatures that normally strike terror in the hearts of others. The densely growing trees let in no light and so the place was covered in a deep darkness; it was frequented by dangerous and predatory creatures, snakes and the like; caves there echoed with the cries of jackals and bears, vultures and other predatory birds. Half-burnt corpses littered the awful place and the ground was pock-marked by pits and holes. In some places the earth was white from the heaps of skulls lying about, while an evil-smelling wind whipped through the place, carrying with it the stench of flesh and fat. There, ghosts and goblins laughed their raucous laugh, and tall trees were encircled by clumps of grass and creepers, like nets encasing their trunks. It was to this horrible burning ground, then, that father and son, their minds pure, chanced to come that June in the course of their monastic wanderings. Free from desires, there they undertook their rainy season fast, living under a tree, subsisting only on the pure water that they strained through leaves. Some time they sat in meditation in the lotus posture; some time they stood stock still in concentration; in these and in other yogic postures, the two passed the rainy season.

Then at last autumn arrived, the season in which men seem more eager than ever for work; like the dawn it brought light to all the world. Some pale, tremulous clouds could still be seen in the sky, like wispy blossoms of the cane plant. In the sky, now free of clouds, appeared the sun, friend to the lotuses, just as the Jina, friend to the righteous, appears at the end of the degenerate age in the cycle of time. The moon was resplendent among the host of stars, like a fine young swan in the midst of a pond of blooming lilies. The world was awash in moonlight, like a sea of milk released from the moon, lord of the night, as if from a dike. The clear rivers, their banks softly marked by waves, spoke gently to the world with the cooing of cranes and kraunca and cakravāka birds. In the ponds, the clusters of lotuses, bees skipping among them, perked up, like righteous people suddenly freed from the stain of false belief. At night men, having enjoyed many objects that delighted their senses, sported with their lovers on the lower terraces of their mansions that were strewn with flowers. Couples, once separated, were reunited and great parties were held, in which friends and family took part.

Now that October had come, all the Jain monks, rich in their austerities, resumed their wanderings, setting out for those places where once the Jinas had performed special acts and now people gathered in worship and celebration. Those two monks, Sukośala and his father Kīrtidhara, completed their rainy season austerities, and in strict obedience to the laws laid down for monks they headed toward human settlement in order to break their fast. The tigress, who had been Sahadevī in its previous birth, saw them and was filled with anger; she shook her mane that was wild and red like blood. Her face was made hideous by her huge fangs and her red eyes sent out sparks; her tail was curled high above her head and she tore the earth with her claws as she walked. Looking like death incarnate, she let out a deep growl. Her red tongue hung out of her mouth and her powerful body trembled. She looked like the midday sun as she advanced to pounce with all her might on Sukośala. The two monks, both exceedingly handsome, saw the tigress about to attack, and with firm resolve they stood there in a posture of meditation. The cruel tigress began to rip the monk Sukośala apart, starting from his head. When she was finished she dropped to the ground. Blood gushed from the tattered body of the monk, which looked like a mountain with waterfalls made red by the minerals dissolved in the water. Then that wicked tigress stood in front of the monk and began to eat him, feet first.

See, O King Śreṇika, what delusion can cause a person to do; the mother devours her beloved son, limb by limb. What can be more painful than to see how relatives, deluded by things that have happened in a past birth, become cruel enemies. That monk, who was as steadfast as Mount Meru, reached the highest level of meditation and became Omniscient. Shortly thereafter he was released from his body. The gods with their king and the anti-gods gathered at the spot where he had died and joyfully worshipped his bodily remains with bouquets of divine flowers.

The tigress was awakened to the Truth by Kīrtidhara's gentle words. She renounced everything and died a pious death. She went to heaven. Kīrtidhara, too, gained Omniscience. The gods celebrated his Omniscience as well, when they came to honour Sukośala. Having bowed down at the feet of the two monks and having celebrated their acquisition of Omniscience, the gods and anti-gods returned to wherever they had come from. Whoever learns about the greatness of Sukośala is free from all troubles and lives happily for a long time.

(from the *Padmapurāṇa* of Raviṣeṇa, Ch. 22)

CELANĀ

There was on this earth a city named Pāṭaliputra, which was like the city of the gods and was the dwelling place of wise men. The famous king Viśākha ruled there, having conquered all his enemies with his sword held high. His wife was named Viśākhā, she had eyes like lotus leaves and feet and hands like lotuses; her lovely face was like a fully opened lotus blossom. They longed for a son and one was born to them; they named him Vaiśākha. He was a veritable ocean of virtue and was humble, although his fame spread far and wide. With all due ceremony Vaiśākha married Kanakaśrī, whose body glowed with the lovely shining golden radiance of her skin.

One day Vaiśākha and his new bride, Kanakaśrī, were chatting together on the rooftop of their mansion. Vaiśākha was busy putting jewels on his beloved, when his childhood friend, now a monk named Munidatta, in the course of his wanderings stopped at their house for alms. As soon as he saw the monk, Prince Vaiśākha left his wife's side and went to greet him, feelings of joy and devotion rippling through his body. He bowed down to the monk and led him into the house, where he gave the monk all kinds of food to eat. When the monk finished his meal and was about to leave, the prince bade his wife farewell and went with him.

He realized that worldly existence is worthless; he realized that the body is perishable and subject to disease, and knowing these things Vaiśākha wasted no time in becoming a monk under the guidance of Munidatta. Kanakaśrī realized that her husband had become a Jain monk, practicing austerities; but she clung fiercely to false religious beliefs. She died and became a troublesome demi-goddess.

One day this demi-goddess saw a monk. Using her supernatural knowledge, she recognized him as her former husband. She was filled with anger as she thought, 'This cruel and shameless man abandoned me when I was in the prime of my youth. Now that I am angry, let us see what kind of austerities he can perform.' When it was time for the solitary monk, frail from a month-long fast, to take some food, she caused him to have an erection. The monk, who had performed severe penances, had fasted for a month and was ready to break his fast. He had entered the city of Rājagṛha and stopped at some house.

Celanā saw the ascetic, emaciated from his fasting, coming into her courtyard. She got up at once to welcome him. The demi-goddess, who had been Kanakaśrī in her past birth, saw the ascetic standing there ready to break his fast and she caused his organ to swell. Celanā, filled with devotion, realized that the monk was in trouble and she concealed him from public view with a piece of cloth, afraid that people would speak ill of him. The monk, thinking only of his disgust for things of this world, finished his meal, and honored by Celanā, who bowed down to him, he quickly left her house.

This lord of monks went to Mount Vipula. There, through the power of meditation, he destroyed all the obstructing karmas and attained Omniscience. The kings of the gods felt their thrones tremble and they knew that the monk Vaiśākha had attained Omniscience; they hastened to the spot. All the gods, including Śakra, worshipped the Omniscient one with flowers and incense, their hands held above their heads in reverence. When Celanā and the other people heard that the ascetic Vaiśākha had attained Omniscience, they too joyfully went to bow down to the Omniscient One. There, in the assembly of gods, Celanā, filled with devotion, asked, 'Tell me, why were you subjected to such a torment?' The monk, hearing Celanā's question, replied, 'There once was a terribly cruel woman named Kanakaśrī, who had lively darting eyes. Someone named Vaiśākha, overcome by great lust, married her. This Kanakaśrī was evil and terrifying, like a poisonous snake. One day the monk Munidatta, in the course of his wanderings, came to my house. We had been friends before and so I treated him to a meal of excellent food. I followed that monk and left the house of Kanakaśrī. Shortly thereafter I became a monk under his guidance. When she heard that I had become a monk, that wicked woman at once embraced false views. She died and was reborn as this terrible demi-goddess. That treacherous creature used her supernatural knowledge and recognized that I, her former husband, was the ascetic performing penances; driven by the force of her undying hatred for me, she caused me to have an erection. I had fasted for a month before I came to your house. As I stood there waiting to eat, she caused me to have an erection. But you knew that I had fasted for a month, and in your great devotion, you protected me by placing that cloth there. I ate in your house and was saved from that trial. I practiced meditation here on this mountain, where I stood motionless in concentration. Through the fire of my meditation I burned up the obstructing karmas, that were like so much firewood, and I attained Omniscience, which reveals everything in the universe.

'I had abandoned this woman, a new bride in the full blossom of her youth, after only seven days, in order to become a Jain monk. She died, clinging to false beliefs, and became a troublesome demi-goddess.It was she who created this torment for me. I have told you everything that happened in answer to the question that you asked; firm in the right belief, you have protected me.'

When the Omniscient One had thus explained what had happened to him, the gods and anti-gods were astonished, and they bowed their heads to him in worship. Indra and the other gods, having bowed down to the Omniscient One in joy, and Celanā and the other people, all returned to their homes. The Omniscient Vaiśākha then destroyed all of his remaining karmas, so that they were like burnt pieces of rope. He attained Liberation, which is an ocean of Bliss. Just as Celanā protected this monk, so should others protect all of those who practice the true religion.

(from the *Bṛhatkathākośa* of Hariṣeṇa, Ch.8)

5

BHADRABĀHU AND VARĀHA

In the South, in the city of Pratiṣṭhāna, lived two young brahmin boys called Bhadrabāhu and Varāha, both without a penny to their names and with no one to look after them, and both gifted with much native intelligence. Now the Jain monk Yaśobhadra, who was one of those rare individuals to possess knowledge of the fourteen ancient scriptures, chanced to come to that city. Bhadrabāhu and Varāha heard him preach. This is what he said:

'Pleasures, in all their many forms, are treacherous and impermanent, and from them arises this cycle of births. O see here now, all you people, why do you look for what is eternal and true in all of this? Your doings are in vain!

'Make your mind pure and calm, free from the snares of all your desires, and concentrate it in meditation on that highest abode of eternal bliss, if you trust in my words.'

As soon as they heard these words they were awakened

to the truth, and when they got home they took counsel with each other. 'Why do we lead our lives in vain? To begin with we have no money to get pleasures for ourselves; we should instead practice religion.

'Listen, O mind of mine, let him lust after the taste of worldly pleasures, before whom walk bards, singing praises; let him hanker after sensual delights, who walks in step with gifted poets from Southern lands, bantering with them in well-honed verses, and who hears behind him all the while the enticing jangling of the bracelets of the young women who wave ceremonial fans over him in honour. But if a man lacks all this, well then, O mind, he should direct you at once into the stillness of meditation on the Supreme Truth.'

Thinking this, both the brothers became monks.

Bhadrabāhu became a famous monk, a leader in the monastic community, conversant with the fourteen ancient scriptures and possessed of the thirty-six qualities of a holy man. He was celebrated as the author of commentaries to these ten texts: the *Daśavaikālika*, *Uttarādhyayana*, *Daśāśrutaskandha*, *Kalpa*, *Vyavahāra*, *Āvaśyaka*, *Sūryaprajñapti*, *Sūtrakṛta*, *Ācārāṅga*, and the *Ṛṣibhāṣita*. He also wrote a text which was entitled the *Saṃhitā* of Bhadrabāhu. Now at that time there also lived the Jain monk Ārya Sambhūtivijaya, who was also one of those rare individuals gifted with knowledge of the fourteen ancient scriptures. It came time for the Glorious monk Yaśobhadra to sojourn in Heaven. Bhadrabāhu and this Sambhūtivijaya, cherishing great affection for each other, wandered separately around the land of India. They were like suns that make bloom the lotuses that are the fortunate souls ready to accept the true doctrine.

Now Varāha was also a learned man. But he stood high atop the mountain of terrible pride and he kept asking his brother Bhadrabāhu to install him as a leader of the group of monks. Bhadrabāhu told him, 'Brother, true it is that you are learned and that you carry out all your duties with care, but you are stained by pride. I cannot give the office of a leading monk to someone who suffers from pride.' Though these words were true they did not appeal to Varāha, for it is said that the words of a teacher, even when they are crystal clear like pure spring water, sting the ears of a disciple who is not fit for receiving the true doctrine. And so it came to pass that Varāha abandoned his monastic vows. He returned to his earlier false beliefs and began to dress and behave as a brahmin once more.

He boasted that he had written a new text known as the *Saṃhitā* of Varāha, which in fact was based on the knowledge that he had acquired during the time he had been a Jain monk. But he told everyone, 'I have been studying the position of the planets and heavenly bodies ever since I was a child. And I have always been totally absorbed in this pursuit. Once, just outside the city of Pratiṣṭhāna I happened to draw an astrological calculation on a rock. When evening came I left my calculations there and went home to sleep. In my dreams I suddenly remembered that I had not erased my scribblings. And so I went back there to erase what I had written. There on the rock on which I had written my astrological calculations sat a lion. No matter, with one hand I stroked his belly and with the other I erased the notes I had made. At that the lion turned into the Sun God right before my very eyes. He spoke to me, 'Son, I am pleased with your firmness of determination and your devotion to the science of astrology. I am the Sun; ask of me some boon.' I, for my part, then replied, 'O master! If you are pleased with me, then let me ride in your chariot awhile and show me all the heavenly bodies in their courses.' And so it came to be that I was permitted to roam the heavens with the Sun in his very own chariot. And partaking of the nectar of immortality that he magically transferred into my body, I felt no pang from hunger or thirst or any other unsatisfied bodily need. And when I had accomplished my task, I bade farewell to the Sun and I returned to this world to roam around and serve the earthly realm with my knowledge. That is why I am called 'Varāha of the Sun, Varāhamihira.'

He did not hesitate to spread all sorts of tales like this. And because there was just the slightest grain of possibility in all of his stories he came to be greatly honoured in the world. In the city of Pratiṣṭhānapura he won over the King Śatrujit with his many talents. And the king made him his own court priest. So it is that they say:

> A man's fine qualities lead him to a position of respect, not any fiddle-faddle about his birth and family; we treasure a flower grown in the woods, but throw away in disgust the dirt that comes from our very own bodies.

Now he began to abuse the Śvetāmbaras, saying, 'What do those old crows know about anything? Like naughty schoolchildren confined to their rooms they mutter and mumble to themselves, buzzing like flies, wasting all their time. Oh well, let them do what they want. Why should I care anyway what they do?' The lay disciples who heard his taunts were pained by his words; why, their heads throbbed as they heard them. They gathered together and said, 'What use is it to be alive if we must just stand by and hear our teachers being abused? What can we do? The king honours this Varāhamihira, considering him to be a man of many talents, and people do say, "He who is honoured by kings is honoured by the world." There is nothing we can do about that. But we can summon Bhadrabāhu, at least.' And this is exactly what they did. The Glorious Bhadrabāhu arrived there. The lay disciples welcomed him with a great celebration in his honour, and with such pomp and ceremony as to excite the envy of anyone watching. They lodged their teacher in comfortable quarters. The members of the king's court were daily treated to a feast of lectures delivered by Bhadrabāhu. Varāha was not a little chagrined by Bhadrabāhu's arrival; nonetheless there was nothing he could do against him.

In the meantime a son was born to Varāhamihira. Delighted at the birth, he spent a vast sum of money entertaining his friends and making donations to the poor. And for all of this he was even more greatly honoured in the community. He proclaimed before the king and all the courtiers in the royal assembly hall, 'My son will live a hundred years.' And at his house he gave party after party in celebration of the birth. One day Varāha publicly declared, 'Now see here. Even though he is my very own brother, Bhadrabāhu did not come to the party I gave in honour of the birth of my son. Henceforth he shall be an outcast amongst us, never to be invited to any of our family festivities.' When they heard these words, the lay disciples told Bhadrabāhu, 'This is the kind of thing he is going around saying. You must go to his house one day. It is not right that the enmity between you should grow any more.' The Glorious Bhadrabāhu instructed them, 'Why do you make me undertake not just one but two difficult tasks? This child that has been born to Varāhamihira will be killed by a cat in the middle of the night when he is just seven days old. And when he dies I shall have to go anyway to express my condolences.' At this the lay disciples said, 'But that brahmin proclaimed before the king himself that the child has a life span of one hundred years. And now you say otherwise. What are we to believe?' The Glorious Bhadrabāhu told them, 'Truth depends on corroboration. For that is something that cannot happen if what a man says is untrue.' The lay disciples were silent.

It was seven days after the birth. And on that very day, when the night was only two watches deep, the wet-nurse sat down with the baby to let it nurse. A heavy iron door bolt fell from the top of the door lintel as someone opened the door to come into the room. And it struck the baby on the head. The child was dead. There was much wailing and crying then in Varāha's house. A crowd gathered. And Bhadrabāhu told his lay disciples, 'It is a monk's sacred duty to relieve people of their grief. I must go there at once.' The teacher then went there, accompanied by hundreds of his lay disciples. Varāha, though dazed and wounded by grief, was properly respectful to him and rose to greet him. And he said to him, 'Teacher! Your prediction has come true. The only thing that was not exactly right was that you said a cat would kill him, but the door bolt has killed him instead.' Bhadrabāhu said, 'There is a line drawing of a cat on the tip of that iron door bolt. I did not speak untruthfully.' They brought the door bolt and examined it; it was exactly as Bhadrabāhu had said.

Varāha then said, 'I am not as pained by the death of my son as I am by the fact that the prediction, which I made before the king, that my child would have a life-span of a hundred years, has turned out to be false. I curse those books of mine which I trusted so when I boasted of my great knowledge. They are all a bunch of liars. I'll wash their filthy mouths with soap and water.' And with these words he had the servants fill cauldrons with water. As soon as he was about to carry out his threat and wash the books with water, Bhadrabāhu grabbed him by the arms and stopped him: 'Why should you be angry at the books when the fault was yours alone? It was your own failure to understand them that led you to make false conclusions. These books do in fact record what the Omniscient One said, only it is not so easy to find someone who understands them correctly. I can show you the very places where you went astray; it is you yourself whom you should be cursing. You know yourself what people often say:

> The favour of the king, youth, riches, good-looks, high birth, valour in battle, learning, all these things make a man drunk even though they are not wine.

'And how can a drunkard have the subtle understanding that is necessary to comprehend a difficult treatise? You must not destroy these books.'

With these words Varāha was restrained from his rash act; nonplussed at the turn of events, he did nothing more. At that point a lay disciple, who had been quite upset by Varāha's denunciation of the Jain doctrine, stepped forward and said,

'Wretched little worms you are, who glow in the deep darkness of night. Now the world is aglow with the brilliance of the midday sun. Even the moon does not dare to show its light. Wretched little glow worm, look what's happened to you now!'

And with these words he beat a hasty retreat. Varāha was exceedingly pained. By this time the king himself had arrived on the scene. The king told him, 'Do not grieve. O wise man, this is the way of the world.' At that a minister of the king, who was a Jain devotee, spoke up, 'The new teacher is also here, the one who predicted that the boy would live only seven days. He is indeed great, for his words have proved to be true.' Someone then pointed out Bhadrabāhu to the king, saying, 'This is the one.' With those words the brahmin was made even more miserable; he alone could have described his own mental torment. The king departed; Bhadrabāhu too departed, and finally the crowd dispersed. The king accepted the Jain doctrine and became a lay disciple.

Varāha in his humiliation became a Vaiṣṇava monk and endured all sorts of penances out of ignorance. On his death he became a demi-god who was hostile to the Jain faith. With all his hatred, though, he was not able to trouble any of the monks, for it is true what they say, "Austerities are like a suit of armour made of the hardest diamond; they permit a sage to repel the attacks of others just as armour repels swarms of arrows deftly shot at it." And so Varāhamihira began instead to torment the lay disciples. He caused disease to occur in every house. Distressed and suffering, the lay devotees approached Bhadrabāhu, 'O Blessed One! That even while you are here with us we are so tormented by diseases is proof of the saying, "Even when he is mounted on an elephant, a man may still be gnawed at by mice".' The teacher answered them, 'Do not be afraid. You remember that Varāhamihira. Now he seeks to harm you all because of the hatred he nourished for you when he was alive. I can protect you even from the hand of the Wielder of the Thunderbolt, Indra, the King of the Gods, should he wish to strike you down.' And then, taking from the ancient scriptures such hymns as the hymn which begins with the words, "Lord Pārśva who removes obstacles", he wove a hymn of praise which contained five verses and he recited it before everyone. All of their troubles instantly ceased. Even today those who desire to be rescued from some difficulty recite this hymn. It is like a wonderful wishing jewel with unimaginable powers. It is said that after Bhadrabāhu his student the Glorious Sthūlabhadra also possessed knowledge of the fourteen ancient scriptures and defeated many rivals in debate.

(from the *Prabandhakośa* of Rājaśekharasūri, p. 2)

THE GLORIOUS JĪVADEVA

There is in Gujarat a prosperous town named Vāyaṭa, which was founded by the God Vāyu, God of the Wind. In that town there lived a wealthy merchant named Dharmadeva. His wife was called Śīlavatī; she was like the Goddess of Domestic Prosperity and Bliss incarnate. They had two sons, Mahīdhara and Mahīpāla. Mahīpāla only wanted to amuse himself; he never studied any of the traditional skills. Scolded by his father, he left home in anger and went abroad. The merchant Dharmadeva passed on to the other world. And Mahīdhara also left the world; he became a Jain monk under the tutelage of the Glorious Jinadatta, who belonged to the lineage of monks known as the Vāyaṭa Gaccha. He became a leader of the monastic community and his name as a monk was Rasillasūri.

Now it happened that Mahīpāla, too, became a monk; in the East, in the city Rājagṛha, he became a Digambara Jain monk and he was honored for his learning and known as a great teacher. His name as a monk was Suvarṇakīrti. His teacher Śrutakīrti gave him two magic spells, the one enabling him to summon the protecting Goddess Cakreśvarī, and the other enabling him to enter into someone else's dead body and reanimate it. When Dharmadeva went to heaven, Śilavatī was deeply saddened, for what they say is true:

> Like a river without the ocean, like the night without the moon, like a lotus pond without the sun to make it bloom, so is a good woman without her husband.

She learned from someone who had come from Rājagṛha that her son, who was now called Suvarṇakīrti, was there, and she went there to see him. She found Suvarṇakīrti. Both son and mother felt great affection for each other. One day she told Suvarṇakīrti, 'Your father has gone to heaven. You are now a monk here. But your brother, Mahīdhara, has also achieved fame as a monk; he occupies a position of great respect in the Śvetāmbara Jain community and is known as the monk Rasilla. He is active in Vāyaṭa. You two should get together, settle your differences and espouse the same faith.'

She brought Suvarṇakīrti back to Vāyaṭa and the two brothers were reunited. Suvarṇakīrti's mother told him, 'Son, become a Śvetāmbara. Suvarṇakīrti replied, 'Let Rasilla follow in my footsteps and become a Digambara monk.' When things had come to this impasse, the mother prepared two dishes for them to eat. Now one of the dishes she made had been specially prepared for them and it was rich and delicious. The other was nothing special; it was just taken from the usual cooking that she had done for everyone else in the household. She summoned the Digambara first. He ate the first dish, the specially prepared rich food, to his heart's content. He didn't even so much as cast a glance at the ordinary food in the second dish. Two students of Rasilla then arrived. They both took the ordinary fare, desirous of burning off the effects of the bad deeds they had done in the past through the correct observance of their monastic vows. After everyone had eaten, the mother said to the Digambara, 'Son, these Śvetāmbaras are pure. You don't seem bothered by any rule that says that a Jain monk cannot accept food that has been specially prepared for him. These Śvetāmbaras, on the other hand firmly declare:

> The monk who accepts food that has been specially prepared for him and does not refuse such delicacies, indeed hankers after them, must be considered as outside the pale of the true Jain community. Such a monk fails in his duties.

'And these Śvetāmbaras steadfastly practice what they preach. For this reason, you should join their group if you truly are seeking final release from the bonds of this world.'

Suvarṇakīrti, brought to his senses by these words of his mother, became a Śvetāmbara monk. His name as a monk was Jīvadevasūri, and it was a name that soon became known all over the world. He wandered from place to place, accompanied by five hundred monks. And this Glorious Monk, a leader among monks, destroyed forever the disease of false belief for those noble souls whose time had come for them to accept the true faith, showering on them the magic healing elixir of his preaching of the true doctrine.

One day a strange ascetic showed up at one of his lectures. In fact he was trying to master a certain magic spell that would enable him to conquer all the three worlds, heaven, earth and the nether world. To that end he was in search of a man who possessed the thirty-two marks of greatness. Now at that time in history there were only three such men alive. One was King Vikramāditya; the second was the Glorious Monk Jīva, and the third was the ascetic himself. There was no one else on earth who was so great as to bear the entire thirty-two marks of greatness on his person. Now he could not kill the king, but he needed to eat his one daily meal by begging for it with the skull of such a great man as his begging bowl for a full six months in order to accomplish the magic spell. That was why he had come to the Jain monk to try to work black magic on him so that he could murder him and get his skull. But because the monk had an even more powerful spell, a Jain spell, although his monastic robe turned black and rotted, his body was untouched by the ascetic's magic. Then the ascetic paralyzed the tongue of the monk who was standing next to the Great Jīvasūri and whose duty it was to recite the sacred texts. The Great Jīvasūri in turn paralyzed the ascetic's speech in retaliation. Then that one wrote on the ground with a piece of chalk:

'Everyone does a good deed to the person who has done him a service. There's nothing to that. But rare indeed is the man who helps out someone who came to do him harm.

'I came here to work black magic on you. You figured that out and have taken away my powers of speech. Show mercy on me. Release me from your grip. Take pity on me.'

Anyway, this was the gist of what he wrote there. And so, out of compassion, the noble monk released him; the ascetic left Vāyaṭa and took up residence in a monastery just outside the town. The monk called together all the members of his own monastic group and told them, 'That wicked ascetic is staying in a monastery over there. Take care that no monk or nun goes near the place, no matter what.' They all accepted this prohibition without any dissent. But then two nuns, simple souls, got curious and they went to that very place that had been forbidden to them. The ascetic saw them there and brought them under his control with some magic powder so that they never left his side. The Jain monk, Jīvadevasūri, remaining right there in his own lodgings, made a grass effigy. When he cut off the hand of the effigy, the ascetic's hand fell off. The ascetic released the two nuns. They were restored to their normal selves after they washed their heads, removing the last vestiges of the ascetic's magic spells.

Now one day in Ujjain, King Vikramāditya decided to start a new era which bore his name. In commemoration of that great event he sent the minister Nimba to Gujarat as part of his larger plan to free all his territories of poverty and make every place in his realm rich and prosperous. That Nimba built a temple to the Glorious Mahāvīra in Vāyaṭa. The Glorious Jīvadevasūri performed the consecration ceremony for the image in this temple.

At exactly that time there was in Vāyaṭa a merchant named Lalla who was a devout follower of the false faith. He began right then and there to carry out a costly and lavish Vedic sacrifice. All the brahmins gathered. Oppressed by the smoke from the sacred fire, a snake fell out of a nearby tree and landed on the edge of the fire pit. The cruel brahmins picked up that poor creature and hurled it right into the fire. Seeing that, Lalla was suddenly disgusted with the brahmins. He said, 'Look how cruel they are; they actually enjoy taking the lives of living beings. I do not need to make men such as these my teachers in matters of religion.' And with those words, he dismissed all the brahmins and returned to his own home. He looked everywhere for a religious teacher. One day at midday a pair of monks who were the disciples of the Glorious Jīvadevasūri came to his house for alms. He was pleased with their demeanour and the way they took only pure food. He asked the two monks, 'Who is your teacher?' They told him it was the Glorious Jīvadevasūri. Lalla went to see him. He formally became a lay devotee, accepting the twelve rules of conduct for a lay disciple. One day Lalla told him, 'I had set aside a lakh of gold as a donation on the occasion of the festival to the Sun God. I have spent half of that sum. Please take the other half.' The teacher did not accept the money, for he was without any greed or desire for worldly wealth. Lalla was ever more pleased with his new teacher than before. The teacher instructed him, 'You must bring to me the gift that you will receive tonight while you are in the middle of washing your feet.' Obedient to his teacher's words Lalla went home.

That evening someone brought him a gift of two bulls. Lalla brought them to his teacher. The teacher told him, 'Let these bulls go on their own. Build a temple on the spot where they stop.' Again, obeying his teacher's words, Lalla released the bulls. The two bulls then went as far as the village Pippalana and then just stopped somewhere there. At that very place Lalla began to construct a temple. When it was finished, a strange Śaiva ascetic arrived on the scene. He declared, 'There is a flaw in this temple.' The people asked, 'What is the flaw?' He said, 'There is a woman who will haunt it.' Lalla had heard all of this and he went back and told his teacher what was happening. The teacher said, 'You must rid the spot of that offending ghost and then rebuild the temple. Lalla! Do not worry about where the money will come from. The Goddesses whose task it is to look after the temple will provide all the money that you will need.' They began to dismantle the temple. They heard a voice, 'Do not take down this temple.' They told the teacher Jīvadevasūri about the voice. He withdrew into meditation. The superintending Goddess appeared. She said, 'I am the daughter of the king of Kanyakubja. My name is Mahaṇīka. A long time ago, when I was living in Gujarat, Muslim armies invaded. I fled, but the soldiers pursued me and in my terror I jumped into a well. I died and became a demi-god. I will not permit you to clear the ground by digging up the bones of my body. Make me the superintending Goddess of your temple and I shall make your temple rich and prosperous.'

The teacher agreed to do as she said. On a spot of land that she showed them they built a small shrine to her. And on that very spot they found all the money they needed, so much that they could not even begin to count it. Lalla became the happiest man in the world; no one could have vied with him for that distinction; the Jain community was also pleased. Angry at Lalla, the brahmins placed a dying cow in the Jain temple. It died there. The lay disciples told the teacher about this. Through his magic powers the teacher moved the dead cow and put it in the temple of the brahmins. As they say, 'Plot against another and it happens to you.' Desperate, with no other recourse, the brahmins sought to appease the Glorious Jīvadevasūri, crying out, 'O Jīvadevasūri, rescue us.' The Glorious Jīvadevasūri scolded them and then told them, 'If you all worship in my temple like faithful Jain lay believers and show my successors respect, if you donate a sacred thread made of gold on the occasion of the installation of my successor, and if you promise that you will carry his sedan chair on your own shoulders, then and then only will I remove this cow from your temple.' And they were so desperate that they promised all that he asked. They even fixed the agreement between them in writing, with seals and all. Then the teacher, with his magic, removed the cow from the brahmin temple. All the four castes were pleased at this.

Later when he knew that it was his time to die, the Jain monk, fearing that ascetic who had sought his skull to accomplish his evil magic, instructed the lay disciples to break his skull. He was afraid that if the ascetic succeeded in his designs he would trouble the Jain community. They did exactly as he asked. The ascetic, deprived of any hope for success, cried for a long time.

(from the *Prabandhakośa* of Rājaśekharasūri, p.7)

7

AMARASĪHA

In the midst of the southern sector of Bharaha, which lies in Jambūdīva, there is a fine city called Amarapura, "City of the Gods", which is, in truth, as lovely as the city of the gods and could be described in the same words, if only you know how to play with their meanings. For if the city of the gods has the treasures of Kubera, including the conch, this earthly city has many bards; the greatness of heaven may be proclaimed in thousands of religious texts, while this city has become great on account of the thousands of women who have been exemplary in their faithfulness to their husbands; the city of the gods has Jayanta, son of Indra and the other princes, while this city has victorious princes galore. And finally, if heaven is resplendent with radiant Viṣṇu and the other deities, this city is resplendent with the rays of light that come from shining pearls.

Suggīva was king there.

The sword in his hand glittered like the dark tamāla tree; it looked like the braid of hair that had once belonged to the Goddess of Victory and that he had rudely taken from her in battle.

He had two queens, chief among all the ladies in his harem. Their names were Kamalā and Vimalā. Now it happened that Queen Kamalā became pregnant.

Her pregnancy made her want to see people dying in battle. The king satisfied her pregnancy craving by staging a mock battle in which warriors were cut to pieces with sharp swords. Next she wanted to see a hunt. This desire was fulfilled by staging a hunt in which many animals were slain with all sorts of different weapons. In time the queen gave birth to a boy. The king held a celebration in honor of the birth, and in keeping with the kinds of longing the mother had displayed during her pregnancy, he named the child Samarasīha, "Lion in Battle".

Queen Vimalā also became pregnant. Her pregnancy made her want to save creatures that were being killed by others. The king fulfilled her pregnancy craving by issuing a proclamation that there was to be no taking of life in his realm. She gave birth to a son who brought delight to the hearts of all the people. He was named Amarasīha, "Lion of the Gods". The children were nurtured and taught the arts, and in time they became young men.

Samarasīha was violent, cruel, heartless and evil; the people rejected him, for he had no virtues, only vices.

Amarasīha was compassionate, kind, always eager to aid others. On account of all his virtues the people loved him very much.

Now because all things are impermanent, Suggīva was stricken with a terrible disease and died.

Samarasīha proclaimed himself king, thinking that he was, after all, the older of the two brothers. It is true that a person lacking virtue does not realize how unworthy he is to occupy a position of importance.

Samarasīha was utterly without compassion and did not care about protecting his subjects. He was addicted to hunting and could not be bothered with the affairs of the kingdom. Amarasīha, on the other hand, was filled with compassion for all living beings. He was devoted to helping others and he scrupulously avoided sin, which is the cause of going to hell, as if it were a chain to bind him. Now one day prince Amarasīha went out of the city to exercise the horses. He exercised all the different horses that had come from many different countries, all of them swift and handsome. He then stopped to rest under a tree. There he saw a goat being led away by some man. The goat was talking in its own language. Out of compassion the prince made the man let it go. The goat kept on bleating; it did not stop.

At that the prince, his compassion further aroused, said to the man, 'Where are you taking this goat?'

The man replied, 'If you kill a beast in the sacrifice you get to go to heaven, and so I am taking this goat to kill it.'

The prince said, 'If you can get to heaven by killing an animal, then what could possibly cause a man to go to hell? For they say there is no greater sin than the taking of a life.'

At that moment a Jain monk named Soma, possessed of divine knowledge, arrived on the scene. His gaze was directed at the ground to avoid his doing harm to any living creature, moving and not moving.

When the prince saw the monk, who was like the true religious doctrine incarnate, who was like calm dispassion in motion, he said, 'This sage will settle our dispute.'

Bowing down to the monk, the prince said, 'Remove our doubt. Can a person gain the happiness of heaven by killing a living being that has five sense organs?'

The monk explained, 'O Prince, the torments of hell or rebirth as an animal await a person who slays a living being. In no way can that lead to the happiness of heaven. What more need I say? This goat right here will dispel your doubt.' With this the monk turned to the goat.

'You had this tank dug yourself; you had the trees planted yourself; you made a sacrifice yourself. Now why do you go on bleating in this idiotic way?'

When it heard these words the goat fell silent. The astonished prince said, 'Blessed One! Why did this goat become silent as soon as you recited that verse?' The monk said, 'Noble sir! This man's father was named Ruddasamma. He had this tank dug and he had these trees planted around its borders. Every year he performed a sacrifice in which goats were slain. In time Ruddasamma died. He was reborn as a goat. He was killed by this very man, his very own son, right here in a sacrifice. He was again reborn as a goat and again he was killed. This happened five times. This is his sixth rebirth. Now he does not have that much karma left, having exhausted much of his karma through his repeated suffering. Seeing his own son this goat has remembered his former births; it has been crying, "Son! Why do you kill me? I am your father Ruddasamma. If you do not believe me, I will give you a sign. I will show you a treasure that I buried and hid from you."'

The man said, 'Blessed One! If what he says is true, then let him show me the treasure.' When it heard these words, the goat went inside the house to where the treasure was buried. It began to dig up the ground with its hooves. When it dug at a certain spot the treasure was revealed. The man was convinced; he listened to the Jain doctrine from the monk and became a pious lay Jain. The prince said, 'Blessed One! If this is the result of killing an animal, even when it is enjoined in some religious texts, then I must always show compassion to all living beings.' The goat also heard the true doctrine from the monk and renounced all food. It kept on repeating the words of praise to the five Jain worthies, to the Jinas, to those who have attained Liberation, to the leaders of the monks, to the teachers among the monks and to all the Jain ascetics. It died in meditation and was reborn among the gods. With his supernatural knowledge this god knew his previous births; he recognized the great service the prince Amarasīha had done him and constantly kept watch over the prince. Thus did time pass.

Now one night the goat that had become a god, adorned with a shining crown of jewels and glittering earrings, appeared in the sky and spoke to Prince Amarasīha:

'The king is extremely cruel hearted and cannot bear to see how much all the people love you. He is planning to kill you. You must leave this city and go elsewhere. In time you must return and save the kingdom.'

When the prince heard these words of the god, he left the city with Vimala, the son of the minister, and wandered the earth.

Everywhere he went he received honour from the people on account of his most excellent virtues, as sandalwood is appreciated for its special properties, wherever it may be. In time Prince Amarasīha came to the city Kuṇḍiṇapur.

There the only thieves were the eyes of the lovely fawn-eyed women, which stole the hearts of the young men, for the citizens of that town were to a man all honest.

In that city reigned King Bhāṇu. He cut down his enemies with his dark sword, that was like the lotus the Goddess of Kingship twirls playfully in her hand.

At that time a great plague raged in the city. The king asked the brahmin priests how the plague might be stopped.

They told him, 'Worship the city gods by sacrificing animals to them.' The king's men proceeded to slay the sacrificial beasts.

When Prince Amarasīha saw that slaughter he was moved by compassion and he told the killers, 'Do not kill these animals.'

They replied, 'Who are you to stop us? We are killing these animals on the orders of the king; you would stop us merely by your own say-so?'

With those words, the men set to their task with even greater determination. The prince implored the goat-god, 'Stop this slaughter.'

The god then caused the men's arms with swords poised to strike to stop in mid-air; when the people saw this miracle they quickly reported it to the king.

Astonished King Bhāṇu rushed to the scene. He saw the prince, as handsome as a god.

The prince bowed down to the king and asked, 'Why are these animals being killed? Killing these animals will not stop the plague; the plague will only spread more, just as a fire spreads when fed with grass and chaff.'

King Bhāṇu said, 'Good man, what will put an end to this plague?' The prince replied, 'Lord of men! The power of my magic spell will make a god descend into a suitable receptacle; the god will then tell us clearly how to stop the plague. There is no need for me to say anymore.'

The king had a young virgin brought there and the prince positioned her inside a magic circle. After she was worshipped with various flowers and sandalwood, she pronounced these words:

'This will stop the plague: the water that was used to wash the feet of a person, in whose mind there dwells compassion for all living beings, as the royal swan dwells in a lotus pond.'

At that King Bhāṇu said, 'Good man! How will we know in whose mind dwells compassion for all living beings?' The prince answered, 'There is a way. Call a gathering of people of different religious persuasions.' The king did so.

The prince gave them this portion of a verse to complete:

'. . . whether the eyes of the woman, though she was right in front of me, were marked with collyrium or not.'

Because they had lust in their hearts, all the representatives of religions other than the doctrine of the Jinas completed the verse in such a way as to make it describe the body of the young woman; for example:

'My eyes and lips were on her full round breasts; that is why I did not notice whether the eyes of the woman, though she was right in front of me, were marked with collyrium or not.'

Now as fate would have it, it just so happened that the Jain monk Soma, who had told Amarasīha about the previous births of the goat, arrived on the scene. Here is how he completed the verse:

'Intent as I was on watching where I stepped lest I bring harm to any living being, moving or not moving, I did not notice whether the eyes of the woman, though she was right in front of me, were marked with collyrium or not.'

The prince asked, 'In the mind of which one of these men do you think there is compassion for living beings?'

The king replied, 'If compassion for living beings existed in the minds of any of these, except for the Jain monk, then their words would not be filled with the sentiment of erotic love, as indeed they are.'

And so the entire city was sprinkled with water that had been used to wash the feet of the Jain monk. The plague stopped. The king was pleased.

He said to the prince, 'I can tell in a general way that you are exceptional. But now I would like to know more specific things about you, for example, your place of origin and your family history.'

Vimala then told the king all about the prince, the city he came from, his family, his father and so on. The king gave to the prince his own daughter Kaṇagavaī in marriage.

The king also gave him gifts of horses, elephants, gold and fine cloth. The prince lived there happily, enjoying the pleasures of the senses.

One day messengers came from the city of Amarapura. This is what they told the prince: 'Prince! After you left the city, that Samaraṣīha, addicted to the vice of hunting, failed to protect the kingdom and it was overwhelmed by our enemies. The king was a tyrant and the people turned against him. One day, the ministers, pretending to take aim at a wild beast, let fly their javelins at the greedy king and killed him. You must come now and rescue your kingdom that has no king to protect it.'

When he heard these words, the prince set out for Amarapura, accompanied by a complete army of elephants, horses, footsoldiers and chariots.

When he got there the ministers placed him on the throne. He ruled for a long time, intent on following the doctrine of the Jinas, and when he died he attained a good rebirth.

Samarasīha, devoid of compassion for living beings in this world, was himself slain.

Amarasīha, practicing compassion for all living beings, obtained hundreds and hundreds of pleasures.

(from the *Kumārapālapratibodha* of Somaprabhasūri, p.23)

8

ABHAYASĪHA

The person whose mind trembles at the thought of sin and who protects all living beings out of compassion for them never has anything to fear himself, just like Abhayasīha.

The king Kumārapāla asked the monk Hemacandra, ' 'Blessed One! Tell me, who is this Abhayasīha?' The monk explained, 'O lord of men! Listen and I will tell you.'

'Right here in the land of Bharaha, in the charming village of Kusatthala, was a man of good family, who was in character and in name Bhadda, "Noble". It was a time of great famine and Bhadda was unable to survive. He thought, "I can sustain myself by killing deer and other living beings." And so he took a club and went out of the city. There he saw a rabbit. He rushed at the rabbit to kill it and threw the club straight at it. When the rabbit saw the club coming, it fled in terror. Bhadda threw the club at the rabbit again and again, determined to kill the creature. The rabbit kept running and finally, having no other refuge, it hid between the feet of a monk who was meditating there in the middle of the forest. Now the Forest Goddess, won over by the ascetic's severe austerities, had made a slab of purest transparent crystal and had placed it in front of the monk. The club struck that slab of crystal and with a sound it quickly bounced back and smacked Bhadda right on the forehead. At once Bhadda was knocked unconscious; his eyes shut and he fell to the ground; blood streamed from the wound; his whole body was wracked by pain. Revived by the forest breeze, Bhadda saw the monk in front of him. He said to the monk, 'The evil deed that I committed has borne fruit right here in this very birth. Or perhaps some meritorious deed that I once did has now come to fruition, for somehow this club bounced back and hit me on the forehead; otherwise it might have struck this sage who is deep in meditation. If it had, I would not have found a place even in the seventh hell, after committing such an evil act.'

'At that moment the monk, an ocean of compassion, came out of his meditative state. He said to Bhadda, "O Glorious One, why do you do this sinful deed? Cruel-hearted, why do you kill living beings out of a lust for the taste of their flesh? That sinful act will be the fuel that feeds the fires of hell." Bhadda bowed down to the monk and said, "Blessed One! From now on as long as I live I will never kill a single living being for the sake of its flesh." The monk said to Bhadda, "You are a good soul, destined in the future for release, for you have made a vow never to harm living beings; this is the seed of the tree of the religious life."'

'Bhadda again bowed down to the monk and then returned home. He felt that now that his mind was totally free from any desire to kill a living being, his life was complete. Because of the great merit that he had thus acquired, he somehow managed to get something to eat every day. Now listen to me as I tell you where he was reborn when at the end of his life span he died.

'Here on Jambūdīva, in the central region of the land of Bhāraha, is a city called Seyaviyā, "Made White", which indeed is made white by the rows of its whitewashed mansions. There the golden globes atop the temples look like so many ripe yellow fruits hanging from the trees in heaven.

'Vīrasena was king in that city. He won the affection of all of his subjects with all of his excellent virtues, his fairness, his handsome appearance, his willingness to forgive and his prowess in battle; his virtues were as pleasing to the people as is fine white sandal paste.

'He had a queen named Vappā, who put to shame the women of the gods by her own great beauty. The soul of Bhadda descended into her womb, announced by her dreaming of a lion. She devoted herself to serving all three goals of a human life, the pursuit of wealth, sexual pleasure and religion, and in time gave birth to a son, who brought delight to the minds of the people. The king decreed a lavish celebration be held in honor of the child's birth. When the month of celebration was not yet over, King Māṇabhanga attacked King Vīrasena with a mighty army of elephants, horses, chariots and footsoldiers. Vīrasena went out to meet him with his own army. The battle commenced. As Fate would have it, Vīrasena was killed by Māṇabhanga. Māṇabhanga seized Vīrasena's elephants, horses and encampment. He took possession of the kingdom of Seyaviyā. When Queen Vappā learned of the defeat of the kingdom, she took her son and fled into the forest. There a single footsoldier came upon her. He thought to himself, "I surely am a lucky one; now I have found this fawn-eyed woman, who is as beautiful as a divine damsel. I'll get rid of the child; then I can have all of her love just for myself." And so he said to her, "Lovely lady, abandon this child." Her eyes brimming with tears, she replied, "How could I abandon this child, born from my own womb, the single crowning jewel of all the three worlds?" The soldier told her, "You will have many more children with me." She replied, "If that is to be, it will only be in another birth." And with that she began to weep. The cruel soldier forced her to put the child down. He then grabbed her arm and pushed her forward. He said to her,

'"Why do you cry, O slender-waisted damsel? Forget your despair. Take me as your husband. Do not let your youth go to waste, as useless as a cry uttered in the wilderness."'

'Hearing these cruel words that stung her ears, the queen wept bitterly, tears flowing onto her breasts. She lamented,

'"Alas, O God! What did I do against you in a previous birth, that now you show me no pity and cause me to suffer like this.

'"First there was the death of my husband, the king, who was a treasure of jewel-like virtues, and who was dearer to me than my life.

'"Second was the destruction of the kingdom that was endowed with abundant wealth and a mighty army of elephants, horses, chariots and footsoldiers, that kingdom that was a source of every pleasure a person might desire.

'"Then came the loss of all of those who surrounded me, friends and relatives, whose hearts were full of affection and warmth, and who were imbued with such virtues as humility and goodness.

'"Add to all of this, my wandering alone, afflicted by hunger, thirst and heat, in this desolate forest filled with hundreds of wild beasts, nothing but a torture.

'"But my greatest torment surely was when my jewel of a son was forcibly wrested from my lap and abandoned in that forest.

'"But, wicked Fate you were still not satisfied with all those sufferings you had caused me. Now you want to cast a stain on my chastity, which is as pure as the moon.

'"O my heart! Shameless, heart, unworthy heart! You

must truly be made of diamond not to burst into pieces on hearing the disgusting words this man has said to me."

'As the queen uttered her lament, her heart did indeed break and her breaths left her body.

'The queen died that very instant and became a demi-goddess. With her supernatural knowledge she knew her previous birth.

'She saw her son licking at the base of a rose-apple tree; a ripe fruit, struck by the wind, fell into his mouth.

'That demi-goddess, moved by her love of her child from her previous birth, took the form of a cow and gave him her milk to drink. She protected him from harm.

'A few days later a trader from Seyaviyā named Piyamitta, returning from his journey, stopped his caravan in that forest. He saw the child under the rose-apple tree. He took the child, realizing from the fact that the shadow of the tree did not change its position that the child must have great merit, and realizing from his fair complexion that he was the child of some wealthy and noble family. Delighted, he handed the child over to his own wife Rajjā, who was barren. He let it be known among his friends and relatives that his wife had concealed her pregnancy but had now given birth to a son. When he got back to Seyaviyā he held a celebration in honor of the baby's birth. Thinking that he had found the child, like a lion, unafraid in the forest, he named him Abhayasīha, "Fearless Lion".'

'Sheltered, the child grew up, like a campaka tree in a mountain cave. In time he was entrusted to a teacher, who made him skilled in all of the traditional arts. He reached adolescence, which is like a pleasure grove in which the God of Love roams freely. One night as the boy slept on his golden couch, the demi-goddess, who had once been his mother, spoke to him, "Child! I was once Queen Vappā, the wife of Vīraseṇa, who was the lord of this city. You are the child born of my womb. Your father, Vīraseṇa, was killed by this Mānabhanga. I died too, and became a demi-goddess. This King Māṇabhanga is your enemy, for you are the son of his enemy. Let me give you this magic formula, which will make you invisible as soon as you recite it.' Abhayasīha accepted the magic formula, saying, 'Blessed One, you are very kind to me." The demi-goddess vanished.

'Now King Māṇabhanga was addicted to eating meat. Everything else that a person might eat tasted like straw to him. One day the cook was inattentive and a cat stole the meat that he was going to cook. He could not find any other meat, so he killed a child and cooked him. The king tasted the dish and asked, "Why is the meat so tender and delicious today?" The cook told him the truth. The king in his lust for flesh gave the cook this order, "You must have one prominent citizen killed every day and you must cook his flesh."

'As this command was carried out, the townspeople turned against the king. A man who does evil is his own enemy; it is only natural that others will hate him, too.

'One day this thought entered the mind of King Māṇabhanga, "Is this kingdom firmly established in my line, or is it not?"

'At that moment a fierce wind blew, like the wind at the end of time, destroying all the trees, as Death destroys all hopes and aspirations.

'The sky was covered with the dust raised by the wind, so that nothing could be seen, even gross objects like poles seemed to have fled in fear.

'Darkness, like delusion, spread everywhere, blocking the line of vision, cleverly turning diverse objects into one indistinguishable mass.

'All at once clouds, like wicked men, were everywhere, thundering; lightning flashed, terrifying like the tongue of the God of Death.

'At that instant the king beheld a goblin and his wife in the sky. The duo were chatting to each other, much to the king's great terror and surprise.

'The male goblin said, "O lotus-eyed lady! Let me tell you something that will happen in the future." The goblin's wife said, "My love, tell me. I am all ears."

'The goblin said, "There is no doubt that King Māṇabhanga will fall in just a few days, laden with his many sins of killing living beings."

'The goblin lady asked, "Husband, then who will be king here?"

'The goblin said, "Listen, lovely one! I will tell you right now. That man who will go against the order of the king, who will subdue the best of elephants, and who will abduct the princess Kaṇagavaī, will be our fine king."

'When they had finished this conversation, the goblin pair disappeared. The wind died down. The king had heard what the goblins said; in his mind he was seized with the fear of dying. He gave this order to the city guards, "You must put to death any man who transgresses my commands."

'Now spring came, achatter with the lovely sounds of the cuckoos, that were like the bard of King Love, proclaiming everywhere his great victories.

'The sun with its gentle rays stayed in the north, while even at night a wind blew from the south, fragrant with the perfume of sandalwood.

'The forest was even more beautiful, decked out in new rosy buds, like a lovely lady decked out in a fine red robe, ready for her husband.

'Mango shoots with clusters of bees looked like the blazing flames of passion, ringed with smoke.

'On such a spring night, Abhayasīha was returning from the temple, where he had just seen a dramatic performance. A city guard stopped him, "Sir, halt! Stop a minute. Identify yourself. Who are you?" Abhayasīha did not stop. The guard commanded him to stop in the name of the king. Abhayasīha retorted, "Order your own father about in the name of your king!", and kept right on walking. The city guard unsheathed his sword and ran after him, screaming, "Kill that one! Kill that one!" Seeing him in hot pursuit, Abhayasīha made himself invisible and escaped. The guard was perplexed. The next morning he told the king what had happened. The king said, "What kind a man are you, not to catch him? You're not a man, you're a eunuch!"

'On another occasion the royal elephant, mad with rut, uprooted the post to which it was tied and broke loose. It terrorized the city. Now the king had a daughter Kaṇagavaī, "The Golden One", whose lovely complexion must have put the metal gold to shame. What else could explain why gold is so often melted down by fire; surely, it must willingly immolate itself, humiliated by its defeat! Kaṇagavaī was on her way back from the garden, having worshipped the God of Love, when the mad elephant spotted her. He charged at her and managed almost to grab her. Her retinue began to shout, "Is there anyone in this world who can save our mistress from this terrible elephant, as if from the clutches of the God of Death himself?" As Fate would have it, Abhayasīha heard their cry. Out of compassion he rushed to the spot, shouting, "Scoundrel! You are what your name says; elephant or outcaste, both are the same word! Are you not ashamed to kill a woman?" With those words he struck the elephant on the hind quarters with his fist that was as hard as a thunderbolt. The elephant let go of the princess and began to charge at Abhayasīha. Abhayasīha grabbed him and whirled him around. When the elephant was thoroughly exhausted he jumped onto its back. He grabbed the elephant goad and jabbed it into the elephant's temples. Having brought the elephant under his control he headed for the palace. Word began to circulate among the crowd, "That heroic man is the son of Piyamitta." The daughter of the king looked at him with desire in her eyes.

'Abhayasīha reached the palace; all along the way he was honored by the women of the city with garlands of lotuses. The king saw him and thought to himself, "Judging from his valour and his looks, I would say that he will rule this kingdom. Still, I mustn't give up." And so he commanded his best soldiers, "A mere merchant's son has tamed my elephant. That is an insult to me and to my elephant. Kill him." In the meantime Abhayasīha had brought the elephant back to its post. As he dismounted from the elephant, the warriors rushed at him, shouting, "Kill him! Kill him!" He became invisible and vanished. The warriors, perplexed, retreated. They told the king, "He vanished, just as we were about to strike him." The king said, "You are also a bunch of eunuchs!"

'One day the servant Vasantaseṇā told the king the state that Kaṇagavaī was in and this set the king to thinking. Here is what she said:

'"Kaṇagavaī has seen painted portraits of so many handsome princes, but none of them has made her heart stop.

'"But as soon as she saw him, she fell in love with Abhayasīha, son of Piyamitta, who saved her from the mad elephant.

'"I told her, 'Fawn-eyed lady! He is unworthy of you, a mere merchant's son!' But the princess replied, "I aṃ sure that he is the son of someone from the warrior class.

'"If he were not, how could he have subdued the raging king of elephants, that was like the God of Death himself? A person's nobility of birth is proclaimed by the nobility of his deeds.

'"In truth, if he were not a prince, how could be have stolen my heart? When people are in doubt they must rely on what their hearts tell them.

'"What is more, were I to love someone else, when it was he who rescued me from the danger posed by the elephant, when it was he who gave me my very life, then I would truly be an ingrate."'

'When he heard all of this the king thought, "I still have to kill that fellow." With Vasantasenā right there, he commanded the guard, "Bring Abhayasīha, son of Piyamitta.

He has saved the princess from the danger posed by the elephant. I must reward him." The guard went and conveyed the king's command. Abhayasīha, knowing that the king was against him, nonetheless thought, "The demi-goddess, who was my mother in her past birth, will make sure everything comes out just fine." And so he went to see the king. The king handed him over to his soldiers, thinking, "I will kill him at night when no one is around." They guarded him well. Early the next morning Abhayasīha made himself invisible. The soldiers could not see him, even though he was right there. They said to each other, "He must have fled." The king overheard them. Thinking, "I must take care lest he abduct my daughter," the king hastened to the rooftop apartments of the palace, where Kaṇagavaī stayed. The king fell asleep there and dreamt that Abhayasīha had grabbed Kaṇagavaī by the arm and was making off with her. The king unsheathed his sword and shouted, "Where do you think you are going?" In his anger he forgot that he was on the rooftop and he fell from the building. Before he even hit the ground he was dead. Everyone in the town shouted out with joy, "The wicked one fell by himself."

'As the ministers were debating whom to place on the throne, the demi-goddess spoke to them from the sky, "Place Abhayasīha, son of King Vīraseṇa, on the throne." They all agreed and crowned him king. He married Kaṇagavaī. Having conquered all of the feudatory states, he spent his days enjoying his rule over the kingdom, which never disappointed him, and which gave him everything that he needed to accomplish the three aims of human life, the acquisition of wealth, the pursuit of sexual pleasures, and the perfection of the religious life.

'One day the thought suddenly occurred to him, "What did I do in a previous life that enabled me to get through all of my misfortunes and ultimately attain this happiness of ruling over a kingdom?" A Jain monk named Nāṇasūri, who had exceptional knowledge, came to the city. The king bowed down to the monk and asked him if he could answer this question. The monk explained, "In a previous life you were once about to kill a rabbit, but you did not kill it and you renounced completely the taking of any life. That is why although you went through a time when you had troubles, you eventually attained this happiness of ruling over a kingdom."' At that the king remembered his past birth and he became a pious Jain layman. He supported the Jain mendicants and forbade the taking of life throughout his kingdom. In time he died while intent on meditating on the Jain truths and was reborn in the realm of the gods.

(from the *Kumārapālapratibodha* of Somaprabhasūri, p.33)

9

DURGILĀ

To dissuade her husband, Jambūsvāmin, from leaving her and her co-wives, Padmasenā said to him, 'What happens to people depends entirely on the deeds that they have done. And so you should not renounce this world, but should stay and enjoy yourself with us. What more need I say? There are many examples that could be given to show that one should or should not renounce the world. Listen to this story of *The Clever Lady of the Anklet and the Jackal*.

'"There was a goldsmith named Devadatta in the city of Rājagṛha. He had a son named Devadinna. Devadinna was married to a woman named Durgilā. She was a brazen one, no doubt, and a great beauty. One day she went down to the river to bathe, inflaming with passion the minds of all the young men just by her tantalizing glances. Every inch of her body was covered in gold jewellery and her bright clothes glittered in the sunlight. She made the very bank of the river glow, like some river goddess incarnate. Displaying her two breasts, which were like the fortress of the God of Love, that ample-bosomed lady very slowly took off her clothes. She gave her blouse and her skirt to her friend and then that slender woman proceeded down into the water, with nothing more than a thin bodice covering her breasts. They say that the God of Love was once burnt to ashes by Śiva, but she seemed to revive him fully. Chatting gaily with her friends, she swam from one bank of the river to the other, like some graceful swan. The river seemed to embrace her like a long-lost friend with its wave-like hands that reached out to her from afar. Her eyes darted here and there like the eyes of a frightened doe, and in her eagerness to have some fun in the water she cut through its surface with her hands, like a boat with its oars. As she bathed in the river she scattered the water with her hands, which as they moved looked as lovely as lotuses dancing in the current. As she swam about, her single garment slipped and her hair came loose, while her lips were wet; all in all she looked like a woman just come from the bed of her lover. Some young city-slicker just happened to see her enjoying herself in the river there, looking like some demi-goddess in the water. She had on only a thin garment which was wet and clung revealingly to her body, and that young man felt the stirrings of desire when he looked at her. He called out to her with this verse, 'The river asks you,' 'Are you enjoying your swim? and these trees ask you the same. Likewise, I ask you, bowing my head at your feet.' She replied with this verse, 'Hail, O river! And all the best, O trees. I am at your service, all of you who ask about my swim.'

'"The young man heard her words, which were like a rain of heavenly nectar, making his desire sprout like a blossoming vine. He stood there, rooted to the spot, as if in obedience to the command of his king. And as he stood there wondering, 'Who is this woman?', he saw some children under a tree. They were looking up at its branches, trying to figure out how they could reach the fruit hanging high above them. The young man took a clod of earth and pelted the branches, making the fruit fall to the ground with a loud thud. The children were delighted when he gave them all the fruit they could possibly want, and seeing his chance, he asked them, 'Who is that woman bathing in the river? Where does she live?' In the meantime, Durgilā, thinking only of that young man, finished her swim and went straight home. Day and night both of them kept thinking, 'On what night, on what day, in what place, at what moment shall we meet again?' The young man and the young woman suffered pangs of longing for each other and yearned to be together, like the famed cakravāka birds, who must endure separation from each other each night. And thus they remained, madly in love with each other, for quite some time.

'"One day the young man approached a certain nun, who had been the salvation of many a wanton woman. He won her over by such things as serving her sumptuous meals, and then proceeded to say, 'The daughter-in-law of Devadatta and I are madly in love with each other. Just as the Goddess Fate brings people together, I implore you to bring us together. I approached her once myself and spoke to that lady with lovely eyebrows and I know that she wants me, too. It should be easy for you to fix things for us.' The clever nun agreed to act on the young man's behalf and proceeded to Devadatta's house under the guise of seeking alms. There she saw the daughter-in-law of the goldsmith, busy putting a pot onto the stove. She wasted no time in delivering her message, 'A certain young man, handsome as the God of Love himself, longs to be your lover. He has sent me, O lady with lovely eyes, do not turn me away. Do not waste your youthful beauty; make it count by taking a man who is your equal in looks, age, wit, intelligence and every other quality. Ever since he saw you bathing in the river, O lovely one, he has been like a crazy person; he does nothing but sing your praises. Not even the name of another woman passes his lips.'

'"Durgilā wanted to conceal her feelings and so she cleverly rebuked that nun, shouting at her these harsh words, 'O bald-headed one! Are you drunk that you speak to me in this way? Though I am a woman of good family you speak to me as if I were some slut. O unworthy lady, what are you anyway, a whore yourself, taking everyone else for the same? Get out of my sight. May I never see you again. It is a sin for me just to see you, never mind speak to you!' The nun, having been harshly rebuked by Durgilā, turned to go. Durgilā then pressed her soot-stained hand on the nun's back as if on a white wall. The nun had no idea what Durgilā intended, and she angrily went back to that would-be adulterer and scolded him in turn with these harsh words:

'What a liar you are, telling me "the lady loves me"! That woman is full of herself; why, she thinks she is the very incarnation of wifely chastity. She treated me like a dog. I was a useless go-between, you fool, for you sent me to a woman who is of noble birth and deed. Even the best painter needs a proper wall to paint on. What's more, she was busy in the kitchen and in her anger she slapped me on the back with her soot-stained hand.' When the rogue insisted, the nun showed him the black mark that Durgilā had made on her back. The young man thought to himself, 'Surely this is a secret message that she intends to meet me on the fifth day of the dark half of the month, for she has made a mark in black on this nun's back with all five of her fingers. She really is a clever one, to let me know in this way on what day we shall meet. Courage, courage, I must take heart! But for some reason she hasn't told me where we shall meet. That puts a stumbling block in my path, to be sure.' He spoke again to the nun. 'You did not understand what she was trying to do. There is no doubt of it, she loves me, too. You must go there once more and ask her again to meet me. Mother, do not give up. Courage is the root of all success.' The nun replied, 'She is a chaste woman; she does not even want to hear your name. Your wish is as hopeless as is the prospect of getting water from dry land. While the successful outcome of your desires is in doubt, there can be no doubt about the way she will treat me. But I'll go anyway, even though I know it is no use.' With those words the nun hastened once more to see the daughter-in-law of the goldsmith. She spoke to her once more, with words dripping with honeyed nectar, 'Make love with that young man, who is worthy of you in looks. Pluck the ripe fruit of your youth. That is what the young should do.' Durgilā yelled at the woman and then grabbed her by the neck, as if in anger. She threw her out of the house, pushing her through the back gate that leads to a grove of aśoka trees.

'"The bald nun was consumed with shame and covered her face with her robe. In her distress she rushed back to tell the young man what had happened. 'She insulted me this time, too, just like she did last time. She grabbed me by the neck and shoved me out the back gate, right into the middle of a grove of aśoka trees.' The clever young man thought to himself, 'Now she has given me the sign that I am to meet her in the midst of the aśoka grove.' He told the nun, 'Blessed One! Forgive me for putting you through this. I am sorry that that wicked woman insulted you this way. You need not go to her anymore for me.'

'"And so on the fifth night of the dark half of the month the youth made his way to the grove of aśoka trees outside her back gate. He saw her from afar, making her way there, and she saw him, too. Their eyes met and stayed firmly fixed on each other, as the eyes of a bride and groom do at the wedding ceremony. They stretched out their arms as they had sent forth their glances, and their bodies rippling with joy, they rushed towards each other. Before they had been joined in mind, now they were joined in body, too. They melted into each other as river and ocean merge together. They spent the night with sweet words of affection and in making love in new and exciting ways, immersed entirely in a lake of pleasure. Sleep came to them, closing their lotus-like eyes, as the night causes the lotuses in a pond to shut. They lay exhausted from their love-making, their heads resting on their arms for pillows.

'"Meanwhile, Devadatta woke up to go outside and urinate. He went out to the aśoka grove, where he saw the two of them lying there. He thought to himself, 'Damn that wicked daughter-in-law of mine! Look how she sleeps here with some strange man, totally exhausted from making love.' But he wanted to make sure that the man really was her lover and so he went back into the house, where he saw his own son sleeping peacefully. He went back to where the couple was lying, thinking to himself, 'I will take off one of her ankle bracelets as proof, so that my son will believe me when I tell him what I have seen.' And so like a thief Devadatta slipped off one of her anklets and, retracing his steps, he went back home. The goldsmith's daughter-in-law woke up with a start when he pulled her anklet off. They say that guilty people sleep lightly; their sleep is quick to flee, as if it too is afraid of what will happen. She realized that it was her father-in-law who had taken off her anklet. Trembling in fear, she woke her lover up, 'Go quickly. My mean father-in-law has seen us. You must help me if I get in trouble.'

'"Her lover agreed. In his fear he hastily pulled himself together and beat a quick retreat. That wanton woman then rushed back into the house and lay down next to her husband. As brazen as she was clever, the skilled actress woke her husband up with a firm embrace. She said to him, 'Noble One! It's too hot in here. Let's go outside to the aśoka grove, where the leaves of the trees sway gently in the breeze.' Devadinna, in his innocence, was completely under his wife's thumb; he got up and went to the aśoka grove, his wife's arm around his neck. When they got there she lay down on the very spot where her father-in-law had seen her lying with her lover; this time she held her husband tightly to her. Her innocent husband fell asleep at once; true it is that honest people have no trouble falling asleep. The cheating wife concealed her true feelings, and like a skilled actress she turned to her husband and asked, 'What is it with your family? I hesitate even to speak about their strange customs! As I lay here asleep in your arms, my chest uncovered, your father took one of my anklets from my foot. Decent men would never touch their daughters-in-law, ever; what is this, touching your daughter-in-law, when she lies there making love with her husband?' Devadinna replied, 'O lovely lady, tomorrow you will hear what I'll say to my father about this!' But she broke in, 'You mustn't wait. You must speak to him right now. By tomorrow he will say that he has seen me lying with another man.' Her husband reassured her, 'Don't worry; I am on your side. I will tell my father off for taking your anklet while I was fast asleep.' 'My love, be sure you say that tomorrow morning.' And that clever lady made her husband swear to her over and over again that he would do just that.

'"When the sun came up, Devadinna, angry at his father, yelled at him, 'What did you think you were doing, taking your daughter-in-law's anklet?' The old man said, 'Son! Your wife is unfaithful. Last night I saw her lying with another man in the aśoka grove. I wanted to prove to you that she had been unfaithful to you and so I slipped one of the anklets from her foot.' The son said, 'I was sleeping there with her, not some other man! Why have you done this; your shameless act has caused me great embarrassment. Give my wife back her anklet; don't keep it. You took it from her while I slept by her side. She is an exemplary and faithful wife.' But the father insisted, 'When I took off her anklet, I came and checked on you; you were asleep in the house.' Durgilā now spoke up. 'I will not stand for these false accusations. I will prove to my father-in-law that I have done nothing wrong by asking the gods to clear my name. I am a pure and faithful wife, a woman of high birth; how could I let this stain on my character, even if it is just talk, go unchallenged; it is as ugly as a blot of ink on a pure white cloth. I will crawl between the legs of the demi-god, the yakṣa Śobhanadeva; it is said that a person who is not pure cannot pass through the yakṣa's legs.'

'She was so brazen that she made this agreement with her father-in-law, who knew exactly what was going on, and with her husband, who hadn't a clue. She bathed and donned a pure white garment. Carrying an offering of flowers and incense in front of all her relatives she went to worship the yakṣa. She had given her lover a message that as she was worshipping the yakṣa he was to act like a mad man and grab her so firmly by the neck that she would feel as if she was choking on her very own words. The crowd dragged him off, thinking he was crazy. Durgilā bathed again and continued with her worship of the yakṣa. She proclaimed, 'I swear that I have never touched a man other than my husband. Oh yes, this crazy man clung to my neck right in front of all of you. I therefore swear that no man other than my husband and this crazy man has ever touched my body. I am telling the truth. This yakṣa loves the truth. Let him clear my name.' This put the yakṣa in a bit of a quandary, and as he pondered, 'What should I do?' she quickly crawled between the yakṣa's legs, and passed the test. All the people shouted, 'She's been proven to be pure, she's passed the test!' The king's guards placed a garland of flowers around her neck. To the sounds of beating drums, accompanied by her delighted family and accepted by her husband Devadinna, she returned to the house of her father-in-law in triumph. From that time on the people called her by the name, 'The Clever Lady of the Anklet'.

'"Her father-in-law, Devadatta, was thus defeated by his son's wife's cleverness. From that moment on he was consumed with worry that destroyed his sleep, like an elephant tethered to a post. When the king heard that Devadatta had become like a yogi in that he never slept, he hired him in a suitable post. He made him the guard of his harem.

'"One night one of the queens kept checking to see if the harem guard was sleeping or not. Devadatta thought to himself, 'I'm not quite sure what it is, but there must be some reason why she keeps getting up to check if I am awake or not. I shall pretend to be asleep so that I can find out what she is up to.' When Devadatta lay down, pretending to be asleep, the queen got up again. She was delighted to find him sleeping like that, and she slowly, like a thief, crept over to the window. The king's favourite elephant was tied up just under the window. This elephant was like one of the elephants of the gods; it was always in rut. She was enamoured of the elephant's keeper. She removed the sliding wooden shutter from the window and climbed down. The well-trained elephant lifted her up with his trunk, as he had done many times before and set her down on the ground. The elephant driver was furious when he saw her. His eyes flaming with rage, he asked, 'Why are you so late?' and he struck that queen with the elephant's chain as if she were no better than a servant girl. She cried, 'Don't hit me. The king has some new person guarding the harem and he was awake for a long time. I couldn't come before. I came as soon as I saw he was asleep. O handsome one, don't be mad at me.' When the elephant keeper learned this he was no longer angry. And he enjoyed himself with her, doing as he pleased, unafraid. When the night was almost over, that brazen woman let the elephant lift her once more with its trunk and she went back up to the palace.

'"The goldsmith thought, 'The ways of women are as difficult to fathom as the rumblings of a horse that has the wind. When even queens, whom the rays of the sun never touch, are unfaithful to their husbands, how can anyone expect an ordinary woman to be chaste? How long would it take before a simple housewife, who roams all over the city and must constantly go out to fetch water and do other chores, finds herself another man?' At this thought, Devadatta no longer felt so angry at his daughter-in-law's act of infidelity, and like a man who has paid off all his debts, he began to sleep again, deeply and soundly. When in the morning the old goldsmith still had not woken up, the servants informed the king. The king told them, 'There must be some reason for this. Bring him to me as soon as he is awake.' The servants went back to the harem, but after a long time of not sleeping at all, the goldsmith blissfully slept on. He slept for a full seven days. At the end of those seven days the goldsmith finally woke up. The servants brought him before the king, who asked him, 'Sleep never visited you, as an amorous woman never visits an unfortunately ugly man. Now you have slept for seven full days. Do not be afraid. Tell me what has happened.' And he told the king everything that he had seen that night, what the queen had done, what the elephant driver had done, and even what the elephant had done. The king gave him a gift and sent him back to his own home. He had had his share of suffering and now was happy. Men do find peace of mind in time.

'"The king wanted to find out which of his queens had been unfaithful to him. He had a wooden elephant made and then said to all of his queens, 'I have had a dream that told me that all of my queens are to mount this elephant without their clothes on. I will watch them.' The queens then all did as the king commanded, while the king looked on. Only one queen demurred, saying, 'I am afraid of that elephant.' The king was impatient and struck her with the lotus he was holding in his hand. She pretended to faint and dropped to the ground. The king was no fool and realized at once that she was the one who had cast a stain on his house. She was that wicked one, the unfaithful one, that the old harem guard had told him about. He examined her back and saw the marks of the elephant chain. Snapping his fingers, he smiled and said, 'You play with an elephant in rut, but you are afraid of a wooden elephant. You find pleasure in being beaten with a chain, but you faint when struck by a lotus.'

'"The king burned with rage. He went out to Mount Vaibhāra, not far from the city of Rājagṛha, and summoned to him the elephant driver with the elephant. He made the queen get on the elephant with the elephant driver, and then that king, whose laws could be harsh, commanded that beastly elephant driver, 'Take the elephant to a treacherous area on the mountain and make it go over the edge. When it falls, you two will also be properly punished.'

'"The elephant driver made the elephant climb higher and higher on the mountain until they reached the summit. It had one foot over the edge and was balancing itself with only three feet. The people all cried out, 'O jewel among kings, you must not slay that jewel of elephants, which is obedient to your commands.' The king pretended not to hear their pleas and commanded, 'Drive the elephant over the edge!' Now the elephant driver had the elephant balanced on only two feet. As the people cried out again, 'No, no. Do not kill the elephant!', the king was silent. The driver stopped the elephant with only one foot left on the ground. The people could not bear to see the elephant being killed; they raised their arms and implored the king, 'This is no ordinary elephant. It is the royal elephant, O King. It is perfectly trained and has no equal among elephants. Where will you get another elephant like this? It is as rare as a special conch shell with right-handed whorls. You are the ruler; you take commands from no one and you may do whatever you want. But if you act without restraint your fame will be sullied by an action that was done without careful reflection. For, O master, even a ruler must consider for himself what should be done and what ought never to be done. Consider that now and protect this jewel of elephants, if only for our sakes.'

'"The king then said, 'So be it. Tell the driver that I command him to spare the elephant.' The people then asked the elephant driver, 'Can you save this elephant, after you have brought it so close to the edge?' He replied, 'I will bring the elephant back safely if the king promises that he will not punish us.' When the people reported this back to the king, he agreed to spare them. Carefully, very carefully, the elephant driver led the elephant back from the mountain's edge. The queen and the elephant driver dismounted from the elephant. The king banished them from his kingdom and they fled.

'"At the end of the day they found themselves in a village. They slept together that night in an abandoned temple. In the middle of the night a thief fled the village, and pursued by the police, he took refuge in the temple. The police surrounded the temple, thinking that in the morning they would seize the thief. Like a blind man, the thief felt his way inside the temple and stumbled upon the two of them sleeping there. The elephant driver did not wake up when the thief touched him; sleep clings like glue to a person who is exhausted. But the queen woke up at once at the thief's light touch. And just from his touch she felt desire for him. She whispered 'Who are you?' He whispered back, 'I am a thief. I came in here to save my skin when the police were hot on my tail.' That wanton woman, showing herself to be the slut that she was, then said to the thief, 'I will save you, don't worry, but there is one condition, handsome fellow, and that is that you want me.' The thief told her, 'I have gold and perfumes. If you save my life, you will indeed be my wife. But tell me first, how will you save me, O fair-complexioned lady? O clever damsel, put my mind at rest.' She told him, 'O handsome man! When the police come I will say tell them that you are my husband.' He agreed.

When morning came the police rushed into temple, brandishing their weapons, their brows furrowed in anger. 'Who is the thief?' they asked the three of them. That wanton woman, the very incarnation of deceitfulness, pointed at the thief and said, 'He is my beloved.' She folded her hands in a gesture of humble respect to the police and continued, 'Brothers! We were on our way to another village and stopped here in this temple for the night.' The police were all simple villagers. They huddled together and decided, 'What she says could indeed be true. How would a thief have a beautiful woman like this? She is either a brahmin girl or the daughter of a merchant or maybe, even a princess, or maybe someone else. Whatever the case, her beauty attests to her good character. She would never have a thief as her husband. Besides, she is expensively dressed and has fine jewellery. Her husband would not have to live by stealing. The other man must be the thief.' And so it was that they accused the elephant driver of the other man's crime and had him impaled on a stake. There on the stake he called out pitifully to every passerby, 'Please, please, give me some water to drink.' But everyone was afraid of the king and no one dared give him even a drop of water. People are only prepared to do a good deed if they are assured beforehand that no harm will come to them from doing it.

'"A Jain layman named Jinadāsa was passing that way. When the elephant driver saw him and begged him for water, he said, 'I will bring you water. But you must do as I say. Until I come back with the water you must call out these words, "Praise, praise to the Arhats"'. And the elephant driver, desperately thirsty, began to call out those words. The Jain then brought the water, and the king's men gave him permission to give it to the elephant driver. When the elephant driver saw him coming with the water he felt a surge of relief. He called out even louder, "Praise be to the Arhats", and at that moment he died. Even though he had never even heard about proper conduct according to the Jain doctrine, through the very force of his sufferings he still burned off his karma. As a result of the great power of reciting those words of praise to the Jinas, he became a demi-god.

'That whore of a queen set off with the thief. They came to a river; the water was high, making the river difficult to cross. The thief said, "Beloved! I can't carry you across the way you are, weighted down by your fancy clothes and jewellery. O fair one! Give me your clothes and your jewels. I'll take them across the river first and then I'll come back for you. You'll be easy to carry across without all that excess weight. You can hide in the reeds until I come back for you. You need not fear being all alone; I'll be back in a jiffy. Then I'll put you on my back and ferry you across like a real boat. I'll get you to the other shore. Don't be afraid. Just do as I say."

'The wanton woman did as the thief ordered. She hid in the thicket and that thief, carrying her clothes and her jewels, made his way to the other shore. But when he got there he began to think, "This woman killed her husband because she had taken a shine to me. Her affection surely doesn't seem any more lasting than the color of fresh turmeric. What proof do I have that she will not abandon me at the slightest sign of trouble?" And so that thief took her clothes and her jewels, and looking back at her, he vanished as swiftly as a deer. She raised her arm and beckoned to him, as an elephant raises its trunk. She was as naked as the day she was born as she cried out, "Where are you going, leaving me here like this!" The thief shouted back, "When I saw you naked in the thicket, like some demonness, I was suddenly frightened by the thought of what you have done." And with those words he disappeared, like a bird flying aloft in the sky. And that whore, who had killed her husband, was left there, just like that.

'The soul who had been the elephant driver had been reborn as a god. He used his supernatural knowledge and found that wretched woman there. Wanting to awaken her, for she had been his wife in a previous life, he turned himself into a jackal with a piece of meat hanging from its mouth. The jackal spat out the piece of meat and proceeded to try to eat a fish that was lying there on the bank of the river. The fish jumped right back into the water and a hawk, that the god had also magically made to appear, quickly snatched up the meat and flew off. That naked woman, sitting there in the thicket of reeds, as wretched as she was, still was slightly curious at this turn of events. She said to the jackal, "Fool! Why did you give up the meat that you had out of a desire to eat that fish? Now you have neither fish nor meat. What will you do now, O jackal?" The jackal answered, "You abandoned your husband out of desire for a new lover. And now you have neither, husband nor lover. O naked lady, what will you do now?"

'When she heard those words she was seized with fear. The demi-god then revealed to her his real and marvellous form and said, "O wicked woman, you have done something very wrong. Accept the doctrine of the Jinas, which is like a flood of water to cleanse the dirt of sin. O foolish lady! I am that elephant driver whom you delivered to death. Through the great power of the Jain doctrine I have become a god." When the lady had made the firm resolve, "I too shall become a Jain," he took her to some nuns and under their guidance she renounced the world.'

Padmasenā concluded, 'You need not pay any attention to the many stories like this, which are either meant to stir a man to action or to make him want to renounce the world; in truth, none of them is meant for people like us. Ignore them and devote yourself to a life of proper pleasure.'

(from the *Pariśiṣṭaparvan* of Hemacandra, Ch.2)

10

SUNDARĪ

Here in this very land of Bharata is a city called Sāketa. The king there was Madana, 'God of Love', both in name and appearance. He had a son, Prince Anaṅga. In the city also dwelt a rich merchant Vaiśramaṇa, as rich indeed as his namesake, the God of Wealth, Vaiśramaṇa. He had a son named Priyaṃkara. Priyaṃkara was handsome and virtuous; he was talented, generous and compassionate, and he was a fervent believer in the Jain doctrine. One day Vaiśramaṇa married off his son Priyaṃkara to Sundarī, the daughter of his neighbour Priyamitra. They came to be very much in love with each other. If they had to be apart for even a few minutes, they became agitated in their longing to see each other. But fate so ordained it that one day Priyaṃkara became ill. Grief tore at Sundarī and she would not eat, nor bathe, nor talk, nor do anything at all in the house. All she could do was to be miserable; tears flowed from her eyes, for the thought that her beloved might die only caused the pain in her heart to grow and grow. When Priyaṃkara's lifespan was exhausted, for such was his karma, he went to the other world. His family was despondent when they saw that he had died. His father began to lament,

'O son, abode of all fine virtues! Treasure house of good qualities! Priyaṃkara, where have you gone? Answer me!'

His relatives started to take the corpse out of the house so that it could be cremated, but Sundarī, her mind confused by her love, would not allow them to burn the body. No matter how her father and mother and her friends tried to convince her, she would not relinquish the corpse. Embracing his dead body, the beautiful woman wailed and lamented, despondent over what she saw as a world in which there was no king to see that justice was done. Though her husband was lifeless, she treated him as if he were still among the living. It is clear that love can blind and delude people so that they can no longer distinguish between what is true and what is false.

Sundarī's family was distressed and they summoned those who were skilled in magic spells and practices. But it was all to no avail. Thinking that she was beyond the reach of their ministrations, her family dismissed these people and left her alone for a day. By the next day, the corpse was swollen and beginning to stink. But that did not matter to Sundarī; under the influence of her strong love for Priyaṃkara she continued to embrace the corpse. When the family scolded her and her friends tried to make her stop, she thought to herself, 'My family says that he is dead and I am crazy. It's clear that I must leave this place and go somewhere where they can't find me.' And so Sundarī put the corpse on her head and left her home, making her way to the cemetery, as people stared at her with feelings of astonishment, pity, disgust and amusement. There, wearing an old rag, her body covered in dust and hair all dishevelled and standing on end, she looked like someone carrying out rituals in service of the terrifying god Bhairava. She begged for alms and took the choicest morsels and set them before the corpse saying, 'Beloved, you take whatever looks most delicious and give me whatever looks rotten.' After saying such words, she would eat. Day after day she stayed there at the cemetery, looking like either a young girl devoted to the Kāpālika sect that worships Śiva, or like a demoness or goblin of some kind.

Her father Priyamitra petitioned the ruler of the city saying, 'Master! Please have this proclamation made in the city: "My daughter is like one possessed. I will give whatever he desires to the person who can make her well."' Prince Anaṅga heard this proclamation and thought, 'This foolish girl has been possessed by the demon of love, that is all. I will use my wits to cure her.' When he told the king, the king said, 'Son! If you can cure her, then you should do this good deed to help that merchant.'

The prince found the corpse of some woman and put it down near Sundarī in the cemetery. He did not speak to her and she did not speak to him. Whatever she did to the corpse of her husband he did to the other corpse. One day she said to him, 'What are you doing?' He replied, 'This beautiful charming wife of mine isn't feeling well. But everyone kept telling me, 'She is dead. She should be cremated.' I thought that they were all lying and so I took her away from there and have brought her here to this cemetery.' Sundarī then said, 'You did the right thing. We are both in the same situation; let's be friends. For it is said, "People in the same state of distress become true friends."' Anaṅga said, 'You are my sister. He is my brother-in-law. Tell me, what is his name?' She said, 'My husband's name is Priyaṃkara. What is your wife's name?' He told her, 'Her name is Māyādevī.' The two of them stayed there together in the cemetery, having become good friends.

When she had to go off for a moment to do something urgent, she would say to him, 'Take care of my beloved.'

Whenever she would go anywhere, she would leave the corpse in his care. One day he said to her, 'Sister, your husband said something to my wife, but I didn't quite catch what he said.' She became angry and said, 'O lord of my life! For your sake I abandoned everything, family, home, father and mother, as if it were all as worthless as a blade of grass. And now this is what you do?' On another day she left the corpse with him and went off to do what she had to do. He threw the two corpses into a well. He then went after Sundarī. She asked him, 'Whom did you ask to look after the two of them?' He replied, 'I told Māyādevī to look after Priyaṃkara and I told Priyaṃkara to look after Māyādevī. Let's go back there.' But when they got back they did not see Priyaṃkara or Māyādevī. Sundarī was grief-stricken. Anaṅga pretended to fall in a faint. When he came to he said, 'Sister, what can we do? Your husband has clearly run off with my wife. I guess I did the wrong thing.' The innocent Sundarī thought to herself for awhile, 'There is no doubt that my husband has run off with his wife. What a miserable, wretched person he must be, totally devoid of compassion, ungrateful, to have done such a thing.' Anaṅga asked her, 'Good lady! What should we do now?' She answered, 'I have no idea. You tell me what we should do.' He said, 'Good lady! Listen to this truth. One and the same soul wanders from birth to birth. What does it mean to call someone husband or wife? Everything in this cycle of births is as impermanent as a flash of lightning. You should meditate on such things as the impermanence of all things, the suffering that souls undergo in the cycle of rebirth, and the absolute solitary state of the soul as it goes from birth to birth. Every union ends in parting. Every rise leads to a fall. Pleasures are like diseases. The soul, like an actor, dons different costumes as it goes from birth to birth, among the eighty-four possible states of rebirth in the cycle of transmigratory existence. Knowing this, you should embrace the Right Faith in the Jain Doctrine.' In this way Sundarī was awakened to the truth. She returned home. Her father arranged a great celebration and throughout the town was heard praise for the prince, who had brought Sundarī to her senses.

(from the *Kuvalayamālākathā* of Ratnaprabhasūri, p.74)

11

The Death of Lakṣmaṇa and the Awakening of Rāma

Lakṣmaṇa, Rāma's beloved brother and faithful companion in the fight against Rāvaṇa, was dead. Their trusted allies, Sugrīva and the others, declared, 'King Rāma, let us now make a funeral pyre. Give us the body of Lakṣmaṇa, lord among men, so that we may cremate it properly.' But Rāma was not in his right mind and he retorted, 'May you all burn on that pyre, with your fathers and mothers and even your grandfathers, too. And may all of your friends and relatives die with you, you men of evil heart. Come, get up, get up, Lakṣmaṇa. Let us go somewhere else, where we will not have to hear such cruel words from scoundrels like these.' Rāma then went to lift the body of his brother. The kings, Sugrīva and the others, in a flurry rushed to help him, grabbing the shoulders, back and other parts of the body. But Rāma did not trust them and so he carried Lakṣmaṇa's body all by himself and stole away from them, as a child might steal away with a poison fruit.

Rāma's eyes overflowed with tears as he said, 'O brother! Why are you still asleep? Get up! It's time. Come, come and take your bath.' And with those words he placed the dead body on the throne that had been prepared for his own bath. Overcome by delusion, he gently poured water on the corpse from gold pitchers. Then he adorned the dead body with all kinds of ornaments, with a crown and other jewels. Rāma, whose command was always obeyed, next hastened to order the servants in charge of the kitchen with these words, 'Lay out plates and saucers made of gold and fashioned of various jewels, and bring the finest food. Bring the best of wines and every kind of condiment to stimulate the taste buds.' When they heard his order, the servants, obedient to the desires of their master, carefully did all that he had asked of them. Rāma tried to put a morsel of food into Lakṣmaṇa's mouth, but nothing would go in, just as the words of the lord of the Jinas do not enter the ears of the unfortunate person who is not destined for salvation. When he saw that, Rāma said, 'Lord, even if you are angry at me, why do you take it out on this innocent morsel of food, that tastes as exquisite as the nectar of the gods? O glorious one! This is the finest of wines, which you always loved. At least drink some of it from this lotus-shaped cup.' With those words he tenderly placed the cup on Lakṣmaṇa's lips. But how could that lifeless corpse sip that sweet draught?

In this way Rāma, deluded by the intensity of his love, and clinging stubbornly to the ties that bind people together in worldly life, did everything for Lakṣmaṇa that one might do for a living companion. It was all for naught. Rāma continued to entertain Lakṣmana, though he was devoid of life, in sweet songs that were accompanied by the music of a flute and a lute. Filled with longing, Rāma gently lifted

Lakṣmaṇa's body that he had smeared with sandal paste and placed it on his lap. He kissed Lakṣmaṇa on the head, and then on the cheeks, and then on his hands. 'O Lakṣmaṇa, what has happened to you, that you go on sleeping like this and will not wake up? Tell me now.'

Rāma was possessed by the demon of love; his past deeds had now come to fruition in such a way as to bring him under the spell of a great delusion. While Rāma was behaving so oddly, his enemies came to know of his condition and rose up against him, like the dark clouds that at the time of the destruction of the universe thunder and rage at the sun, the brightest of the heavenly lights. Intent on rebellion and no longer able to contain their wrath, they went to Cāruratna, the son of Sunda, who was the nephew of Rāvaṇa. Cāruratna in turn went to Kuliśamālin, the son of Indrajit, who was the son of Rāvaṇa. Cāruratna declared, 'Lakṣmaṇa killed my father Sunda and my uncle and made Virādhita king of the netherworld. Rāma was suffering from the loss of his beloved wife. He struck up a friendship with Sugrīva, who is like the moon, bringing delight to the army of the Vānara group. When he learned where his wife had been taken Rāma crossed the ocean in chariots that flew up into the sky. In his desire to conquer Lankā, Rāma destroyed many an island. Rāma and Lakṣmaṇa mastered two magic spells and were able to capture Rāvaṇa's son Indrajit and the others. Lakṣmaṇa obtained a magic wheel with which he killed Rāvaṇa, the ten-headed one. Now this Lakṣmaṇa himself has been struck down by the wheel of time. And those Vānaras who were so bold when they had him to stand up for them are now cut down to size and will be easy for us to conquer. For six months now Rāma, stricken by grief, has been carrying around Lakṣmaṇa's dead body. What greater foolishness can there be than this? Even if he once was an unbeatable warrior, who wielded the plough as his weapon and had magic jewels with which to fight, he is ripe for conquering now, sunk as he is in the mire of his grief. He is the only one we need fear, and no one else; for it was his younger brother who destroyed our line.'

When the son of Indrajit, Kuliśamālin, heard this account of all the troubles that had befallen his great lineage, his mind became agitated and he burned with the fiery anger of the warrior. With loud beating drums he summoned his glorious ministers to battle and together with Cāruratna, the son of Sunda, they marched on the city of Ayodhyā. Kuliśamālin and Cāruratna, protected by an army that was as vast as the ocean itself, angry at Sugrīva, marched against Rāma, ready to arouse his wrath.

When the friendly Vidyādhara kings, who all possessed magic powers, heard that Kuliśamālin, the son of Indrajit, and Cāruratna, the son of Sunda, were marching, ready for battle, they all beseeched Rāma to protect them. The entire city of Ayodhyā fell into despair, besieged from every side, trembling with fear as once it had trembled at the onslaught of the warriors Lava and Aṅkuśa, Rāma's own two sons who, ignorant of their true parentage, had once set out to conquer Ayodhyā.

When Rāma, the sun of the Raghu clan, beheld the enemy army approaching, he clasped the body of Lakṣmaṇa tightly in his lap, and still in a state of turmoil, he glanced over at the arrows and the great bow called Vajrāvartta that had been brought to him; the bow was just lying there, curved like the furrowed brow of the enraged God of Death himself.

At that very moment in heaven the thrones of the two gods Kṛtāntavaktra and Jaṭāyu shook. Kṛtānta, once the leader of Rāma's army, had been reborn as a god in that very heaven in which had been born the great god Jaṭāyu, who had once aided Rāma in an earlier rebirth as a bird. The god Kṛtānta said, 'O lord of the gods, Jaṭāyu, why have you become agitated?' Jaṭāyu, who had used his supernatural knowledge and knew what was happening, replied, 'When I was a vulture Rāma cared for me as if I were his own dear son. Now a mighty enemy army is marching against

Rāma, who is afflicted by grief.' When he heard this, Kṛtānta used his own supernatural knowledge to look down onto earth. The radiant god, pained even more by what he saw, then said this, 'Friend! Rāma was also a devoted master to me. Indeed it was his protection that allowed me to indulge myself in all sorts of mischief on earth. He made me promise that I would help him if he were ever in trouble; now is the time. Come, let us go to him at once.'

With those words the two glorious gods, their thick curly black hair waving, rays of light streaming from their crowns, their jewelled earrings ashimmer, went to Kosalā. They were eager to act and skilled in counter measures. Kṛtānta said to Jaṭāyu, 'You go and confuse the enemy army. I will go to protect Rāma, the best of the Raghu clan.' And so the wise god Jaṭāyu, who was capable of changing his shape at will, threw the vast army of the enemy into utter confusion. As the enemy soldiers approached and looked towards Ayodhyā, they saw before them a solid mountain; turning around, they saw behind them a solid mountain. As the enemy army retreated into the distance he filled the heaven and earth with Ayodhyās, so that no space was left empty. Ayodhyās were everwhere; here was Ayodhyā, there was Ayodhyā, everywhere was Ayodhyā. When they saw that all the earth had become Ayodhyā, and the heavens, too, the enemy army was shaken, robbed of all trace of self-confidence.

The enemy soldiers said, 'How shall we save ourselves? This must be the power of some divine being, devoted to Rāma, for ordinary Vidyādharas, though they have magic powers, do not have this ability to create objects at will. What have we done in our rashness? What can fireflies do even if they are angry at the sun, which illuminates the world with a light that even a thousand fireflies cannot produce? Now even though we would flee, there is no way out; the entire world is now one vast army. No good can come of dying; only while he lives may a man find prosperity through the ripening of his own previous good deeds. If like so many bubbles we vanish in the waves of these armies, then what will we have gained?' Thus the enemy Vidyādhara soldiers lamented, one to the other, and their army trembled mightily, thrown into great disarray.

Then Jaṭāyu, having had enough of playing with them by making these magic displays, out of compassion opened up a way for them to retreat towards the south. Their minds atremble and their bodies shaking, those enemy Vidyādharas took off, like so many song birds terrified by a hawk.

Kuliśamālin, the son of Indrajit, was deeply ashamed of his defeat; having seen the greatness of the gods, he was now utterly revolted by his own limited power and wealth. He thought to himself, 'What answer have I now for Vibhīṣaṇa, Rāvaṇa's own brother, who gave his support to Rāma? What glory remains to us, now that we are defeated? How can I show my face to my followers, robbed as I am of all splendour? What happiness lies ahead for us, what contentment in living?' He gave up his anger and along with Cāruratna and his loyal followers he became a monk under the guidance of the Jain ascetic Rativega.

When the god Jaṭāyu saw that the enemy kings had all become naked ascetics, free from sin, in fear he quickly withdrew his magic weapons. Agitated, he used his supernatural knowledge and came to know, 'These men have become great sages, rich in awareness. Once, in my previous birth as King Daṇḍa, I falsely accused many pure-minded Jain ascetics and they were put to death. On account of that sin I had to suffer great torments, being born in hell and as different animals. It is true that I must still endure some residue of that bad deed, which is like a wicked enemy, but now only a trace of it remains and I shall not wander in this ocean of rebirths for much longer.' These thoughts calmed his mind. He revealed himself to the ascetics and bowed down to them, filled with faith. He confessed his wrong doings and begged their forgiveness. After he had done that, he proceeded to Ayodhyā where Rāma, deluded by his great grief over the death of his brother, was behaving like a foolish child.

There he saw Kṛtānta, trying to awaken Rāma by carefully watering a dried-up tree that had been dead for ages. Jaṭāyu took a plough and yoked a pair of dead oxen to it. He whipped the oxen and began to sow seed in a rock. Kṛtānta then took a pot of water and began to churn it right in front of Rāma, while Jaṭāyu began to crush sand with a wheel, just as one might crush sesame seeds to obtain their oil. The two gods did other useless things. Eventually Rāma came and said,

'Fool! Why do you water this dead tree? And why do you yoke corpses to a plough and sow seed in a rock? How will you get butter from churning water? Foolish man, how will you get oil from crushing sand? All you will get for your efforts is exhaustion; you will never get what you desire. Why are you doing these useless things?' They in turn said to him, 'Let us ask you, then, why do you carry around this body that is bereft of life? Surely nothing will come of that!'

Rāma, lord of men, his mind sullied by grief, only embraced more tightly the body of Lakṣmaṇa, which was adorned with auspicious marks. He said, 'Why do you speak ill of Lakṣmaṇa, the best of men? Are you not afraid your ill-omened words will turn into a curse?' While Kṛtānta was thus arguing with Rāma, Jaṭāyu appeared on the scene, carrying a corpse. When Rāma saw him coming towards him he asked, 'Why are you so deluded that you carry a corpse on your shoulder?' Jaṭāyu replied, 'If you are so clever why do you accuse only me of carrying a corpse around; do you not see that this is what you are doing yourself? For you too are carrying around a body that is without breath and motionless. You are quick to see a fault in another, no matter how slight, while you ignore your own flaws which are as enormous as the peaks of Mount Meru! We felt great affection for you as soon as we saw you; it is true what they say, that birds of a feather flock together. We are goblins, who do what we please, and you are the foremost among us. You will be a fine king for us! We wander the earth, waving the royal pennant of madness, subduing all the mad earth that rises up against us.'

When King Rāma heard these words, his delusion weakened somewhat. He remembered what his teacher had once taught him and he felt deeply ashamed. Freed from the clouds of his delusion, King Rāma shone with the light of awakening, as the moon, freed from a host of rain clouds, shines with its radiant light. His mind was pure again, restored to its former clarity, like the autumn sky, restored to its pure state after the rain clouds have all gone. He remembered the words his teacher had told him, which were like the divine nectar of the gods, and was freed from grief; he was as resplendent as before, having regained his mental health, as the garden of the gods is restored by being watered with nectar. That best of men, having been made to take ahold of himself by those two gods, looked as magnificent as Mount Meru does when it is washed by the water used to bathe the Jina at his birth. The pure-minded Rāma, his thoughts no longer sullied, was as charming as a garden of lotuses, freed from the touch of an icy wind. Like a man tormented by hunger, who obtains the most delicious food he could want; like a man confused in the darkness at the rising of the sun; like a man afflicted by a searing thirst, who comes upon a deep lake; like a man suffering from a terrible disease, who obtains a potent drug; like a man who desires to cross the ocean and finds a sea-going vessel; like a young man about town, who had strayed from the right path and then finds his way back; like travellers who yearn to return home and find a caravan to join; like a man who longs for release from prison and suddenly finds his shackles gone, Rāma, recollecting the doctrine of the Jinas, was filled with joy. He became wonderfully handsome, his eyes like wide-open lotus blossoms. He considered that he had been lifted to safety from the bowels of a dark, dank well; he felt as though he had been reborn. This is what he thought, 'O! Human life is as fragile as a droplet of water that clings to a blade of grass; here one moment, gone the next. I wandered from birth to birth, in this round of births which includes birth in hell, birth as animals, as men and as gods. With the greatest difficulty I obtained birth as a human, the only state in which it is possible to gain release. Why then was I so deluded; why did I waste my life? Who cares about wives? Who cares about wealth or friends or relatives? In this cycle of rebirths such things come easily; only True Knowledge is hard to find.'

When the two gods knew that Rāma had found that True Knowledge, they withdrew their magic powers and revealed themselves to him in all their divine splendour, which was a source of astonishment to everyone in the world. A strange wind blew, gentle to the touch and fragrant, and the sky was crowded with heavenly chariots of great beauty. Rāma heard his own deeds, from the past to the present, being celebrated in song by heavenly damsels, as lutes accompanied their song.

At this juncture the gods Kṛtānta and Jaṭāyu asked Rāma, 'O Lord, have you been well and happy these many days?' Rāma replied, 'Why do you ask if I have been happy? Only those who have renounced the world to become Jain monks are truly happy. Now I must ask you, who are you, so pleasing in appearance? And why did you do all the strange things that you have done?' The god Jaṭāyu then answered, 'You know, O King, how I was once a vulture in the forest, but found peace when I saw a Jain ascetic. You and your brother Lakṣmaṇa and your wife Sītā tenderly cared for me. Then Sītā was abducted and I was killed by Rāvaṇa as I attacked him. You were afflicted by grief and whispered in my ear the Jain sacred words, the prayer to the five beings, the Jinas, those who have attained liberation, the leaders of the monks, the teachers among the monks and all the monastic community. Through that act of kindness which you did for me I became a god in heaven, leaving behind me the sufferings I knew in my animal birth. In my ignorance I was deluded by the great pleasures that I had at my disposal, the divine pleasures of the gods, and did not know that you had come to suffer such a loss. In the end I came to remember what you had done for me and came here do something, however little, to help you.' The god Kṛtānta, decked out in finery, also spoke, 'Lord! I was your army commander named Kṛtānta. You once told me that I was to help you if you were in trouble and so I came to your aid.'

The mortals who saw the marvellous splendour of those gods were all greatly astonished and their thoughts became pure. Rāma then said to the commander of his army and the lord of the gods Jaṭāyu, 'You two came from heaven to awaken me. You are great in power and extremely pure in mind.' Thus Rāma took his leave of the two gods and emerged from his prison of grief. He cremated Lakṣmaṇa's body on the banks of the Sarayū river. Awakened to the true state of things, he was freed from despondency. In order to insure that justice and righteousness would continue in the world, he turned to his younger brother Śatrughna and spoke these words,

'O Śatrughna, my brother, now you must rule over the mortal kingdom. I am going to retire to the penance grove. There, with my mind free from all trace of desire, I shall strive to attain the place of the Jinas, Final Release.'

(from the *Padmapurāṇa* of Raviṣeṇa, Ch.118)

12

MAHEŚVARADATTA

There was a famous city named Tamālinī, where the pillars of the lofty temples to the gods seemed to reach so high that they could support the very vault of the heavens, and the many palaces of the rich were like a garland around the city. There lived the wealthy merchant Maheśvaradatta, who was the foremost citizen of the town; he was famed for being like an elephant that sported at will in the ocean of false belief. His wife was like the mistress of the school of wanton women. Her name was Nagilā, and she was famous in the city for being a water channel to make blossom the garden of erotic delights. Now one day, on the occasion of the death anniversary of his father, Maheśvaradatta killed a buffalo as an offering to the dead. And he even fed his son, whom he held on his lap, with the meat of the sacrificed buffalo. Just at that moment a sage came to his house; his face was all wrinkled and he had seen for himself the true nature of things. He recited this verse again and again:

'He feeds his own enemy, whom he holds on his lap, with the flesh of his very own father. And that he considers to be a proper sacrificial offering in honour of his father. Alas, could there be any more deluded act?'

When he heard those words Maheśvaradatta quickly rushed over to the lord of monks. He bowed to him and asked, 'O Lord! What is this strange thing that you say?'

And when he saw that Maheśvaradatta was determined to find out the truth, then that foremost of those who are restrained in speech, knowing through his great wisdom that he could help Maheśvaradatta, and being filled with compassion, replied:

'That lover of Nagilā's whom you once killed long ago is now playing happily in your lap. He died just as he released his semen into Nagilā, and because he was reborn in Nagilā's womb, he became thereby your very own son. And that buffalo, with whose flesh you satisfied your deceased father, was really the soul of your father, Samudradatta. And, O wise one! There is a she-dog by the door that is eating the bones of the buffalo. Know, O wise one, that that bitch is none other than your very own mother named Bahulā. Knowing through my supernatural knowledge that all of these terribly strange and improper things were going on in your home, I hastened here to enlighten you.'

'What proof is there that what you say is true, O Lord?' When Maheśvaradatta asked the monk this question, the monk in turn replied, 'When you take the dog inside the house, it will remember its previous births and reveal to you where some jewels were buried long ago.'

At this the monk took his leave. And the dog that he had told Maheśvaradatta about indeed showed Maheśvaradatta the buried jewels when it was brought inside the house, just as the monk had said it would. And that merchant Maheśvaradatta, like an elephant brought under control by a good trainer by means of an elephant goad, was brought to his senses by the monk, by means of his pointed words. He gave up his wrong religious beliefs and accepted the correct religious beliefs. Knowing that the whole net of relationships, father, son and everything else, was all topsy-turvy, he realized that even he could not save himself, and that of course no son could help him.

(from the *Dharmābhyudayamahākāvya* of Udayaprabhasūri p.73)

13

Kuberadatta and Kuberadattā

There was in the city of Mathurā a courtesan named Kuberasenā. She was so beautiful that it seemed that the moon was just a poor copy of her face, made by the Creator in the same way a sculptor makes a special image of a god that can be used for the bathing ceremony, so that the more valuable image in the temple is not harmed by the eager devotees as they wash it. One day with great difficulty she bore a son and a daughter, just as the sword of a great king gives rise to unprecedented glory and victory. Kuberasenā fought off the harsh words of the madam of the house, who urged her to abandon the twins, and she nursed them for a full eleven days. She made a signet ring for the boy inscribed with the name Kuberadatta, and a similar ring for the girl, marked with the name Kuberadattā. And then the cowardly mother, terrified of the madam, placed the two children in a casket studded with jewels. She set the casket afloat in the waters of the river Yamunā, as if it were the vessel containing all of her own future happiness, and she bade it farewell, washing it with the tears from her eyes, as one might send off a beloved guest with sprays of consecrated water.

It so happened that a pair of merchants were delighted to discover the casket which had floated down the river Yamunā as far as the city of Sūryapura. They quickly opened the box and there they discovered the two children. Like heirs sharing their rightful inheritance, the two merchants divided up equally the contents of the box, each one taking home one of the two children. The brother and sister were raised with loving care by the merchants, and they grew more charming with every day, like the moon and the moonlight in the moon's waxing phase. Those two best of merchants then married off the boy and girl, who were known by the names that had been inscribed on the signet rings found with them, even though they seemed indeed to be twin brother and sister.

Now one day Kuberadatta placed his own ring in his wife's hand, as if to give her a letter that would announce her renunciation of the world. Seeing that ring, so like her own, Kuberdattā was astonished, and she said to her husband, 'How is it that these rings are so like each other, just as our names are so similar? I fear that we are in truth brother and sister, and that we are not the two children of those merchants at all. They must have found us somewhere and out of ignorance of the true state of affairs they married us to each other. We must find out the truth from our parents, no matter how much we have to ask them. We must know the circumstances of our birth.' And after she said this, the two of them together went to the merchants. They asked them again and again about their birth and then realizing that their suspicions were true and that they were indeed brother and sister, they deeply regretted their marriage. They lost all taste for worldly life, which they regarded as without value and as their enemy; filled with the desire for renunciation, they just stood there, heads bowed low, bereft of all their natural beauty, like the moon and the moon-lotus as early dawn breaks.

And then Kuberadattā, being very wise, bid farewell to her brother and her parents and became a Jain nun. She then hid her jewelled signet ring, on which her name was inscribed. The ring was as radiant as the knowledge that would come to Kuberadatta one day.

Kuberadatta, for his part, made his way to the city of Mathurā as a trader, selling various toys. He became the lover of that very Kuberasenā, who had given birth to him, as the moon is said to be the lover of the night. O fie on the creator who makes us all do such things! In time Kuberasenā bore Kuberadatta a son, fashioned as it were by the very stuff of delusion that governs transmigratory existence.

Now Kuberadattā had perfected her knowledge to the extent that she now had the ability to know some things that were beyond the range of the senses. She desired to enlighten her brother, and she knew through her supernatural knowledge the terribly improper things that he was doing. She took leave of her superior, still guarding the signet ring that she had kept concealed all that time. Like a boat to rescue her brother, who was sinking quickly in the ocean of transmigratory existence, she hastily made her way to Mathurā. She asked Kuberasenā for a place to stay and found lodgings there, in that unsuitable place; for religious people will do anything that they have to do in order to help someone else.

Now one day the nun Kuberadattā saw the robust son of Kuberadatta, and knowing how monks and nuns enlighten others, she spoke these absolutely true words, 'Child! You are my brother-in-law, for you are the brother of my husband. And our mother is the same woman, and so you are also my brother! My husband begot you, and so that makes you also my child. But your father is the child of my rival in love, and that would make you my grandson. You are the brother of my mother's husband, which makes you my uncle. And you are my brother's child, which makes you my nephew. Your mother is my mother, who bore us both in her womb. And that woman is also the mother of my mother's lover, which makes her my grandmother. She is the wife of the young man who was born from my co-wife, which makes her also my daughter-in-law. And she is the mother of my husband, which makes her my mother-in-law as well. She is the wife of my brother, which makes her my sister-in-law, and she is the wife of my husband, and so is my co-wife. And as for your father, who is the lover of my mother, I guess that makes him my father, too. You are my uncle, and he is your father, and an uncle's father is your grandfather, so he is my grandfather as well. My mother and his mother are the same woman, and so he is my brother. He is the husband of the woman who bore my husband, and so he is my father-in-law, too. He took my hand in marriage, and so he became my husband in addition to all of this. And he is the son of my co-wife, and so is my son as well.'

Now when Kuberadatta heard these words of the nun, which seemed to contradict themselves at every step, he was amazed, and he asked her, 'What does all of this mean?' And the nun then told everything to that Kubera, who kept asking her what she had meant. And she gave him the jewelled signet ring, which was like a lamp to enlighten the darkness of his delusion. By that signet ring, which was bright like the sun, Kubera became enlightened, and he gave up his deluded beliefs as a bee leaves a lotus. He was ashamed of his own behaviour and he became a monk, and that wise Kuberadatta, though still a young man, renounced the householder's life and went into the forest. The forests were made radiant by that one, who was like a lion to destroy the elephant of karma, and who was like a mountain with natural rushing springs of his own glory; he was like a tree bearing as its fruits one austerity after another. He meditated on the Jain teachings and constantly recited Jain prayers to the tīrthankaras and sages of old, and he went to heaven, a lion that had killed the elephant of sexual desire. Even Kuberasenā saw how topsy-turvy the world of sense objects is, and she became disgusted with life in this world and took on herself the vows of the Jain householder.

(from the *Dharmābhyudayamahākāvya* of Udayaprabhasūri p.71)

14

SIDDHI AND BUDDHI

Jambūsvāmin wanted to abandon his wives and renounce the world to become a monk. His wives tried to dissuade him by telling him stories. Nabhasenā, her hands folded in reverence, said to her husband, 'Do not be like the old lady whose story I now tell you.

'"In a certain village lived two women named Siddhi and Buddhi. They were friends; both of them were old now and both were extremely poor. Just outside their village there was a temple to a famous yakṣa, a demi-god named Bholaka, who had the power to grant people the wealth that they desired. If poverty were a tree, the old lady Buddhi was a veritable forest of those trees, and so she prayed to that yakṣa every day, with all the proper rituals. Morning, noon and night she would sweep clean his temple, and before she worshipped the yakṣa she always presented him with suitable offerings.

'"One day the yakṣa was pleased with her and asked her, 'What can I give you? After all even a bird, if treated kindly all the time, is eventually won over.' The old lady replied, 'If you are pleased with me, O God, then give me the means to leave comfortably and happily.' The yakṣa said, 'Clever old lady, you are advanced not only in years but in wisdom as well. You shall be rich. Every day you will find a coin at my feet.'

'"And from that time on the old lady did indeed find a coin every day at the feet of the yakṣa. With that money she became richer than anyone in her family; in fact, she became richer than anyone else in the village. She soon began to wear new outfits every day, magnificent clothes fit for a queen, such as she had never even dreamt existed. Where once she could not even get enough meagre rice gruel to fill her belly, she now had thousands of cows, their swollen udders dripping with milk. All her life she had lived in a pitiful grass hut, but now she had a palace built for herself, with spreading balconies and lofty pavilions. She, who had subsisted on the pittance she could earn by collecting cowdung from her neighbors, was now waited upon by servants, who stood ready to do her bidding, leaning against every pillar in her house, like so many relief sculptures carved into their surface. She who had once had to worry constantly about whether or not she would have anything to eat now used the wealth she got from the yakṣa to help the poor and needy in her village.

'"When Siddhi saw Buddhi's new wealth she became jealous. She thought to herself, 'How did she become so rich? I know what I shall do. We are friends, after all, and she has always confided in me. I'll just butter her up a bit and then ask her outright how she got so rich.' With this in mind, Siddhi went to see Buddhi. After Buddhi had properly welcomed her old friend, Siddhi asked her, 'Friend, where did you suddenly get all this incredible wealth? From the looks of things, it seems you have found a magic wish-granting jewel! Tell me, is this the favour of the king, or have you won over some god? Did you find a buried treasure or have you discovered the alchemist's secret? I feel rich myself, seeing all your wealth, my friend. I can bid farewell forever to this poverty that has plagued me. You and I are one in our great love for each other. We are so close to each other in our hearts that there is no difference whatsoever left between us. Surely there is nothing that we cannot tell each other. So tell me, then, where did you get all this wealth?'

'"Buddhi had no idea what was really in Siddhi's heart and so she told her the truth, how she had worshipped the yakṣa and how he had given her the wealth. When Siddhi heard all of that she jumped for joy, for she thought to herself, 'Now I know the way for me to become rich, too. Surely there can be no harm in my doing what she has done. In fact I will worship that yakṣa even more fervently than she has; that way I am sure to become even richer than she is.'

'"And so it was that Siddhi began to worship that yakṣa day and night, in exactly the way that Buddhi had instructed her. She adorned the staircase to the yakṣa's temple with various patterns of chalk and was constantly busying herself decorating the temple courtyard with auspicious designs, svastikas and the like, as if she were counting up, with each line she drew, the various ways in which she would display her devotion. Every day she brought water to the temple and bathed the yakṣa with her own hands, having fasted and observed various restrictions to make herself suitably pure. Three times a day she worshipped the yakṣa with offerings of plants and flowers that she picked herself, with basil and wood apple, karavīra and kubjikā. She ate only one meal a day and undertook various other fasts, and she never left that temple, day or night, like some demi-goddess who was madly in love with that yakṣa.

'"After Siddhi had worshipped the yakṣa so intently for

some time, the yakṣa finally spoke to her. 'Noble lady!' he said, 'I am pleased with the way you have worshipped me. Ask me for whatever you want.' At that she declared to the yakṣa, who had inexhaustible wealth, 'Give me twice what you have given my friend.' Saying, 'So be it', Bhola the yakṣa disappeared. And in time Siddhi became even richer than Buddhi. When Buddhi saw that her friend was so rich, she went back to worshipping the yakṣa, and every day the yakṣa gave her twice the money that he had given her friend. Siddhi, jealous as ever, also worshipped the yakṣa. When the yakṣa was pleased with her, that wicked woman thought, 'No matter what I ask from this yakṣa, who is pleased and ready to grant me a boon, Buddhi will get the same thing twice over, having worshipped the yakṣa herself. I must therefore ask for that boon, which when doubled will cause Buddhi great harm. That would indeed be a clever thing to do!' And so it came to pass that she asked the yakṣa to make her blind in one eye. No sooner did the yakṣa say, 'So be it', than she became blind in one eye. Buddhi, thinking that the yakṣa must have given her friend something more than she herself had, again worshipped the yakṣa, wanting twice of whatever the yakṣa had given Siddhi. When the yakṣa was pleased with her she begged of him, 'Give me twice what you gave to Siddhi.' Saying, 'So be it', the yakṣa vanished. Instantly Buddhi became totally blind, for the words of the gods always come true.

'So it was that the old lady Buddhi, unsatisfied with the wealth that she had acquired and impelled by greed, caused her own ruin. Now, you have acquired worldly riches, but you say you want something even greater by becoming a monk. You will end up just like that blind old lady.'

(from the *Pariśiṣṭaparvan* of Hemacandra, Ch.3)

15

LOBHADEVA

The teacher Dharmanandana was known far and wide for his praiseworthy conduct; indeed, if proper conduct were likened to Mount Malaya, he would be the famous sandalwood that grows there, spreading its fragrance everywhere. Master Dharmanandana said:

'That man who does not avoid greed, even though he may be free of anger and the other imperfections, still sinks deep into the ocean of transmigratory existence, like a heavy ball of iron.

'Souls, wandering in the forest of transmigratory existence, are bitten by the snake of greed, which robs them of their very life, that is, their ability to distinguish right from wrong. Thus they cannot tell what is good for them from what is bad for them.

'Even the best virtues disappear if a person is possessed

of greed, as drops of water are repelled from the surface of a heated piece of iron.

'Just as an ordinary fire is never satisfied, no matter how much fuel it is fed; just as the subterranean fire at the bottom of the ocean is never satisfied, even by all the ocean's waters, so is a person never satisfied, no matter how much money he may have.

'A person under the control of greed loses all his wealth; he even slays his friend and surely, he drowns in an ocean of grief. O King Purandaradatta, this is exactly the case with this person that you see here.'

The king declared, 'Blessed One! Which person do you mean, and what has he done?'

The Blessed One replied, 'I mean the person sitting behind you, just to the left of your minister Vāsava; that emaciated person, who is nothing but skin and bones, and who is the very incarnation of greed. Listen carefully now, O King, to what he did because he was overcome by greed. This is his tale.

'Here on the island of Jambūdvīpa, in the central area of the land of Bharata, there is a city called Takṣaśilā, which in its wealth, which is like the wealth of heaven, puts to shame the city of the gods.

'With its lofty turrets, the rampart that surrounds the city makes everyone think that the thousand-headed snake Śeṣa has come and curled himself around the city in order better to admire its great beauty.

'The wall of crystal casts its reflection in the waters of the moat, as if it were about to descend into the netherworld to marvel at the underground city, Bhogāvatī.

'The people of that city could be described by the same words used to describe a splendid garden, each word being taken to mean something a little bit different. The garden has lovely jasmine flowers, while the people are of the most distinguished castes; the garden has handsome thorn apple trees, while the people are of calm demeanor; the garden always has plantain trees in blossom, while the people undertake only good deeds; the garden has many ponds, while the people have righteousness; the garden has pretty abhayā plants, while the people have nothing to fear; the garden has charming asāna trees, while the people have excellent food to eat.

'The lofty mansions, made of the most costly silver, look like so many baby Mount Merus, who had come there to play.

'One might think that the city of the gods was hiding in shame, having seen this splendid city, ever victorious, with its infinitely radiant beauty.

'In that city there was a dharma wheel made of jewels that had a thousand spokes. It had been made by Glorious Bāhubali at the site of the footsteps of the first Jina, Ṛṣabhanātha, the Glorious son of Nābhi.

'There were many wonderful people in that city, people whose minds were filled with affection for others, and there were many outstanding ascetics, whose minds were devoid of attachments. There were wealthy men, who had excellent wives with whom they were deeply in love, and who feasted on the most sumptuous of foods; likewise, there were many sages, who were celibate, assiduously cultivating that state beyond passion, and who ate only those pure and proper foods that were permitted to ascetics.

'There was a village named Uccala situated to the southwest of this city. It was a fine village, with heaps of grain. There in that village lived Dhanadeva, son of a caravan leader, a scion of a fine lineage. He passed his time amusing himself with other sons of caravan leaders.

'Now this Dhanadeva was greedy by nature. He had always been an accomplished cheater, liar and thief. That was why his friends, the other sons of the caravan leaders, did not call him by his real name, Dhanadeva, but instead called him Lobhadeva, "the man whose god is Greed". And so it was that when he was a young man in his prime, his mind was completely overcome by greed.

'Now one day, driven by a desire to make money, Lobhadeva told his parents of his intentions. He made ready some fine horses and wagons and equipped himself with necessary provisions for his journey. He bade his friends farewell and then on a suitable day, when the moon was in the right zodiacal house, and the proper moment, as determined by an astrologer, had arrived, he bathed, worshipped the gods and completed the rituals that were designed to assure him of success. His face beaming with joy, he set off for the South. His relatives escorted him for a short distance. His father said to him, "I know you have studied all the texts on various subjects yourself and you do not need to be told this, anymore than a natural gemstone has to be made, or the Goddess of Learning has to be taught, or a pearl needs to be polished; still my love for you compels me to speak. O son, the place you are going to is very far away and the road is treacherous. People are deceitful and women, especially, are out to trick a man. There are many wicked people, while the good are few in number. It is not easy to protect the goods that you are carrying with you and your young age is against you. You must keep your wits about you. At times you must be wise and at times you must play the fool; at times you must be compassionate and at times you must be cruel. At times you must be courageous and at times you must be a coward. In this way you will arrive successfully at your destination." These were the words of admonition that the father addressed to his son, who was afloat on a gentle milk-ocean of joy, tears streaming from his eyes. Lobhadeva then set out for the South and after a few days of travelling without a stop he reached the port city of Sopāraka.

There in that city the only crookedness to be found was in the lovely eyebrows of the charming ladies, not in the hearts of people; moths may have fluttered, but no ill omens shook people's composure; the only things to tremble were the flags flying high on the lofty mansions; no man or woman trembled in fear there. Argument was confined to philosophical debate and taxes were low; the only squeezing anyone did was the squeezing of women's hands. All was quiet and tranquil; the only churning was of butter; the only thing ever crushed was betel nut. The people in that city were all devoted to performing good deeds and following the proper path; they strove constantly to put a Final End to transmigratory existence. What all could not be said in praise of such a city!

'In that city the people were just like the god Kṛṣṇa, in that the same adjectives, slightly differently interpreted, could be applied to both; while Kṛṣṇa is accompanied by his mother Yaśodā, charming in every way, the people there had great compassion and their fame had spread far and wide; both Kṛṣṇa and the townspeople carried out deeds that were of great benefit to others. The crowd of courtesans of the city and the righteous people were like the God Śiva, husband of Pārvatī; the courtesans all stole men's hearts, as Śiva made Pārvatī fall madly in love with him, and the righteous people kept company with sages who were devoid of passion, as Śiva is often in the company of dispassionate ascetics.

'Lobhadeva dwelt in that city for some time in the home of an elderly and virtuous merchant named Rudra. He sold his horses for a good profit and was soon eager to return home. It was customary there that merchants, whether local or foreign, would gather in the evening and in a friendly atmosphere would tell each other what they had bought and sold that day and what they had thereby earned. They would also describe the goods that they had brought from abroad. Then they would offer each other tokens of honor and friendship, betel, fragrant substances and garlands.

'Now one day Lobhadeva was sitting in the merchants' meeting when someone happened to describe how, in some country or other, he had earned a vast profit from the sale of a relatively inexpensive item. Another merchant who was present said, "I crossed the vast ocean, which is difficult to cross, and travelled all the way to Jewel Island. There I exchanged leaves of the nimba tree for jewels. I traded there for awhile and then I returned safely home." When Lobhadeva heard about this, his mind was seized by greed. He abandoned his former intention to return home and made up his mind instead to travel further in order to accumulate even greater wealth. He went back to his lodgings. After he had bathed and eaten, he told the merchant Rudra everything that he had just heard. "Father, Rudra," he said, "people who go to Jewel Island become very rich, for there one can get jewels in exchange for mere nimba leaves. Why shouldn't I try to do that?" The merchant Rudra told him, "Son, the more a man desires wealth or sex, the greater his desire grows; as it is said, 'Greed is only increased when its object is attained.' Take what you have already earned and go home. What is more, crossing the ocean is fraught with danger. Do not be greedy. You have enough wealth; now enjoy it. Give money to help the poor and others in need. Help those of your relatives who are in trouble and in every way reap the reward of your gain. Control this demon of greed, the desire for more and more money."

'When Lobhadeva heard these words, he replied, "The Goddess of Wealth, like a woman who goes out to meet her lover, embraces that determined man who does not give up, even when his goal is difficult to attain. And so, Father, a man must be determined to see to its end a task that he has begun. Please, come with me to Jewel Island." The merchant told him, "I cannot go. You will have to go alone." Lobhadeva asked, "Why can't you come?" Merchant Rudra said, "I have crossed the ocean seven times. All seven times my ship was wrecked. I have never made a successful voyage and earned any money." Lobhadeva said, "Look at it this way. Even the sun must rise and set every day; that is the way of all things. And that is precisely why a person must always be on the lookout for a means to acquire fortune." To this the merchant answered, "My son, there is still one thing I must say. You must be in charge of the cargo on the ship. I clearly do not have good luck in these things." Lobhadeva agreed to the condition.

'The ship was made ready. The cargo was loaded. Sailors were hired. The propitious day for departure was decided by the astrologers. The moment for setting sail was fixed. The omens were carefully observed and the words of the astrologers noted. The most respected of the townspeople were suitably honoured and the gods were worshipped. The sail was hoisted and the mast raised. Wood was gathered. Everything that was needed was loaded onto the ship, including food. Vessels were filled with drinking water. As all these preparations were being made, the day for departure came. The two, Lobhadeva and Rudra, their minds filled with joy, bathed and adorned themselves with garlands of flowers, fragrant perfumes, fine clothes and jewellery. Accompanied by family and friends, they boarded the ship. The ship set sail. The drums resounded. The oars were set in motion. Thus the ship began its ocean voyage. A favourable wind was blowing. In no time at all, the vessel reached Jewel Island. The two of them disembarked, taking with them some very valuable objects as presents for the king. They presented their gifts at the feet of the king, and pleased to have secured his favour and permission to trade there, they sold some things and bought others and in time were anxious to return home.

'As the ship was carried along smoothly by a favourable wind, Lobhadeva gazed at the ocean. He thought to himself, "I have made even more money than I ever dreamt of making. The boat is filled with jewels. The only thing that bothers me is that when we reach the shore, I will have to share my wealth with my companion." And with this thought, Lobhadeva threw decency to the winds; devoid of any trace of compassion, he pushed the merchant Rudra into the sea as Rudra was squatting to answer the call of nature. Only when the boat had gone a distance of a good three furlongs, did Lobhadeva raise the alarm, "Help! Help! Come quickly! Come quickly! My friend has fallen into the depths of the ocean that swarms with vicious crocodiles." When they heard this, the crew and the friends and servants who had accompanied them began to search for Rudra. They asked, "Where did he fall in?" He cried, "I think he fell in right here. He must have been swallowed by a crocodile. What use is my life to me now? I cannot live without him. Let me die too." When they heard this, the crew and the others all thought that he must be in earnest and they did everything they could to dissuade him from committing suicide. The boat continued on its voyage.

'The merchant Rudra, through his suffering, burnt off his karma. There in the ocean he was swallowed up by a gargantuan crocodile with terrible jaws like a mighty saw. Thus he met his end. He was reborn as a demon, with modest wealth and splendour, in a particular realm of such beings. Using his supernatural knowledge, he saw his own body that had been devoured by the crocodile; he also saw the boat sailing away. He thought to himself, "That wicked Lobhadeva cast me into the sea. Just look at what that evil one has done. He did not care at all about the bonds of friendship and affection between us. He did not even care about all the help I had given him. He had not the slightest bit of compassion." And as he thought about all of this, anger burned in him like a raging fire. This is what he decided: "I shall kill him and take all the wealth for myself. I shall make sure that neither he nor anyone else gets a penny of it." And with that in his mind, the demon went to the middle of the ocean. When he spotted the ship, he began at once to make trouble.

'In the sky there appeared a mass of dark threatening clouds, as if angry at having seen the merchant Rudra bereft of life.

'Clouds spread out over the sky; lightning flashed across them, like darting glances trying to catch a glimpse of the merchant Rudra. The clouds were filled with water, as if with tears of affection for Rudra.

'Torrents of rain poured from the clouds onto the ocean, like showers of sharp arrows released from their bows by warriors in battle.

'Everything was covered in darkness because of the masses of clouds that rose all around; clouds are born of black smoke, and the darkness they caused only seemed to prove the saying that children take after their fathers.

'The demon's anger caused the ship to be buffeted by one rolling wave after another; it caused the ship to be tossed by violent winds, striking terror in the heart of everyone on the boat. In the middle of the ocean the boat, filled with all of its many goods, suddenly split apart.

'As fate would have it, Lobhadeva found a plank of wood, as one might find an island in the sea or water in the desert. He clung to the plank and floated on the ocean.

'After seven days and seven nights he came to an island. For a moment he felt revived by the cool wind that blew from the coast. But then he was seized by some of the natives, men with black shining bodies and red eyes, looking for all the world like messengers of Yama, the God of Death. Lobhadeva cried, "Gentlemen, what do you want with me?" They lied and said, "Fine sir! Do not worry. Do not be afraid. It is simply our custom that whenever we find a merchant who has been shipwrecked, we welcome him to our island." Saying this and other things like it, they escorted Lobhadeva to their home. They bowed to him respectfully and offered him a seat. They let him bathe and then fed him and gave him fresh clothes. Then it was that they said, "Sir! Trust us! Do not be afraid." When he heard their words, Lobhadeva thought to himself, "These people are really kind, even to a stranger." But no sooner did this thought cross his mind, than those cruel men tied him up and began to cut off pieces of his flesh with a sharp knife. They collected the strips of cut flesh and the blood. Then they smeared his body with a paste that allowed his wounds to heal. When six months had gone by they did the same thing again. Then they fixed him up again. Twelve years went by like this. He lived there on that island, reduced to a skeleton by their constantly stripping him of his flesh and blood.

'One day when Lobhadeva had just had his flesh cut off and his body was dripping with fresh blood, a gigantic Bhāraṇda bird spotted him. Thinking that he looked like a tasty morsel, the bird swooped down and snatched him. As the bird that carried him off was flying over the sea, another bird descended on it. The two birds fought, and as fate would have it Lobhadeva fell from the bird's beak into the sea. The salt water stung him, as the cruel words of a wicked person sting a good person. Lobhadeva, tossed here and there by the rolling waves, was cast onto the shore. It was as if the ocean could not stand to harbour such a wicked man, whose heart was stained by the sin of killing his friend. Lobhadeva, there on that shore, was instantly refreshed by a cool breeze. He wandered off into a forest, where he came upon a banyan tree. When he saw how the ground there was fashioned into a jewelled floor made of emeralds and how it was strewn with all kinds of fragrant blossoms, he thought to himself, "I have heard in the religious texts that the gods live in heaven. Surely they are not the connoisseurs we think them. Otherwise, why would they reject a place like this, the most beautiful place in all the three worlds, heaven, earth and the netherworld, and live in a place like heaven?" He sat down under the banyan tree, and wracked by intense pains, he thought, "What are the good deeds that the gods performed so that they now live happily in heaven?And what is the sin that I have done, that causes me now to suffer in this way?" As Lobhadeva wondered about this, with a jolt of pain he recalled the merchant Rudra. He thought to himself:

'"Alas, what use is the life of a person like me? I have slain my friend, who was kind to everyone. He was a cultured man, the merchant Rudra, while I was so wicked that I killed him out of greed for wealth. Now I must go to some pilgrimage place and kill myself in one way or another, putting an end to my life, for I am so polluted by the sin of killing a dear friend."

'Preoccupied with this thought, Lobhadeva dropped off to sleep for a second. When he woke up an instant later he heard the pleasing sounds of some language coming from somewhere. He thought to himself, "This is not Sanskrit, nor is it Prakrit or Apabhraṃśa. It must be the fourth language, the language of the demons. Let me listen." Some demons were talking to each other. One of them said, "The best place to practice austerities and get rid of sin is a place called Pavanābhoga." Another one said, "Mount Meru is even better than that." Still another one said, "The Himālaya mountains, whose rocks are cold from the snow, is even better." Another said, "What are you talking about? The best place to remove sin is the Ganges, the river of the gods." When he heard that, Lobhadeva set off for the Ganges, having given up every trace of greed and feeling a sense of satisfaction in his complete lack of desire for anything of this world. O King Purandaradatta, eventually he came to this place and sat down among us.'

When Lobhadeva heard everything that Dharmanandana related, he was filled with a mixture of shame, joy and sorrow. He bowed down at the feet of the guru and said, 'Everything that you have said is true, O Blessed One, whose lotus feet are worthy of worship. Now what should I do?' Dharmanandana, the lord of sages, then replied, 'Son, in order to destroy the sin produced by killing your friend, you must first slay the huge demon of greed with the sword of renunciation of all desires. Then, in order to destroy the karma that you have committed in the past, you must be deeply humble and practice severe austerities. As a swan adorns a lake and makes it even more appealing to those who see it, practice asceticism as set down in the Jain texts in such a way that others will want to follow in your footsteps. Direct your desires towards serving the lady Forbearance. Practice meditation. Shun the subjects and the servants of Emperor Sin. In that way you will attain Final Release, a place that is pure and ever blissful, where there is no old age, no death, no illness, no pain and no suffering.'

When he heard these words Lobhadeva said, 'Blessed One! If I am worthy of following this way, then show favour on me by ordaining me as a monk.' Lobhadeva fell at the master's feet, his eyes suffused with tears, all of his greed now gone. The master, Glorious Dharmanandana, then bestowed upon Lobhadeva the vows of a monk.

(from the *Kuvalayamālākathā* of Ratnaprabhasūri, p.21)

16

DECEIVING THE DECEIVER

Two men had become good friends. One day they just happened to find a buried treasure somewhere. But one of the men was deceitful. He said to his friend, 'Let's wait until tomorrow to take the treasure home; the stars will be more favorable then.' The second man, who was by nature quite innocent and trusting, agreed. That night the deceitful one returned to the site of the buried treasure and took it for himself; he buried some coals in its place. The next day the two men went together to the treasure site, but all they found there were the coals. The deceitful man made a great show of beating his breast and wailing loudly at the loss. He shouted, 'Ah! See how little merit we have! Fate gave us eyes to see and then plucked them from us; where we once saw buried treasure now we can see only coals!' And he kept looking over at the other man, who at once realized, 'That scoundrel has stolen the treasure.' But he didn't let on and pretended to comfort his deceitful friend with words like these, 'Do not despair. All the crying in the world will not bring the lost treasure back.' The two of them returned to their own homes.

The honest man had a likeness of his deceitful friend made from clay. It was truly life-like. He caught two monkeys and put things that monkeys like to eat all over the statue, in its lap, in its hand, on its head and shoulders and wherever else he could. The monkeys were starving and they greedily ate the food that was all over the statue. The honest man did this every day until the monkeys were trained to jump all over the statue. And then at the first opportunity, at the very next holiday, he invited the two sons of his deceitful friend for dinner. He fed them a grand meal and then hid them somewhere in his house, where they could play without anyone seeing them. It was not long before the deceitful friend came to claim his children. The honest friend said to him, 'My friend, your children have turned into monkeys.' The deceitful man, both amazed and distressed at this news, entered his friend's home. The honest man had taken the clay statue away and now motioned for his deceitful friend to sit down exactly where the statue had been placed before. He let the monkeys go and screeching and chattering they jumped all over the deceitful man, clinging to his lap, his head, his shoulders and even his hands. The honest friend said, 'My friend, you can tell that these are your sons. See how much they love you.' The deceitful one said, 'My friend, how can human beings suddenly turn into monkeys?' The honest man replied, 'It must be because you have so little merit and thus your karma was unfavourable; after all, isn't that why the gold we found turned into coals? How could that have happened if not for our unfavourable karma? And now you see that for the same reason your sons have turned into monkeys.' The deceitful man thought to himself, 'He has figured out what I have done. If I raise a hue and cry the king will arrest me as a thief, but how else am I to get my sons back?' And so he decided to confess everything that he had done. He gave his friend his rightful share of the treasure that he had stolen, and his friend returned to him his two sons.

(from the *Avacūri* to the *Nandīsutta*, p.111)

17

MOHADATTA

The monk Dharmanandana said to King Purandaradatta and all the others who were present,

'Delusion is deadly. If discrimination were a lotus, with fame as its fragrance, then delusion is the killing frost that makes it wither away and die.

'O King! The Jains say that worldly existence is nothing but suffering. Those who are afflicted by delusion do not understand its real nature.

'Of immeasurable merit is the person who is not carried off by the horse of delusion and keeps to the straight path; he is an ornament on this earth.

'King Delusion conquers everyone in the three worlds, heaven, earth and the netherworld, except for the Jain monks, who keep to their strict vows.

'Delusion is like a deep ocean; just as long bamboo poles

cannot fathom the depths of the ocean, so even men of good families cannot get to the bottom of delusion.

'A man whose mind is overcome by the delusion of lust cannot distinguish between a woman he can have and a woman he should never touch. Such a man even goes after his own sister. He kills his father, O King, just like this person right here!' The king asked, 'Master! This assembly is full of people. Which person do you mean?' The monk understood and replied, 'I mean the one who sits somewhat apart from you, to the right of the minister Vāsava. He is handsome enough, but he sits there like a post; like a statue of clay, he is devoid of the ability to discriminate between right and wrong. Just listen to what that person did, his mind overcome by great delusion.

'There is a country named Kośala, which is charming with its many villages, all inhabited by prosperous and happy people. There in that country is the city called Kośalā, invincible in the face of attack by enemy kings. Its splendid mansions shine white from the light of the moon-like faces of the alluring women in them.

'The temples there seemed to be trying to wipe the stain off the face of the moon with their flags, which were tossed about by gentle winds that wafted over the river of heaven.

'The women in that city outdid the Goddess of Fortune a hundredfold in all their qualities that made them so attractive to their men.

'There the heavenly Ganges with its three streams seemed to flow in a hundred streams, its waters scattered by the white flags on the lofty temples, waving in the breezes.

'King Kośala, a jewel among warriors, ruled there. He was extremely pure in mind and wise, skilled in dealing with his enemies.

'The dust that his armies raised as they went forth covered the sun and hid its light; even the Lord of the Snakes with his many tongues could not succeed in describing his many valorous deeds.

'The light of the sun was obscured by the dust that was raised by the hooves of the horses in his cavalry. Rivers made of the copious juice that oozed from the temples of his elephants in rut flowed on every path; the echoes of the snorting sounds made by his elephants were like the thunder of clouds. As this king set forth with his army, the trumpeting of his elephants caused enemy kings to flee.

'As he marched out with his army, the enemy kings were deafened by the roaring and snorting of his elephants that echoed throughout their fortresses; they were blinded by the dust that was stirred up. Even the Lord of the Snakes with his thousand tongues could not praise all of that king's valorous exploits.

'That lord of the earth had a son, who was like Jayanta, the son of Indra, king of the gods, except that he lived on this earth and was of noble human parentage; he was mighty like the king of beasts, though he did not fight with claws, nor did he even need to use fierce weapons; he was like the sun, which gives light to others, but unlike the sun, his light, which streamed from his fame and glory, was gentle and not harsh; he was like the moon, bringing joy to everyone, but unlike the moon which has a mark on its surface, he was without blemish of sin. This son was named Tosala and he was the foremost of the famous and worthy.

'One day as this Tosala, distinguished by all of the virtues just named, was sauntering about his own city, it so happened that he caught a glimpse of the pretty face of some young woman peering out of the lovely jalousied window of her palace, like the moon peeping out from behind a curtain of clouds, though this face, with its two long eyes like lotus leaves, was without any blemish. This young girl was the daughter of one of the prominent merchants of the city. And she saw him, too, handsome as the God of Love, and at once her mind was adrift in an ocean of the most intense passion and desire. As he looked at her, his mind was shot through with arrows by the God of Love, who, though he carries only five arrows, as if angry at the young man's desire for another person's wife, used those five arrows to pierce his mind a hundred times, so that it had as many holes in it as a sieve. Overcome by the suffering that the cruel blows from the God of Love were causing him, the young man touched his chest with his right hand and raised the forefinger of his left hand to just near the region of his navel. The young woman, staring at him, made the shape of a sword with her right hand. Seeing this gesture that she had made, the prince set out for home, thinking to himself:

'"Surely the moon, shamed by the auspicious beauty of her face, has plunged a dagger into its own breast. That would explain the dark spot that we see on its surface. Her face, like the moon as it rises, causes an ocean of beauty to swell. As the ocean carries within it the nectar of immortality, from her face come words, as sweet and vivifying as that nectar. Her eyes are like fish, swimming in the ocean of her loveliness, while her lips are like pieces of coral and her teeth are like pearls. Her breasts are like turtles and her arms are like reeds. She is the epitome of woman's seductive beauty; she is like the capital city of King Love, where youthfulness is the leading citizen and charm is the ornamental pond.

'"O, she is so very beautiful, beautiful beyond compare! She has some inexpressible allure that draws me to her! And how clever she is! O! How utterly, totally ravishing she is!"

'With these thoughts occupying his mind, the prince finally reached his palace.

'When the king's son had disappeared from her sight, the merchant's daughter was afflicted by pain in her every limb, struck by the arrows of the God of Love, the God who carries an odd number of arrows; her hot sighs misted over the paintings on the walls of her bed chamber. She threw herself onto her bed.

'Thinking only of that son of the king, as one might

meditate again and again upon a sacred formula, that young girl, with eyes like a doe, remained there in her bed for a long time.

'She took no pleasure in lying down nor in the company of her mother or her other relatives; nothing pleased her, not the moon, not her jewels.

'Everything was topsy turvy; the moon burned her like the fierce sun, and sandalwood was as hot as fire; night was like day, passing without sleep. Everything turned into its opposite, for it is said:

> The cooling substances that please lovers when they are together burn their bodies when they are apart from each other.

'One day as the prince was trying to figure out a way to be with that woman, who had stolen his heart, so that he might quench the terrible fire of longing for her, which now consumed his body, the sun with its fierce rays climbed to the peak of the Western Mountain, ready to set. As darkness spread over the world, the prince was afflicted by the arrows of the God of Love, the God whose arrows are flowers. He came to this conclusion, "There is no happiness in this world without suffering." And he got up. Prince Tosala wrapped his lower garment tightly around him; at his waist he tied a dagger that was black like the leaves of a lotus and as fierce as the tongue of Yama, God of Death, and in his right hand he took his jewel of a sword that had destroyed hosts of enemy heroes; he slung another sword over his shoulder. He then put on a dark blue cloak. When he reached her mansion he employed his magic skill to climb up to her window. From there he could see that woman, who had eyes like a doe; she was lying on her bed, her face turned away from the window, her body revealed clearly in the bright light of a standing lamp.The prince put his swords on the floor and stealthily crept to her side. He covered her lovely eyes with his hands. She felt waves of joy ripple through her body and thought to herself, "My whole body shivers with joy at the touch of these slender hands, which are soft as new lotus leaves. I am sure it is he, the thief who has stolen my heart." She said, "Treasure house of charm, let go of me." The prince laughed and uncovered her eyes. She then proceeded to welcome him as one welcomes an honored guest who has come to one's home.

'"The prince sat down on the seat she brought for him. He told her, I want to make love with you." She answered, "I can see that, but, my lord, women of good families must preserve their chastity at all costs." When he heard these words the prince said, "If all you care about is your chastity, well then, I guess I had better go." With that he picked up his swords and quickly got up to leave. She grabbed the corner of his garment and said, "Where do you think you are going, young man, having stolen my heart like some common thief? I'll tie you fast in my arms, as if binding you with strong ropes." When the prince heard those words, he stayed. She said, "O Prince! First listen to what I am going to say and then decide what you wish to do.

'"There is a merchant named Nandana living right here in Kośalā. His wife's name is Ratnarekhā. I am their beloved daughter named Suvarṇadevā. My parents gave me in marriage to Haridatta, the son of Viṣṇudatta. He married me and then boarded a ship bound for Śrī Lankā to do some business there. More than twelve years have passed since he left here. No one knows if he is alive or dead. All this time I myself have safely navigated the vast deep ocean of youthfulness, which is difficult to cross with its whirlpools of desire and its predatory fish and sea turtles that are the objects of the sense organs. Because it is difficult to conquer the objects of the senses and because the sense organs are indeed hard to control, I did once entertain this thought, 'The only happiness to be had in this life, which is filled with the suffering of sickness, old age and death, comes from being with a person you love. That has been taken from me. My life is now as useless as the nipple that hangs from a goat's neck, or as a jasmine flower that blooms in the wilderness, or as a sentence whispered into the ears of a deaf man.' This was what I had been thinking and for a long time I was determined to kill myself. I had gone to the window to bid farewell to the world of the living, when I saw you. And as soon as I saw you I was bound fast by the snares of passion. You touched your chest and raised one finger. I knew at once that you were giving me some kind of sign. I realized that by touching your heart you were telling me, 'You are my heart's desire.' By raising one finger you were saying, 'Make love with me, just once.' I in turn made my hand into the shape of your sword, as if to say, "When you come to conquer me with your sword then I will be yours, and not otherwise!" From that time on, O Prince, I have lived in the hope of being together with you, but afraid lest anyone should know. When I had made up my mind to die, you came to me. From that moment on I lost all knowledge of anything else; gone is the respect I once had for my elders; you have stolen from me the precious jewel that was my ability to tell right from wrong. Being with you I have forgotten all of the religious teachings I once knew. But if I do sleep with you, then my family will scorn me, saying I am unchaste, and there will be a great scandal. If we are prepared to endure the consequences, that's fine, but if not, it is better for me to die."

'"As the young woman with sparkling teeth said these words, the prince embraced her ever more tightly, as the moon hugs the Lady Night, and he gave her the pleasure that is the natural reward of youth. The next morning, out of love for her, he gave her his signet ring to help her get through the loneliness of their impending separation. As ruddy dawn adorned a corner of the sky, the prince quickly vanished from her mansion, using the same magical means by which he had let himself in. Eight months passed, during which he visited her in this way every night. Because of the workings of fate and her own karma, she became pregnant.

'Her father, the merchant Nanda, heard about her pregnancy from his wife Ratnarekhā, who had learned what was happening from her daughter's friends. Angry, he went to King Kośala and told him everything. The king said, "Go home. I will find him." The king's minister, following the king's orders, looked everywhere and finally found Prince Tosala. He informed the king. His lips trembling with the might of his fury, the king ordered, "Minister! I will not forgive anyone who commits a crime, even if he is my son. Seize him at once." The minister replied, "As my master commands." But he then spirited the prince away to a cremation ground somewhere. The minister was skilled in reflecting on right and wrong; he said to the prince, "Prince, your father is furious at you for what you have done. He has sentenced you to death. But as the son of my sovereign, you are also my master. How can I kill you? I have served your family and will continue to serve you and your descendants. Go now and never let anyone hear another word about you." With those words the minister released the prince. The prince hastened away, and traversing many a city he came at last to Pāṭaliputra. At that time King Jayavarman reigned there. The prince was taken into the king's service.

'In the meantime, back in Kośalā, Suvarṇadevā's relatives discovered that she had been unfaithful to her husband, and they and everyone else in the city scorned her and reviled her for being unchaste. Her heart burned with a fire of longing for the absent prince, while her body was afflicted by the many discomforts of her pregnancy. She kept thinking, 'Where is that prince? How could he have abandoned me?' 'Her friends told her, "On account of you the king condemned the prince to death, and the minister has carried out the sentence." Because she was pregnant she did not follow him in death. One night she snuck out of her house, and as fate would have it, she joined a caravan bound for Pāṭaliputra. That lovely girl, suffering from the burden of her womb and unaccustomed to walking, went very slowly and soon fell behind the caravan. She lost her way and found herself in a deep forest filled with fruits and leaves and hundreds of different types of trees: tāla, hintāla, tamāla, kadamba, jambū and jambīra. Lost in that forest, she was unable to find her way out. Her terrible thirst clouded her thoughts and she was wracked by pangs of hunger. Her face was wan; she was weary from her journey.She was terrified at the roaring of the lions and her heart beat in terror at the sight of the tigers. Having gone astray in the dense jungle, she began to lament, "O Father! Why did you not save me, your most beloved daughter? O Mother, you too did not come to my rescue. O my beloved, it was for your sake that I gave up everything, my chastity, my family, my good name, my modesty, and my friends, as easily as one shakes off a blade of grass clinging to one's clothes; as easily as one discards the dust after sweeping the house. And now you too ignore my plight!" As she lamented her fate, she dropped to the ground in a faint. In the meantime, the moon, lover of the night lilies, as if it was overcome by grief at the thought of her death, withdrew its rays and sank into the Western ocean.

'Darkness spread everywhere, black as a herd of huge elephants, black as the string of mountain peaks of the Vindhya range. A cool wind revived her, as if moved to pity for her.There in that terrible forest, totally alone, with no one to help her, Suvarṇadevā gave birth to twins, a son first and then a daughter.

'At the very same moment, joy at the birth of a son and terror at having no place to go took hold of her mind; just as both bright light and the dark shadow of the earth's surface can take possession of the sun's disc at the time of an eclipse.

'She began to lament:

'"O my son! I have no one, no father, mother, husband, nor relatives. You are my refuge.You are my support. You are my guiding wisdom.

'"A father takes care of a woman when she is a child, and a husband looks after her when she is in her youth; her son protects her in her old age. A woman is never without someone to care for her."

'In time, the sun reached the summit of Eastern Mountain, as if it wanted to protect her at least from the harm that evil creatures might do her.

'The lord of light rose, red as if in anger at the darkness of night, which had committed the terrible sin of erasing colors, as wicked people erase the distinctions between the castes by their indiscriminate behavior.

'As dawn broke in this way, she began to think, "What shall I do now? I cannot die; if I die there is no doubt that these two babies will also die. I have to take care of them." And so she made her way to the outskirts of some village. She tied the signet ring that Prince Tosala had given her around the neck of the boy and a signet ring marked with her own name around the neck of the girl. She then bound the two children separately with a single piece of her upper garment. She left the two babies and went to clean herself in a fresh mountain spring at the foot of the Vindhya mountains. While she was gone, a tigress that had just given birth and was looking for something to feed her cubs was attracted by the smell of fresh blood and found the twins who were tied, one at each end of the cloth. The tigress dragged them both off, but unbeknownst to the tigress, as she carried them, the baby girl fell out of the cloth onto the ground. An emissary of King Jayavarman of Pāṭaliputra and his wife found the baby girl lying there. The emissary picked up the baby and gave it to his wife, who had no children of her own. Eventually the emissary and his wife took the girl back with them to Pāṭaliputra. They named her Vanadattā, "Gift of the Forest".

'The tigress did not get very far. She was slain by Śabaraśīla, a son of King Jayavarman, who found himself there on some errand. He thought she was a male as he mercilessly struck her with his javelin. Then, he saw the baby boy, his body tender and soft like a lotus fiber, his two feet like red lotuses, his eyes like fully opened blue lotus blossoms and his face like the full moon. Śabaraśīla was delighted. He gave the baby to his wife to raise as her own son and she accepted the baby as her own. The prince organized a celebration in honor of the birth of his son, and on the twelfth day he gave him the appropriate name, Vyāghradatta, "Gift of the Tiger". Throughout the city everyone said that his wife had concealed her pregnancy but had now given birth to a son. Śabaraśīla and the child returned to Pāṭaliputra. There the child played with princes of the same age, but because his mind was always afflicted by delusion, everyone called him Mohadatta, "Delusion's Gift", in this case no doubt meaning the one who was delivered over to Delusion. And so Mohadatta grew up, maturing in years, in his mastery of the arts, and in his good qualities.

'When Suvarṇadevā got back from washing herself, she could not find the children and she fell into a swoon. Once more she was revived by the breeze. She cried and wailed for a long time, but eventually she calmed herself and went on. When she saw the tracks made by the tigress she was convinced that it must have eaten both her son and her daughter. She followed the tracks right to the door of the hut of some cowherd woman in a small village. The woman welcomed her warmly, as if she were her own daughter. She stayed there only a few days and then wandered from village to village until she eventually reached Pāṭaliputra. Through the workings of karma, she came to the very home of that emissary of King Jayavarman, who had found her daughter in the forest. The emissary's wife hired her to look after her daughter. Suvarṇadevā had no idea that the baby was in fact her own child, but she raised it lovingly, as if it were her own. In time the girl became a young lady in the prime of her youthful beauty, exceedingly lovely, and most clever.

'It was spring, the season that brings great delight to the minds of everyone; the soft buzzing sounds of bees filled the air. On the thirteenth day of the month, the day sacred to Kāma, the God of Love, Vanadattā and her mother and friends went to the garden just outside the city to watch the festivities. Mohadatta saw Vanadattā wandering freely in the garden; she saw him as well. And when they saw each other, they fell in love at once. The two of them stood there for some time, just looking at each other, the tree of their affection watered by the glances that they exchanged. Suvarnadevā, realizing that Mohadatta had fallen madly in love with Vanadattā, said, "Daughter! You have been here a long time. Your father will be worried about you. It's time to go home. If you are that eager to see the God of Love, my daughter, then we can come back some time after the festival is over, when the garden is empty, and you can look at the God of Love all you want." With these words she escorted Vanadattā out of the garden.

'Mohadatta thought to himself, "Surely she is in love with me, too." He was also firmly convinced that Suvarṇadevā's words were meant as a secret message to him. In this frame of mind he left the garden. Vanadattā returned to her home in body only; her mind was with the young man she had just seen. Her body was possessed by Love as if by a strong demon. There, her body burning from the raging fires of the terrible separation from the object of her longing.

Lying on a bed strewn with sprigs of Kankeli flowers,
moaning oddly, afflicted by the terrible fever of love;

Covered with lotus stalks and plantain leaves to cool her, all of her body smeared with wet sandal paste;

Her lips cracking from the heat of the hot breaths that escaped them, having abandoned her practice of any of the arts, and indifferent to the pleasures of flowers or betel or adorning herself;

Her face pale and wan like a withered lotus, like a moon beam in the full light of day, she was uncomfortable whether lying on her couch or sitting on the ground.

'One day, after the festival to the God of Love was over, Prince Tosala saw Vanadattā when she was on her way to the garden, accompanied by her mother and some friends. Tosala had changed greatly in appearance from his stay in this land that was not his place of birth; he was also no longer in the prime of youth nor as strikingly handsome as he had once been; his complexion and his physique had altered. Thus it was that Suvarṇadevā did not recognize him. He did not recognize her either, for it would never have occurred to him that she could be here in this distant land. Now Prince Tosal'a was smitten with Vanadattā. He thought to himself, "I have to marry this girl, by whatever means necessary, even if I have to fight for her or pay money to get her, no matter what I have to do. If only she would go to the garden. Let me follow her." And off he went.

'Vanadattā, with a graceful gait like the walk of an elephant, eventually reached the garden. Prince Tosala, his heart abandoned to the mighty feelings of passion that gripped him, indifferent to scandal, casting all sense of shame to the winds, not even caring if he lived or died, and having not a shred of fear, thought, "This is my chance!" Drawing his terrifying sword, his mind clouded by great delusion, he shouted, "Lady! If you care for your life, then give yourself to me. If you do not, I will take your life with one swift blow of my sword." Her friends raised a hue and cry when they saw the turn of events. Suvarṇadevā cried out to those who were there, "Help! Help! Come quickly, come quickly!

Someone is about to slay my innocent daughter, as a hunter slays a deer in the forest!"

'At that Mohadatta emerged from a bower, sword unsheathed. He cried, "Vile wretch! You whose name should not even be spoken! Shameless man! You dare to attack women? I will protect this lady. Show yourself to me." When he heard this, Tosala rushed to confront Mohadatta. He struck Mohadatta with his sword. Mohadatta was a skilled swordsman and he deftly parried the blow. With a counter-strike he delivered Prince Tosala into the saw-like jaws of Death. Mohadatta then went towards Vanadattā. She accepted him as her husband, for he had just saved her life. Suvarṇadevā rejoiced that her daughter was safe. Mohadatta said, "Lovely lady, rest easy. Stop trembling. Do not be afraid." Mohadatta then took her in his arms and as he was about to consummate his love for her, he suddenly heard a deep and melodious voice.

'"You have slain your father right before your mother's eyes and now, O foolish one, you are about to make love to your very own sister."

'Mohadatta looked around him; there was no one there. When he heard the same voice three times in a row he began to have some doubts. His mind was filled with a mixture of astonishment and anger. Brandishing his sword, Mohadatta began to search everywhere in the garden. His eyes lighted upon a holy man, the very incarnation of Religious Practice, the best of renouncers. Thinking, "This lord of monks must have spoken those words," Mohadatta bowed down at the feet of the Jain ascetic and then sat down a short distance from him. Suvarnadevā, Vanadattā and her friends did the same. Mohadatta declared, "Blessed One! Why do you say, 'You have slain your father right before your mother's eyes and now are about to make love to your sister?' How is it that that man was my father? How is it that this woman is my mother? And this one is my sister?"

'The lord of monks then clearly explained everything to them, starting with the events in Kośalā and ending with the death of Tosala. "The first sin that you committed was to kill your father, Tosala. Your second grave sin is that you desire your own sister. In every way one must condemn the workings of great delusion." When Suvarṇadevā and Vanadattā heard these words, they both lowered their heads.

'Mohadatta, disgusted by the very idea of sexual pleasure, thought of how human existence was filled with impurities. He was ready to walk the path of total withdrawal from this world. Mohadatta now said:

'"Ignorance is the root of endless sufferings, which spring from it like so many trees from their own roots. Sin is nothing but ignorance; fear is nothing but ignorance.

'"And so, Lord of monks, tell me what I must do, unlucky person that I am, so that I shall destroy all of my sins by their very roots."'

'The Blessed One replied,

'"Abandon forever your wife, sons and friends. Abandon everything forever. Undergo ordination as a monk; ordination is the only boat that can take you safely across the ocean of rebirths."

'Mohadatta said, "Blessed One! Ordain me as a monk." The ascetic replied, "I am a solitary wandering monk. I do not belong to any lineage. I cannot confer on you the monastic vows.

'"Those who know the Jain doctrine proclaim that there is a mountain that is ten, eight and fifty furlongs in extent, in elevation, and around its base.

'"There stayed the Glorious son of Nābhi, Ṛṣabhadeva, the first Jina, who purified the three worlds. It is the crest jewel among mountains.

'"Karma is active, driving people this way and that, just as long as they have not seen the Glorious son of Nābhi.

'"It was on this mountain that the Glorious sage Puṇḍarīka put an end to all his karma, as a fever destroys a mighty elephant; there, surrounded by five crores of other sages, Puṇḍarīka attained Liberation.

'"It was there on this mountain that Nami and Vinami, kings in the Vidyādhara line, along with two crores of sages, went to the Highest Place.

'"There Glorious Rāma and Bharata and ten crores of the Vālakhilyas, along with others, who numbered three crores, Prince Pradyumna and the like,

'"There Nārada and the five Pāṇḍavas, and many other distinguished ascetics, having destroyed their karma, all attained Final Liberation, the state that puts an end to all suffering.

'"A place where even one person attains liberation is thereby holy; what need I say of this mountain where crores of monks attained Liberation?

'"That mountain with its peaks made handsome by rows of trees seems to mock the other mountains, which have never experienced the touch of the feet of the Jina.

'"That mountain seems to murmur to everyone around, with the sounds of its cascading waterfalls, 'Why do you visit other holy places, when I am here?'

'"I think that mountain must have some secret herb that brings women under its power; for the lady Liberation, devoid of any desire, has chosen this mountain for her lord.

'"As I was flying through the sky, on my way to that mountain I have just described to you, Mount Śatruñjaya, I used my supernatural knowledge and came to know that you had killed your father. I thought to myself, 'This person has committed a great sin. I must bring him to his senses before he commits yet another grave sin.' Again I reflected, 'He is a good soul, destined for release, but his mind is under the control of delusion and so he has done this terrible act. For:

'"Even the Jinas, those great men, best in all the three worlds, on heaven, on the earth and in the netherworld, are subject to the dictates of karma.

'"Even those great men, who without the slightest difficulty at all can make into a churning stick the Golden Mountain, which measures a lakh of furlongs;

'"Even those great men, Lords of the Jinas, who can swim across the ocean Svayaṃbhūramaṇa without any trouble at all;

'"Even those great men, who can hold aloft the entire earth with all its mountains, like an umbrella over their heads;

'"Even those great men are subject to karma.

'"What to say of you, Mohadatta, poor wretch?"

'"And so I descended from the sky and awakened you."'

'Mohadatta declared, "Blessed One! How can I be ordained as a monk?" The sage said, "Go to Kauśambī. There, just south of the city in the garden that belongs to King Purandaradatta, you will see the Glorious Dharmanandana, the best of monks, head of his lineage, who is staying there preaching in the garden. You need not say a word; that most excellent leader of monks will know your story and will ordain you.' With these words, the monk flew back into the sky, which was blue like the leaves of a lotus."'

Dharmanandana continued, 'O King Purandaradatta! Hearing those words, Mohadatta renounced life as a householder and came here looking for me.'

When Mohadatta heard this, he said, 'Blessed One! Everything you have said is true. Now allow me to receive ordination.'

And so the Master Dharmanandana, worthy of the greatest respect, conferred the ordination proclaimed by the Jinas on Mohadatta, whose mind was pure since all delusion had left it. He conferred on him ordination, which leads to that place in which all happiness is achieved.

(from the *Kuvalayamālākathā* of Ratnaprabhasūri, p.24)

18

SANATKUMĀRA

The story begins as follows. In the continent of Bharata, in the city Viśoka was a king named Anantavīrya. He had a queen named Sitā. Their son was Sanatkumāra, the fourth World Emperor. Sanatkumāra had conquered the earth with its six divisions; he possessed the nine treasures and the fourteen jewels that signify lordship over the world. He reigned over his kingdom with great splendor. One day during his reign, the king of the Saudharma gods was sitting in his court and talking with his courtiers about the nature of physical beauty among men. The gods asked him, 'Lord, it there any mortal in the continent of Bharata who has such great beauty or not?' The king of gods replied, 'The physical beauty of the World Emperor Sanatkumāra on earth is not to be found even among you gods in heaven.'

Now when they heard that, two of the gods, Maṇimālin and Ratnaćūla, decided to go and see for themselves just how handsome this Sanatkumāra was. The Emperor was in the midst of his bath and so they could see his natural beauty that was like the beauty of the gods; the magnificence that pervaded his every limb struck wonder in their hearts. And when they saw his beauty they shook their heads in astonishment and said, 'Such beauty is not to be found even among the gods.'

Maṇimālin and Ratnacūla then made themselves visible to mortals at the gate of the king's palace. They spoke to the gatekeeper, 'Ho! Gatekeeper! Tell the Emperor, "Two gods have come from heaven to see your beauty!" Now when the Emperor heard this, he adorned himself in all his regal finery; he sat on his throne and called the two gods into his presence. But when they saw him this time, they were totally dejected. "Alas! The beauty that we beheld when we hid ourselves in the bath chamber is no longer. Everything is impermanent. Nothing lasts for ever!"'

Now when they heard these words, the servants responsible for decking the king out in his finery spoke up. 'We don't see a mite of difference between the king's appearance now and his appearance earlier.' At this, the two gods were determined to prove to those servants that indeed the king's beauty had faded. They had a vessel full of water brought in and placed before the king. They showed the full vessel to the servants and then told them to go outside. As the Emperor looked on, they removed one drop of water from the pot with the tip of a blade of grass. Then they called the servants back in and showed them the pot. They asked them, 'How would you compare the pot now to the pot you saw a moment ago?' And the servants replied, 'The pot is full of water, exactly as it was before. There is no difference at all.' When they heard this response, the two gods said, 'King! Just as these men do not notice that a drop of water has been taken out of the pot, so they cannot perceive how your beauty has faded ever so slightly.'

The Emperor, on hearing these words, lost all interest in

the pleasures of the world and was seized with a desire to renounce the world. He gave the kingdom to his son Devakumāra and began to practice religious austerities under the guidance of the Jain monk Trigupti. He practiced the most severe penances and carried out all the five-fold duties of a monk, renouncing violence towards living beings, renouncing lying, renouncing taking what is not given, renouncing sexual desires, and renouncing attachment to all possessions. But because he ate the wrong foods, numerous diseases, including skin rashes, began to afflict his body. Nonetheless, he paid no mind to what was happening to his body, for he had reached the pinnacle of non-attachment to all things, including the body. He continued to fulfil his vows as a monk with total single-mindedness.

Now it so happened that this time the king of the Saudharma gods, seated in his court, was discussing the five-fold religious conduct of Jain monks. The god Madanaketu asked him, 'Lord, is there anyone in the continent of Bharata who actually practices the kind of religious life you describe?' The king of the gods replied, 'The World Emperor Sanatkumāra, who gave up lordship over the earth with its six divisions and is totally indifferent to his body, practices to perfection the vows of a monk.'

When he heard these words Madanaketu went to see for himself. He came upon the monk Sanatkumāra practicing difficult austerities in the deep jungle. His body was overcome by numerous diseases. In order to test the firmness of this indifference to the body that Sanatkumāra displayed, Madanaketu took on the form of a physician and said to the monk again and again, 'I can cure each and every one of your diseases and make you a divine body free from any taint of illness.' He walked to and for in front of the blessed monk, saying these words, when the monk asked him, 'Who are you? And why are you making all this ruckus here in the jungle where there is no one to listen?' At that Madanaketu replied, 'I am a physician and I can cure all of your diseases and give you a body that is as radiant as an ingot of gold.' The monk said, 'If you can cure diseases, then cure this disease of mine, which consists of my repeated rebirths in the cycle of transmigratory existence.'

When he heard that request, Madanaketu said, 'That is something I cannot cure. Only you can cure the disease that is transmigratory existence. I can only cure bodily ills.' The monk said, 'What good would it do me to have the ills of my body cured, when my body is by nature impure, without any merit, and impermanent, destined to perish? I have no need to seek out a doctor to cure my bodily ailments. I can cure them by the mere touch of my spit.' And no sooner had he said this than the monk spat, and with that saliva he cured himself of his physical ailments. He showed the god his arm, which was like a golden bar. At that the god withdrew his disguise and bowed down to the monk, saying, 'The king of the Saudharma gods had praised your perfect religious conduct one day in his court, singling out the way in which you are indifferent to your body. And now, having come here for myself, I see with my own eyes that it is exactly as the king has described. Fortunate indeed are you to have such virtue! You have truly made your human birth worthwhile.' After praising him in this way and bowing down to him, Madanaketu went back to heaven. And for his part the monk Sanatkumāra, totally disinterested in the pleasures of this world, practiced the five-fold vows of the monk. Displaying to all the greatness of the religious life, he eventually rid himself of his destructive karmas. These karmas had once caused him to fail to understand the true nature of the soul and to be subject to hatred, passion, anger, pride, deceit and greed. With this he attained Omniscience. In time he exhausted the rest of his karma that kept him alive and achieved final release.

(from the *Kathākośa* of Prabhācandra)

19

THE PRINCE WHO LOVED SWEETMEATS

In the glorious city of Rājagṛha reigned the wealthy and righteous King Sumitra. He protected his subjects so well that they all dwelt in peace and happiness. His beloved wife Padmā gave birth to a most wonderful son on the night of the dark half of the month of Jyeṣṭhā. The birth of this son had been announced to her in a dream, in which she beheld an elephant entering her mouth. The God Indra first performed the festivities to celebrate the child's birth, and then his father did the same and gave his son the name Muni Suvrata. In time the son became a Jain monk and cast off all of his karma. He achieved perfect Omniscience and became the Jina Muni Suvrata.

Glorious Muni Suvrata, having enlightened many who were ready to receive the truth on earth, went to Mount

Siddha, where he preached to a combined assembly of all creatures, including holy men and gods. When everyone had taken his and her proper place in that gathering, the Glorious Muni Suvrata preached the law to all those worthy souls. Here is what he preached:

'In the city of Kalyāṇa, King Bhāṇu's wife Rukmiṇī gave birth to a most excellent son, who was endowed with every auspicious mark. The king, having performed the festivities to celebrate his son's birth, gave him the name Rūpa, "Handsome". He handed the baby over to a group of nurses, including a wet nurse, who raised him by giving him her own milk. The son was taught various things and eventually grew to be a young man. His father arranged his marriage to the daughter of King Bhīma, and with his new wife Rūpa began to enjoy a life devoted to the pursuit of sensual pleasures.

'Now this prince was particularly fond of rich sweets, to the exclusion of just about everything else. He became known in the world as "The Sweet-freak". One spring day, Sweet-freak woke up bright and early. He summoned his male dancers to him and had them dance for him along with the dancing girls. When midday came, the prince's mother sent him some fabulous rich sweets. He first gave some of them to his retinue and then he ate a bunch himself. For as it is said:

> A person never comes to harm by associating with the noble, conversing with the wise and being friends with those who are not greedy.
> Sitting around a fire in the cold season, eating rich cream, receiving honor from the king, seeing someone you love, all of these are as nourishing and sustaining as the drink of immortality.

To return to the story. The prince, having made those sweets his evening meal too, dismissed all the dancers and retired for the night along with his retinue. The prince recited to himself a hundred times the prayer to the five beings worthy of honour in the Jain tradition, the Jinas, those who have attained liberation, the leaders among the monks, the teachers among the monks, and the entire monastic community. The prince then fell asleep, and no sooner had he drifted off than he began to fart. When that offensive smell penetrated his nostrils, Sweet-freak immediately realized that all things are equally impure. In the body even the most delicious sweets turn to shit and even the drink of immortality turns into piss. Who would ever commit a sin for the sake of a body like that? The body is the abode of blood and lymph, flesh and fat, bones and marrow, entrails, semen and faeces, all these impure substances. How could the body ever be considered to be pure? That the body, which drips disgusting ooze from all its nine openings, is something beautiful—such a notion can only be the greatest delusion. (Here the storyteller should recite some verses on the impurity of the body.)

> If in this way the finest sweets turn into a foul odour, then won't this body, too, become nothing but a pile of stinking odours?
>
> Even though the body may be anointed with fragrant unguents like perfumes made from the rare musk of the musk deer, all of these perfumes can turn in an instant into a foul stench. Behold, this is the way of worldly things.

In this way Sweet-freak came to think of everything in the world as impure, and he abandoned all his royal accoutrements, his horses and his elephants, and became a Jain monk under a proper teacher. He made the firm resolve never again to eat rich and dainty fare.

For it is said:

A king may give up great wealth in a second, while
a miserable foolish beggar clings to his coarse fare.

Sweet-freak, now a Jain monk, performed great austerities and soon came to have great knowledge; he awakened many fortunate individuals to the truth. Eventually he came to Mount Śatruñjaya. There, concentrating on auspicious thoughts, he reached Omniscience and attained Ultimate Perfection.

(from the *Śatruñjayakalpavrtti* of Dharmaghosa, p.68)

20

Nala and Damayaṃtī

The Jain monk Hemacandra explained to King Kumārapāla: 'A person addicted to gambling loses everything he has, just like Nala, who lost his entire kingdom.' The king asked, 'Who was that Nala?' The monk replied, 'Listen.

'There is in this land of Bharaha, in the country of Kosala, a city called Kosalā. There is something strange and wonderful about this city, if you are clever enough with words to spot it; for were I to tell you that you need to be virtuous to live in the city of Kosalā, you could twist my words to make them say that in the city of Kosalā virtues were the direct cause of vices, an unusual situation indeed! King Nisaha ruled there; he was from the famous lineage of the Ikkhāgu. He was a just ruler, possessed of incomparable bravery and generosity, and a scourge to his enemies. He had two sons from his queen Sundarī; their names were Nala and Kūbara, and they brought joy to the minds of all the people. There is also a city named Kuṇḍiṇa, ornament of the land of Vidabbha. There reigned King Bhīmaraha, who destroyed his enemies as the mythical Śarabha beast is said to destroy lions. He had a queen Pupphadaṃtī, who was the blossom on the tree of his entire harem. As they enjoyed pleasures together a daughter was born to them, who was the ornament of all of the three worlds, heaven, earth and the netherworld.

'She was born with a beauty mark on her forehead, radiant like the orb of the sun, like the auspicious mark that is said to adorn the chest of great men.

'When she was still in her mother's womb, her father conquered all his enemies, and so he named her "Damayaṃtī", "Conqueress". She grew up, a source of joy to all the people who saw her, like the waxing crescent of the moon. In time her parents entrusted her to a teacher of the traditional arts.

'Her teacher was only the witness to the process as knowledge of all the arts just naturally appeared in her mind, as a reflection appears on the surface of a mirror.

'Through her service to the Jain ascetics, she became a pious lay Jain, skilled in understanding the vicissitudes and nature of karma, though such things are difficult to grasp.

'She explained the Jain doctrine to her mother and father in her sweet voice and they, too, came to have faith in the Jain doctrine.

'The Goddess of Liberation, moved by her great merits, gave her a golden image of the future Jina Sāṃti and told her, "My child! You must always worship this image." Damayaṃtī accepted the image and began to do just that. She soon became a young woman, the time of life that is like a pleasure grove for the God of Love. When her parents saw that she was growing up, they thought:

'"She is unparalleled in her beauty; one has to marvel at the creator's skill to have been able to fashion such a splendid creature.

But there is no suitable mate for her, equal to her in physical beauty. Or if there is, we do not know who he might be. It is best to summon all the eligible princes and arrange for her to choose her own mate. That way at least she cannot blame us for having chosen an unsuitable husband for her."'

'And so they dispatched messengers and summoned kings and princes. They all came, accompanied by their armies of elephants, horses, chariots and foot soldiers. Nala, too, of incomparable valour, arrived for the ceremony in which Damayaṃtī would choose her husband. The kings and princes were all suitably honored by King Bhīma and lodged in excellent quarters. A special pavilion was constructed for the ceremony; it was adorned with gold pillars, and in its splendour was capable of putting an end to the pride that the gods felt in their own palaces. The whole pavilion seemed to strike up a dance with its flags that swayed in the wind. The pavilion was equipped with well-fashioned lion thrones; from the rays of their many jewels shimmered rainbows of variegated light. One after another the kings and princes sat down on these thrones, each one trying to outdo the other in his show of wealth and power. They then began to reveal by their various gestures just how smitten they were with Damayaṃtī.

'Damayaṃtī's father then invited her into the assembly; she came, adorning the pavilion with her loveliness; her forehead was decorated with the beauty mark from which emerged a garland of light rays, and she shone like the eastern sky, cradling the newly risen sun; her face was radiant, making her look like a full-moon night, beautified by the full disc of the moon; with her full breasts she resembled a lake for the God of Love to dip in, with a pair of love birds floating on its surface; her hands and feet were rosy pink, like lotuses; her tender body was like a kaṇkeli creeper with tender new buds; wearing a garland of large pearls she resembled a sprig of jasmine adorned with fully opened blossoms; she wore clothes of the finest white diaphanous silk, which made her look like the Beauty of the Heavens incarnate, veiled in the thin wispy clouds of autumn; she cast her alluring glances here and there, stirring up the atmosphere, as the ocean is stirred up by schools of fish that dart in and out of its waters. When the assembled kings saw her they were struck with wonder and their eyes all fell upon her.

'At the command of the king, the harem servant Bhaddā began to describe the valour of the kings and princes to Damayaṃtī. "This is the King of Kāsī, whose arms are mighty and strong; choose him as your husband if you wish to see the river Ganges with its lofty waves!"

'Damayaṃtī answered, "O Bhaddā, I have heard it said that the inhabitants of Kāsī are given to cheating others and so my mind takes no pleasure in this one. Please, keep going."

'Bhaddā did just that and said, "This is the lord of Kuṃkana, a lion to destroy elephants in the form of his enemies; his name is Lion. Choose him and you will enjoy yourself in the summers in groves of plantain trees."

'Damayaṃtī said, "Bhaddā! The Kuṃkans have a reputation for being easily angered. I could never keep him happy all the time. Tell me about someone else.'

'Moving along, Bhaddā now said to Damayaṃtī:

'"This great king is lord over the land of Kashmir. He is as handsome as the God of Love. If you want to play among fields of saffron, then choose him for your husband."

'The princess replied, "Bhaddā! Don't you know how my body trembles at the very thought of mounds of snow? Let us go on.'

'The maidservant continued on. She said, "This is King Jayakosa of Kosaṃbī, who has a vast treasury. He is as handsome as the God of Love; O fawn-eyed lady, doesn't he steal your heart?"

'The princess only said, "Kaviṃjalā, look at the pretty

garland they made for me to put around the neck of the man I choose." Bhaddā took this as a rejection of the king she had just described and walked on. She soon said,

'"O lady with the sweet voice! Put the garland on the neck of this king Jaya of Kaliṇga. His sword has swallowed up the fame of his enemies, just as Rāhu, the demon, swallows up the moon at the time of an eclipse."

'The princess replied, "I offer my respectful greetings to the gentleman, who is old enough to be my father."

'At that Bhaddā walked on to the next king and said:

'"Lady with the charming gait of an elephant! Does this man, king of Gauḍa, a crown jewel among heroes, please you? The entire universe seems to split asunder from the noise made by the bells on his many elephants."

'The princess replied, "I had no idea until now that a man could be so ugly. Why, the universe could be destroyed by his looks alone, never mind his herd of elephants! Quickly, quickly, move on. My heart trembles in fear." Bhaddā could not resist a laugh and moved on.

'"Lotus-eyed lady! If you wish to play in the forest groves that line the banks of the river Sippā, then make this man your lord; he is Paumanāha, lord of Avaṃti."

'The princess replied, "Oh, I am getting exhausted walking around this pavilion. How much longer is Bhaddā going to go on prattling like this?" Bhaddā thought to herself, "The princess is trying to tell me that she does not like this one, either. I must go on." And that she did. Now she said:

'"This is Prince Nala, son of Nisaha. If Indra, the god with a thousand eyes, were to gaze on his beauty, he would finally think that he had found a purpose for having so many eyes."

'Damayaṃtī was astonished. She thought to herself, "His every limb seems to be the perfect example of physical beauty; his charm is unlike anything I have ever seen. He is indeed handsome and his every gesture enchants. Heart! Accept this man as your husband and you will find perfect satisfaction!" And she placed the garland, signalling her choice, around Nala's neck.

'A cry arose from the people, "Good choice! Good choice!" But king Kaṇha unsheathed his sword and rushed at Nala to strike him, shouting, "Ho, Nala! You will never marry Damayaṃtī! She was wrong to have chosen you. I am the only one here worthy of her! Give her up or prepare yourself for battle!" Nala replied, "O vile man! Is it my fault that Damayaṃtī did not choose you? Now that she is mine, are you not ashamed to desire the wife of another man? Have you no concern for the stain you cast on your family? Do you not fear the opprobrium? Are you not afraid of the next world? You have strayed from the path of the righteous and it is my duty to chastise you." At that Nala grabbed his own sword and stood up, his anger like a raging fire. Their two armies prepared to fight, terrifying with their many weapons. Damayaṃtī thought to herself, "Alas, what a wretched woman I am; this destruction of life is about to take place just because of me." She prayed, "If I have had true faith in the Jinas, then I beg the protecting goddess of the Jain Faith to allow Nala to be my chosen one and to prevent their fight." As she pronounced these words she took a pitcher and sprinkled water from it three times. When the water hit King Kaṇha's body, the flames of his anger cooled down; he became like a lump of spent charcoal, the fire of his wrath gone. His sword fell from his hand, like a ripe fruit dropping from a tree. Like a snake without its poison, no longer angry, King Kaṇha thought to himself, "I spoke wrongly to Nala. He is no ordinary man. I should bow down at his feet." And that he did. He confessed his sin to Nala and begged his forgiveness.

'Nala spoke to King Kaṇha, who bowed down to him, and then gave him leave to go. It is true what the wise men say, that noble men treat those who submit to them with kindness and affection.

'Bhīma, pleased with Nala's behavior, honoured the other

princes and kings and sent them on their way. He had Nala's marriage to Damayaṃtī celebrated with great pomp and splendour.

After the wedding he gave Nala many gifts, elephants, horses, jewels, fine clothes, and the like. Nala stayed in Bhīma's palace for a few days, while Bhīma continued to honor him with gifts. Then King Nala set out for his own city. Bhīma accompanied him part of the way.

'As Damayaṃtī was preparing to leave with Nala, her mother gave her this advice:

'"You should say only what is pleasant to hear and you should always be respectful and humble; my daughter, you must never speak ill of others and you must always stay close by him, like his own shadow, even in times of trouble."

'Damayaṃtī accepted her mother's advice; she bowed down to her mother and father and they sent her on her way. Nala helped her onto the chariot and sat her on his lap. As Nala then made his way home, obstructing the sky with the clouds of dust raised by his army of elephants, horses, chariots and foot soldiers, the sun, the jewel of the heavens, set. The world was covered in a dense darkness that prevented the eyes from seeing. It was impossible to distinguish water from dry land, trees and mountains from deep pits. But Nala, eager to reach his own city, did not stop.

'When Nala saw how his army was unable to see anything, how it stumbled and fell into the pits, losing its way, he said to his beloved:

'"Queen! Wake up! Let shine the light from the sun-like mark on your forehead, for my entire army is blind in this darkness and can go no further." Damayamtī got up and rubbed her forehead with her hand. Her beauty mark, home to dazzling rays, shone brightly, destroying the darkness. The army then proceeded along the road without any obstacles. When they had reached the outskirts of the city Kośalā, Nala said to Damayaṃtī, "Queen! This is my city, which is adorned everywhere with temples to the Jina." She said, "Fortunate indeed am I, for having obtained Nala as my husband I shall always be able to worship in the Jain temples."

'On a propitious day Nala entered the city with Damayaṃtī. The city had been decked out for the occasion, fitted with benches for people to sit upon as they watched the royal couple; flags danced on the homes of the wealthy, kissing the heavens; drums resounded, filling the city with sound, while young women danced and the bards recited verses of praise as the couple made their way to the palace. Nala and Damayaṃtī bowed down to Nala's mother and father, who welcomed them with joy.

'Nala and Damayaṃtī enjoyed themselves, sometimes swimming in pools, sometimes swinging on swings, sometimes arranging braids of fragrant flowers and sprigs in each other's hair; occasionally they amused themselves playing dice. Once when they were alone, Nala played different musical instruments and had Damayaṃtī dance for him. And so Nala and Damayaṃtī, never apart, spent their time in pursuit of ever new amusements.

'Eventually King Nisaha installed Nala on the throne, appointed Kūbara crown prince and renounced the world to become a Jain monk.

'Nala ruled over his kingdom; he was a veritable fire to his angry enemies, his valour the unbearable flames that engulfed them. Kings bowed their heads at his lotus feet.

'One day Nala asked his ministers, "Will I rule over just the territory that my father acquired or over an even greater territory?" They replied, "King Nisaha ruled over all but one third of the entire half of Bharaha; you will rule over that third as well. It is only right for a son to surpass his father. But there is one thing that you must know. There is a city named Takkasīlā, which is two hundred furlongs away from here. Its king, Kayaṃba, does not submit to your commands.

'"The moon in the sky bears a dark blot on its surface;

if the fame you will have earned from ruling over the entire half of Bharaha is bright and shining like the moon, this rebellious king is its one dark spot.

'"If you ignore him, then like a disease that only spreads when left untreated, he will become more and more difficult to conquer. If you make up your mind to defeat him, then he is as easily destroyed as a pot that falls from a mountain and shatters to bits. First you must send a messenger to him and find out his intentions. Then you must do whatever is necessary."

'King Nala dispatched a messenger skilled in the clever use of speech, having instructed him in what to say. The messenger wasted no time in making his way to Kayaṃba. He said to him:

'"You are thus commanded by King Nala, who is a veritable forest fire to the forests that are his enemies. "Accept my overlordship and rule over your own kingdom. If you do not do this, then like a monk who has faltered in his observance of his vows and is lost forever, you will be cast out of your kingdom with all that belongs to it. I have sent this messenger with your welfare in mind; otherwise I would have just descended on you in a surprise attack."'

'When King Kayaṃba heard the messenger's words, ignorant of his own weaknesses, he bit his lips in anger and replied,

'"Is your king a fool? Is he crazy? Is he insane? How can he not know that I am like a Garuḍa bird; as the Garuḍa bird is the natural and mighty enemy of the snakes, I destroy all my snake-like enemies.

'"Does Nala not at least have some ministers who are capable of knowing a proper course of action from one that should not be pursued, and who might have prevented him from speaking in this outrageous manner?

'"O messenger! Go. Tell your master to prepare himself for battle, if he is tired of his life. I am ready!"

'The messenger went back and told Nala what Kayaṃba

had said. Nala was furious and marched out against him with his full army of elephants, horses, chariots and footsoldiers.

'He surrounded Takkasilā from all sides. He ringed the city with a line of elephants, as if with a second impenetrable city wall.

'Kayaṃba, unable to endure Nala's insult, armed himself and marched out of his city. Their two armies met in battle. In that battle the flash of their many weapons doubled the intensity of the sun's rays; the sky was packed solid with the hosts of arrows that they shot; there was a glow from the flames of the fires that were sparked when their swords clashed; gods, demi-gods and goblins watched as the headless corpses danced, while the severed heads of the warriors looked like so many lotuses afloat on rivers of flowing blood. Nala said to Kayaṃba, "What is gained by the death of all these footsoldiers, dying here like flies? Let just the two of us fight each other." And so the two of them like two gargantuan mountains in motion began to fight, using arm wrestling and other close means of combat. Kayaṃba called the shots, but Nala defeated him at every type of fighting that he demanded. Finally Kayaṃba fled; he renounced all desires and stood fixed in meditation.

'When Nala saw him like that, he said, "I am the loser, you are the victor, for you have chosen the path of righteousness. Come and rule your kingdom." Because he was without desires, Kayaṃba ignored Nala as if he did not even exist, as if had no more substance than the wind. Nala was impressed by Kayaṃba moral strength and placed Kayaṃba's son Jayasattī on the father's throne.

'The kings celebrated Nala's consecration as emperor over the entire territory of half of Bharaha; once the great King Viṇhu had similarly been installed as world emperor. Back in Kosalā Nala spent his days enjoying himself with Damayaṃtī in pursuit of various pleasures, while his treasury was filled with more and more wealth, coming from the tribute that other kings brought him in submission, and heavenly damsels sang praises of his might.

'But Nāla's brother Kūvara, a blot on his own family, coveted Nala's throne and lay in wait for Nala, watching for him to make some mistake. As Fate would have it, just as the moon is marred by a dark mark on its surface, Nala became addicted to the vice of gambling. Kūvara was thrilled, for he thought to himself, "I can win the kingdom from Nala in a dice game." The two of them gambled together for a long time, victory going to the one and then to the other, as the knot in the rope on a drum moves from side to side. But Fate so ordained it that eventually Nala just could not defeat Kūvara. Although Nala was not a bad player, the dice fell against him. The cruel Kūvara beat him again and again. Kūvara wrested from Nala cities, towns, villages and settlements. Like a lake in summer, its water dried up by the sun, Nala was stripped of all of his wealth. The people watched in horror as Nala was blinded by his lust for the game. Kūvara was delighted as he saw his dreams being realized. The people, devoted to Nala, cried out in grief. When Damayaṃtī heard their lament, she came running.

'She said, "My lord! I beg of you, do this for me. Stop playing. These dice have become your enemy; they will give you nothing but grief.

'"Give the kingdom to your younger brother Kūvara; do not give him the chance to make fun of you, having stolen your kingdom by force.

'"My heart is pained that this kingdom, conquered by valour in battle, should be gambled away in a game of dice, thrown away, like learning that is imparted to a person of the lower classes."

'"But as a mad elephant in rut ignores the jab of the elephant goad, Nala ignored her words. She turned to the ministers and cried, "Stop Nala from gambling."

'They too told Naḷa again and again to stop playing, but

Nala kept on. When a person has a fatal disease, medicine is of no use to him.

'Nala lost his entire kingdom; Nala lost even Damayaṃtī and the other women in his harem; he lost the very jewellery that adorned his person. Kūvara shouted at Nala, "Leave my kingdom at once. You cannot stay here. Father gave you the kingdom, but the dice have now given it to me."

'Nala said to Kūvara, "Fortune is never far from men who are strong and mighty, my good man! Do not be so sure of yourself." Taking with him only the clothes on his back, Nala left with a smile. Even in adversity the steadfast never falter.

'Damayaṃtī followed Nala, but Kūvara blocked her way. "Fawn-eyed lady!" he said, "you must not go. I won you at dice. Now you must adorn my harem." At this the ministers said to Kūvara, "Damayaṃtī would not even touch the shadow of another man, so chaste is she. Do not put her in your harem. A man should look on his older brother's wife as he looks on his own mother.

'"If you force her then she will reduce you to a heap of ashes. A chaste woman can do anything.

'"Do not rouse the anger of this chaste woman; do not bring disaster on yourself. She would follow her husband; let her go. Why do you try to stop her? You need not give Nala a village or a settlement. Give him provisions for the journey and a single chariot with a charioteer."

'"When Kūvara heard the words of the minister, he let Damayaṃtī go with Nala. He gave Nala the chariot as the minister had asked. But Nala said, "I have given up all the wealth and glory that I had acquired in conquering half of Bharaha and I felt no pain at their loss; what do I need with a chariot?" The ministers said to Nala, "We have served you for a long time and would follow you now, but Kūvara prevents us. And there is another thing,

'"It is our tradition that we serve whoever is king in your

lineage. Now that you have given Kuvāra the kingdom, how could we abandon him?

'"Now Damayaṃtī alone must be your wife, your minister, your friend and your footsoldier. Her body is as tender as blossoms of the sirisa tree; how will she be able to walk with her soft lotus-like feet on the road that is rough with dirt and pebbles; how will she be able to go, burned by the rays of the sun? Lord! Take the chariot. Please, do this for us. Get on this chariot with the queen." When the ministers begged him in this way, Nala mounted the chariot with Damayaṃtī. When the women of the city saw Damayaṃtī in a single garment, as if she were going for her bath, they cried such large tears that it seemed that they wore two necklaces of pearls.

'As Nala proceeded through the city he saw, in its center, a pillar five hundred cubits high. Without a moment's sad thought for the loss of his kingdom, he playfully lifted up the pillar as if it were a plantain stalk. Then, as if to show that, though uprooted from his kingdom, he would plant his feet there firmly once more, he put the pillar back where it had stood. When the townspeople saw that they all said, "Strange indeed are the workings of Fate, if even Nala, with his strong arms, can lose his kingdom. Once when Nala and Kūvara were playing in the city garden a monk with divine sight and knowledge came into the garden. He told them, 'In the future Nala will be the ruler of the southern half of Bharaha. He will move the five-hundred cubit pillar that stands in the center of the city.' Now with our very own eyes we have seen both of these predictions come true. The only thing that seems wrong is that although Nala still lives someone else has become king of Kosalā. On the other hand, the words of a sage can never prove false. If Kūvara does not please his subjects, then surely Nala will be king here again." And so Nala left the city, listening to words like these from the townspeople. The chariot was wet with tears that fell from Damayaṃtī's eyes as she wept.

'Nala asked the daughter of Bhīma, "Queen, where shall we go?' She said, 'King! Let us go to Kuṃdiṇapur, where you may honor my father by being his guest." And so the charioteer at Nala's command spurred on the chariot's horses in the direction of Kuṃḍiṇapur. In time Nala came to a forest; there the roaring of fierce tigers terrified travellers, while deer fled in fear at the cruel calls of the leopards; everywhere there slithered snakes puffed up with poison, panicking the other creatures, and all around could be heard the cries of many a predatory beast. There Nala and Damayaṃtī were set upon by wild men who carried bows and arrows. Nala jumped off the chariot and stood boldly in front of them, brandishing his sword. Damayaṃtī got down from the chariot and grabbing his arm, stopped him, saying, "Why do you waste your efforts on the likes of these creatures, like a lion attacking jackals? Is your sword not ashamed to strike at those men, who are little more than beasts; that sword is the palace in which the Royal Goddess of Victory dwells, the Goddess of Victory over half of Bharaha." Damayaṃtī let out a loud cry; no one could have stood there in the midst of that cry which was imbued with all the power of her chastity. The wild men fled in every direction, like so many deer at the roar of a lion. Damayaṃtī and Nala followed them deep into the forest.

'In the meantime other savage men of the forest made off with their chariot; when fate is against a person even all of his heroism is for nought.

"Nala took Damayaṃtī's hand as he led her through the forest, reminding her of the time when he first took her hand in his at their wedding.

'Drops of blood dripped from Damayaṃtī's tender lotus-like feet as they were cut by the sharp tips of the grass; as she walked, the path behind her seemed to be studded with lady-bugs.

'When he was king, Damayaṃtī had wound a turban on

Nala's head; now with pieces of his garment he bound her sore feet.

'As Damayaṃtī sat under a tree, exhausted from the journey, King Nala fanned her with the edge of his garment.

'Nala gathered water in his cupped hands for the thirsty Damayaṃtī to drink. She asked him, "How much farther must we go in this forest today?"

'Nala answered, "Queen! The forest is a hundred furlongs deep. We have gone five furlongs already today. Take heart." As they talked there, the sun, as if ashamed that it could do nothing to help them, hid behind the peak of Sunset Mountain. Nala made a bed of kaṇkeli blossoms for Damayaṃtī there in the forest. He said to her, 'Queen, lie down here and give sleep a chance to seal up your sufferings for a time. Do not be afraid that anything will happen to you. I will keep watch over you.' Nala then took half of the garment that he wore and spread it down on the bed of flowers. Damayaṃtī prayed to the Jinas and recited the prayer of praise to the five Jain holy ones, the Jinas, others who have reached Final Liberation, the leading monks and teachers among the monks, and the entire monastic community. Then she fell asleep there on the bed that Nala had made for her. As she slept Nala thought to himself:

'"Men who must turn to their fathers-in-law for help are not real men at all. How can I go to Damayaṃtī father's house in this pitiable state?

'"I must steel myself and leave Damayaṃtī, even though I love her. Like a beggar I will go somewhere else on my own.

'"Nothing will happen to Damayaṃtī; she will be protected by her chastity. Their virtuous conduct, a suit of armor covering every limb, protects chaste women."'

'And so Nala took his dagger and cut off half of his garment. On a corner of Damayaṃtī's clothes he wrote these words in his own blood:

'"The road to Vidarbha lies just south of this fig tree; or

if you prefer, the road to Kosala lies to the north of this tree.

'"I must go elsewhere.'

'And then Nala tiptoed away, crying silently. He looked back and saw his beloved wife sleeping there, but then he went on a short distance before he began to think, "What will happen if a hungry tiger or lion in search of food should see her sleeping there alone? I will wait here until the sun comes up. At dawn let her go where she will." And so Nala retraced his steps back to her, like a beggar who has nothing left. When he saw her lying there asleep on the ground, he thought to himself, "Alas, Damayaṃtī sleeps here alone in the forest, clad in only a single garment. The women of Nala's harem never even saw the sun. It is because of me that this lotus-eyed lady has been reduced to this state. What can I do, I am lost! Shameless, I must be made of stone that I can look on my beloved wife lying here on the ground and feel no guilt. When she wakes up here in the forest without me, she may even prove herself to be better than I am by dying. I cannot bear to abandon her; she was a faithful wife to me. Let me die or live, whatever happens, as long as we are together. No, I should be the one to suffer here in this forest, which is filled with hundreds of dangers, not Damayaṃtī, too. When she reads what I have written, surely, she will go home to her father and live happily there." Convinced of this, Nala somehow got through the night. In the morning when it was time for his beloved wife to awaken, Nala vanished with swift steps.

'In the last hours of the night, as a pleasant breeze blew carrying with it the fragrance of lotuses, Damayaṃtī had a dream. She had climbed a mango tree with lovely blossoms and fruits. She had eaten its juicy ripe fruits, when a wild elephant tore the tree up by its roots and she fell to the ground, like the egg of a bird from its nest. At that Damayaṃtī woke up. When she did not see Nala there, like a deer that has been separated from the herd, she looked for him everywhere. She began to think, "Oh no! The worst has happened. I have been abandoned here in the forest with no one to protect me. No, no it can't be; my beloved must have gone to find some lake to get water for me to wash my face. Or maybe some demi-goddess has kidnapped Nala so that she could make love with him. The trees are still here and the mountains, and this is the same forest; only Nala is not here, with his face as lovely as the moon." Damayaṃtī searched everywhere, her mind confused by all of these conflicting thoughts. When she could not find Nala she grew frightened and began to think about the meaning of her dream. "The mango tree laden with fruits and flowers was King Nala. That I ate the fruits was my enjoyment of the pleasures of being a queen. That a wild elephant uprooted the tree corresponds to Nala's losing his kingdom on account of Fate, and that I fell from the tree, that is my abandonment by Nala. This dream tells me that it will be hard indeed for me to see him again."

'Damayaṃtī began to weep and wail in loud sobs. After all, women are cowardly at heart and are not strong in times of trouble.

'"My lord! Why have you abandoned me? Was I too heavy a burden for you? Surely the skin that a snake sheds was no great weight on its back.

'"O Goddesses of the Forest! I beg you, show me my husband, or show me the path that has been purified by the touch of his lotus feet. Even better, O Earth! Split open like a ripe fruit that I may enter through the crack and find some peace in the world below.'

'As Damayaṃtī lamented, watering the forest trees with her tears, unable to think of any place, anywhere, that would make her happy now that Nala had left her, she suddenly noticed the words written on the edge of her garment. Her face beamed with delight as she read them out. She thought to herself, "My beloved has abandoned me in deed but not in thought; otherwise he would not have shown me this favor of leaving me this message. I shall carry out his words as I would the words of my elders; in that way no harm will come to me in this world. I shall go to my father's house. In any case, for a woman who is without her husband, her husband's house is a place of scorn." So Damayaṃtī decided; she took the path that lead south of the fig tree. She kept her eyes on Nala's words as if they were Nala himself, walking by her side. Through the power of her unblemished chastity, no danger was able to touch her. Thus:

'A lion, claws stretched out in anger, hideous to behold with its terrible fangs, was unable even to get near her.

'A herd of angry elephants, with noisy bees buzzing around the rut juice oozing from their temples and with trunks held high, kept as far away from her as it could.

'A forest fire, having darkened the skies, licking the heavens with its surging flames, died out before it even reached her, not causing her the slightest pain.

'Poisonous snakes, their hoods raised, spitting drops of poison in their ever growing anger, were not able to strike her.

'As soon as they spotted her, goblins and demons and the like, their great pride humbled, turned their backs on her and marched off in the other direction.

'As she wandered, her body washed with sweat from the exertion of her journey, her feet dripping blood from the thorns that pierced them, her beauty concealed by the veil of dust that covered her, Damayaṃtī came upon a large caravan. She thought to herself, "Oh, my merit has led me to this vast caravan, which will be my way out of this forest." But no sooner had she consoled herself with this thought, then the caravan was attacked by highway robbers, brandishing all sorts of fearful weapons. Everyone was terrified. Damayaṃtī cried out, "Do not be afraid," and she shouted at the thieves, "You wicked men! Do not attempt to loot this caravan which is under my protection! If you do you will suffer the consequences." But that did not stop the thieves. And so she let out a loud cry into which she had infused all the power of her chastity. At that the thieves dispersed like a flock of crows at the sound of the twang of a bowstring. The members of the caravan all said, "This woman who has saved us must be some goddess, who is here in response to our merits." The leader of the caravan bowed down to her with all the respect he would show to his own mother. He asked her, "Goddess! Who are you? Why are you wandering here in the forest?" She wept and told him everything that had happened to her, just as she would have told a good friend. He said, "As the wife of the great king Nala you deserve to be honored by me. Besides that, I am indebted to you, for you have saved me from those thieves. And so I ask you to honor my dwelling with your presence." With those words he led Damayaṃtī to his encampment. There the caravan leader waited on her as if she were indeed a goddess.

'Soon the rainy season was upon them; the entire universe was filled with the roaring thunder of the clouds; rainbows appeared in the sky, while flocks of peacocks danced in joy; the heavens were covered with thick dark clouds, and the torrents of rain made everything feel cool; the earth was adorned with streams of running water. It rained without a stop for three days and three nights. Damayaṃtī, staying with the caravan leader, felt no inconvenience. When the rain finally let up she left the caravan and went on her way. She soon saw a frightful demon with yellow hair; he looked like a mountain ablaze with forest fires; he was black like a cloud; he was like a second embodiment of the God of Death; in his hideous hand he brandished a sword that flashed like lightning across the dark cloud of his body. He said to her, "I am hungry for flesh and blood; you will be my dinner. I will eat you." She said, "Sir! Death comes to every living being. Only the person who has not fulfilled his life's goal fears death. I have fulfilled my goal by worshipping the gods and my elders. I do not fear death. What is more:

'"Afflicted with so many sufferings I seek death as a way out of my misery.

'"Eat your fill of me, for I burn with the fire of longing for Nala.

'"Eat me; why do you hesitate? I give myself to you. How can I put an end to my sufferings if not by dying?"'

'The demon was pleased by her fortitude. He said, "Lady! I am pleased. What can I do for you?" She said, "If you are pleased with me, then tell me, when shall I meet my husband again?" The demon used his supernatural knowledge and then said this to her, "When twelve years have elapsed since the day that you went into exile, you will be reunited with your husband while you are staying in your father's house." Then he added, "Why should you tire yourself with such an arduous journey? Just say the word and I will deliver you to your father's home in the wink of an eye." She replied, "It is enough for me that you have told me that I will see Nala again. I do not want to go anywhere with a man who is not my husband. Go home." Displaying a divine body, ablaze with countless rays of light, the demon vanished.

Damayaṃtī now knew that her husband's period of exile would be twelve years; she undertook to renounce certain things. She vowed, 'I give up wearing red clothes and eating betel; I will not wear jewellery or apply fragrant unguents to my body; I renounce eating rich foods like ghee until I am with my husband Nala again.' Damayaṃtī devoted herself to practicing severe penances; she would break her fasts by eating only fruits devoid of seeds. In a mountain cave she meditated on the image of Sāmtinātha that was always in her thoughts.

'The caravan leader was worried when he realized that she was gone; he searched everywhere for her and found the mountain cave. She emerged from her state of meditation and spoke to him. Some ascetics overheard their conversation; they too came to her cave. They were transfixed; they stood there, intent on listening, mesmerized by the sound of her voice as deer are said to be mesmerized by song. It had begun to rain; indeed rain fell in torrents. Pelted by the heavy downpour, which struck them as mercilessly as a shower of arrows, the ascetics began to ask each other, "Where can we go to get out of the rain?" Moved by compassion Damayaṃtī said to them, "Sirs! Do not be afraid." She dug a trench all around them and then made this truth-oath that was a proclamation of her chaste conduct, "If my chastity has never been sullied, then let the clouds rain down outside this trench." As soon as she said this, water stopped falling inside the area of the trench, as if the area were protected by a roof. Everywhere else even the rocks were washed away in the rush of the falling water. When they saw this, the ascetics were astonished. They said, "Her beauty is not that of a mortal woman and the power of her chastity goes beyond mortal power. She must be some goddess."'

'The caravan leader asked her, "On whom do you meditate? How is that you are not afraid to be here?" She answered, "I meditate on the Jina, who is my god. Through his power I am not afraid." She told the caravan leader all about the nature of god, the teachers, and the religious doctrine according to the Jinas, and thus brought the caravan leader to accept the Jain faith. Those ascetics too accepted the doctrine of the Jinas and cast their own doctrine aside with contempt, as a person who has tasted sweet milk scorns a drink of sour gruel. The caravan leader had a city built on the spot. It became known as "Tāvasapura", "City of the Ascetics", since the five hundred ascetics were awakened to the truth there. He had a beautiful temple made for the image of Sāṃtinātha. And they all spent their time together there, devoted to the doctrine of the Jinas.

'One night Damayaṃtī saw a light like all the rays of

the rising sun coming from a mountain peak. She also saw gods descending to the peak and ascending back into the sky. Their shouts of joy woke everyone up. Damayaṃtī and the people of Tāvasapura climbed the mountain. The gods were celebrating the occasion of the achievement of Omniscience by the monk Siṃhakesari. Damayaṃtī and the others bowed down to the monk and then sat down in front of him. The teacher of that monk, named Jasabhadda, had also come to see Siṃhakesari. He, too, bowed down to the Omniscient One and sat down. The Omniscient One gave a sermon on the Jain doctrine, in which he described the true nature of transmigratory existence as without inherent worth.

'A god joined them, lighting up the heavens with his radiance. He said to Damayaṃtī, "Lady! In this very penance grove I was once the disciple of the chief of these ascetics. I devoted myself to the practice of the severest penances. My name was Kappara. Although I practiced the five-fire penance, exposing myself to the sun and to burning fires all around me, the other ascetics did not appreciate me. That made me angry and I decided to go elsewhere. At night, when dense darkness covered the world, I stumbled in a declivity of the mountain. I struck my teeth on the hard surface of the rock and broke them. Overwhelmed by the pain of breaking my teeth, I dropped to the ground right there. I lay there like that for seven days and seven nights. The other ascetics did not even try to find out what had happened to me, let alone try to take care of me; they were no more eager to know where I was than a person is to know where a nightmare has gone once he awakens from it. I imagine the ascetics were perfectly content there in the penance grove without me, the way a person breathes a sigh of relief when a snake has been chased from his house. My anger at the ascetics smouldered inside me; I died and was reborn as a snake in their penance grove. Once, raising my hood, I even made a dash to strike you. When you saw me you immediately recited the Jain prayer to the five groups of people worthy of honour. I was stopped dead in my tracks when those words reached my ears. I went back into my hole. On another occasion I heard you expounding the Jain doctrine to the ascetics.

> The creature who kills a living being because he is under the influence of anger, pride, deceitfulness or greed, attains the most terrible suffering in his next birth.

"That made me think, Oh, what will happen to me? I live by killing living beings. I also had the feeling that I had seen these ascetics before. I reasoned it all out and came to remember my past birth. Disgusted with worldly desires and worldly gains, I confessed my sins, voluntarily renounced all food, and died a pious death. I was reborn in the realm of the gods as the god named Kusumappaha. I came here now because I wanted to see you; you had done me the greatest service, for it was only because I heard you preach the Jain doctrine that I became a god. I am your son in the faith." The god then said to the ascetics, "Forgive me for what I did in my anger. Observe with care the vow you took to be pious lay Jains." He then dragged the dead body of the snake out of the mountain cave and hung it on a tree. He declared, "Whoever harbors anger, like Kappara, will become a snake in his next birth."'

'The leader of those ascetics, his mind trembling in fear and loathing of this worldly existence, said to the Omniscient One, "Blessed One! Ordain me as a monk." The Omniscient One replied, "My teacher Jasabhadda will ordain you." The head of the ascetics again spoke up, "Why did you become a monk?" The Omniscient One answered, "I am the son of Kūvara from the city Kosalā. Kesari, the lord of the city Bhaṃgā, gave his daughter Bandhumaī to me in marriage. My father advised me to marry her and so I did. When I was on my way back home with her, I saw an ascetic who was preaching to a gathering of people. I bowed down to him and then listened with great faith to his sermon, which was like a river of heavenly nectar. I asked him, 'Blessed One! How long do I have to live?' The teacher used his supernatural knowledge and replied, 'Son! You have only five days to live.' Having learned that I was soon to die, I asked again, 'Blessed One! I have little time left to live. What should I do now?' The teacher felt pity for me and said, 'Son! Do not despair. Renounce the world and become a monk, for even one day as a monk is the cause of a sojourn in heaven or Final Release.' And so I became a monk. My teacher instructed me to come here. Through the fire of my final pure state of meditation, I burned off all the fuel of my karma and attained Omniscience." With those words, Siṃhakesari stopped the influx of further karma, and having now put an end to all of the karma that causes a person to be reborn, he attained Final Release. The gods cremated the body of that Omniscient Sage. The chief of the ascetics renounced the world under the guidance of the Jain monk Jasabhadda.

'Damayaṃtī also asked Jasabhadda, "Please ordain me, too." Jasabhadda replied,

'Lady! You still have pleasures to enjoy with Nala. You should not renounce the world yet.'

The next morning Jasabhadda descended the mountain and went to Tāvasapura.

'Damayaṃtī spent seven years in the mountain cave, devoted to the practice of religion, her body covered in dirt. One day she heard some traveller say, "Damayaṃtī! I saw your husband in such and such a place." She was satisfied; she left the cave. She ran in the direction of the voice, covering a vast distance. She stumbled back into a forest. When she did not see Nala, she began to cry. She lamented, "Alas, What shall I do? Where shall I go?" When she turned to go back to her mountain cave she saw a demoness, mouth wide open, ready to eat her. But because of the great power of Damayaṃtī's chastity, the demonness was not able to devour her. The demoness vanished like something seen in a dream. As Damayaṃtī went on she came to a river without water. She was parched with thirst and struck the dry river bed with her foot; through the force of her chastity water appeared in the river. She drank her fill and then went on again.

'Damayaṃtī grew exhausted and stopped to rest under a fig tree. Some merchants from a passing caravan saw her there. "Lady!" they asked, "who are you? You look like a goddess." She told them, "I am a mortal woman. I was separated from the caravan in which I was travelling and have been wandering here in this forest. Show me the way to Tāvasapura." They replied, "We have come in search of water. The sun has reached the peak of Sunset Mountain; we cannot show you the way right now, but if you come with us you can join our caravan and we will take you to some city or other." She agreed. When the leader of the caravan, a merchant named Dhaṇadeva, saw her, he asked, "Who are you?" She replied, "I am the daughter of a merchant. I was on my way to my father's house. I fell asleep in the forest and my husband abandoned me. Your men brought me here to the caravan, treating me with the affection and respect due a family member." The caravan leader said, "I am on my way to Acalapura. My daughter, come along with us. I will take care of you and see that you come to no harm." She was given a place of honor in the main wagon.

'The caravan set off. They stopped for the night in a mountain grove that was redolent with pollen from the blossoms of the flowering trees. That night Damayaṃtī heard a member of the party reciting the Jain prayer to the five beings worthy of honor. She said to the caravan leader,

'"The person who recites this prayer is a lay Jain. I am also a Jain. I wish to speak to him." The caravan leader, feeling for her the affection a father feels for his own child, took her to the person who was praying. She saw the Jain lay devotee worshipping a painted likeness of the Jina that was dark like the color of the leaves of the tamāla tree. Damayaṃtī, too, bowed down to the likeness. She then paid her respects to her fellow Jain and said, "Sir! Which Jina's likeness is this?" He replied, "Let me tell you. I am a merchant from the city of Kaṃcī, 'Bodice', which is indeed like the jewelled bodice of the Lady Earth. One day a Jain monk named Dhamagutta, who was possessed of extraordinary knowledge, came to Kaṃcī. I bowed down to him and asked him, 'When will I achieve Final Release?' He replied, 'After a sojourn in heaven, you will descend from there and be born as King Pasannacanda in the city Mihilā. You will conceive a desire to renounce the world in the presence of the nineteenth Tīrthaṃkara, the Jina Mallināha, and you will then attain Liberation.' From that day on I have felt great devotion for the Jina Mallināha. I worship this painted likeness of the Jina Mallināha." He asked Damayaṃtī about herself and she told him all that had happened to her. He then said, "This caravan leader is like your own father and I am your brother. You must not despair."

'The next morning the caravan reached the city Acalapura. They left her there and went on. Damayaṃtī was thirsty and went to the town reservoir. The women who saw her there thought she must be the Water Goddess.

'As she stood there on the bank, a crocodile grabbed her by the left foot.

'Suffering follows upon suffering; everything in nature is eager to be with its own kind!

She recited the Jain prayer to the five who are worthy of honor. She freed her foot and got out of the water. Depressed, she sat down at the water's edge.

'The king of Acalapur was Riupanna, and true to his name he was like a Supanna bird to destroy the snakes, his enemies. His queen was named Caṇdajasā, 'The One whose Fame is like the Moon', and her fame was indeed as glowing as the moon. Her serving maids saw Damayaṃtī. They were astonished by her great beauty and told the queen about her. She had Damayaṃtī brought to her. When she saw Damayaṃtī she exclaimed, "Oh, there is such a sweetness in her beauty!" She embraced her. Damayaṃtī fell at the queen's feet. The queen asked her, "Lady! Who are you?" She answered, "I am the daughter of a merchant; I was abandoned by my husband in the forest." The queen told her, "You will be like my own daughter, Candavaī. You must stay here in the palace with me. Do not worry about anything."

'Now every day just outside the city the queen arranged for food and other things to be given to the poor and the needy. One day Damayaṃtī said to the queen, "I want to give out the food in the poorhouse; I think that maybe my husband just might show up there some day in search of something to eat." The queen agreed to let Damayaṃtī serve in the poorhouse. Eager to see her husband, Damayaṃtī distributed the food. She would ask all the people who came to receive alms, "Have you ever seen a man who looks like this?" Now one day when she was working in the poorhouse, she saw a thief bound and being led in by guards. She asked the guards, "What did he steal?" They told her, "He stole the jewel box that belongs to the princess Candavaī. He has been sentenced to death." The thief, biting on his fingers, bowed to Damayaṃtī and said, "I am at your mercy. Make them release me." Damayaṃtī was moved by compassion and made a truth statement about her chastity. Through the power of her chastity, the fetters that bound the thief broke. The guards were perplexed.

'When the king heard about the event he rushed to the poorhouse. He asked Damayaṃtī, "Daughter! Why did you do what you did? It was wrong A thief should not be spared. It is the duty of kings to punish the wicked and protect the good. If kings do not do this, then there will be chaos and anarchy; the big will swallow up the little and there will be no regard for justice." Damayaṃtī replied, "King! Forgive my wrongdoing; I acted out of compassion. For like some contagious disease, his pain touched my heart and I was stricken." The king then freed the thief. Every day the thief bowed down to Damayamti and said to her, "You are my mother." One day she asked him, "Who are you? Where did you come from?" He told her, "I am the servant of the caravan leader Vasanta from Tāvasapura. My name is Piṅgala. I was addicted to gambling and I broke into Vasanta's house and stole his most valuable possessions.

'"With his valuables in my hand I ran for my life, but I was then robbed myself. True it is that the wicked have scant luck.

'"I came here and entered the service of the king; somehow I happened to see Candavaī's jewel box.

'"I felt temptation in my heart; there arose in my mind a desire to steal the jewel box. It is generally true what they say, that a wicked person never changes.

'"Taking the jewel box, I tried to conceal myself under a thick cloak; but the king knows how to read a person's gestures and he recognized me for the thief that I am.

'"The king had me bound by the guards. I saw you as I was being led off to the execution grounds. I recognized you and sought your protection, and you caused me to be set free. There is more that I have to tell you. After you left Tāvasapura, the caravan leader Vasanta refused to eat for seven days. On the eighth day the Jain monk Jasabhadda and everyone else finally convinced him to eat. One day Vasanta went to see Kūvara and brought him some of his finest goods as gifts. Kūvara was pleased with him and gave to him lordship over Tāvasapura, along with the right to carry the royal insignia, like the umbrella. He returned to Tāvasapura to the sound of drums that filled the heavens, and there he reigns." Damayaṃtī convinced Piṅgala to renounce the world; renunciation is the thunderbolt that cleaves the mountain of sins.

'One day Damayaṃtī's father Bhīma heard that Kūvara had defeated Nala in a game of dice and was now sitting on his throne. He heard, too, how Nala had taken Damayaṃtī and gone into a vast forest. But no one could say where Nala was or even if he was still alive; perhaps he was dead. When Damayaṃtī's mother Pupphadaṃtī heard this she began to cry; her large tears wet her breasts. Bhīma sent the Brahmin Harimitta in search of Nala and Damayaṃtī. Harimitta was skilled in performing the tasks his master asked of him, and in time he reached Acalapura and King Riupanna. Queeṇ Candajasā asked him, "How is my sister Pupphadaṃtī?" Harimitta replied, "As always the queen is well, but ever since she heard how Nala and Damayaṃtī had been expelled from their kingdom she has been greatly troubled in her mind." Candajasā asked, "What? What are you talking about?" Harimitta then told her everything about Nala's gambling match and its consequences. Candajasā burst out crying and the courtiers cried too when they saw how she wept.

'The brahmin Harimitta, seeing them all overcome by grief, was himself overcome by hunger and so he went to the poorhouse, where strangers and travellers could also go to get a meal. He sat down to eat. When he saw Damayaṃtī there in charge of the almsgiving, he felt such joy that he knew at once she must be Damayamti. He bowed down to her and said, 'Queen! What has brought you to this state, like a creeper withered in the summer's heat? At least you are still alive! Now everyone will rest easy." As he spoke to her he forgot his own hunger and hastened back to Candajasā. He said to her, 'Queen, all is well! Damayaṃtī is right here in your own poorhouse.'

When she heard what Harimitta said, Candajasā ran to the poorhouse. She hugged Damayaṃtī tightly and exclaimed, 'What a fool I was! I should have recognized you at once from all the auspicious marks on your body; such marks never appear on the body of an ordinary person. Daughter! Why did you not tell me who you are; you must know how much I care for you. What had you to be ashamed of in front of me? But tell me, did you abandon Nala or did he abandon you? It must have been Nala who abandoned you. If you were to forsake your husband when he was in distress, then surely the sun would rise in the west. Alas, Nala! Are you not ashamed to have abandoned this woman of such impeccable virtue? Does that befit a man of your breeding? I shall take away your suffering, Damayaṃtī. I shall make an offering to the gods to remove your pain. Forgive me that I did not recognize you. But where is the beauty mark on your forehead with its radiant glow?' And as she asked this, Candajasā used her own saliva to wipe Damayaṃtī's forehead.

'The mark on Damayaṃtī's forehead began to shine, like the sun released from the clouds, like a lump of gold just taken out of the fire.

'Queen Candajasā then bathed Damayaṃtī with her own hands, as one might bathe the image of the god. She dressed her in the finest silks and then seated her by her side.

'As Candajasā and Damayaṃtī sat there together with the king, the sun, light of the world, went down.

'The world was coated in darkness as a pot is smeared with lampblack; but there was not a trace of darkness in the king's court.

'The king said, "The sun has set and there is no lamp here. There is no fire, either. Where does this light come from?"

'The queen then showed him the birthmark on Damayaṃtī's forehead, from which streamed a mass of light. Curious, the king covered it up with his hand. At once the court was enshrouded in darkness like a mountain cave. The king took his hand away. He then asked her about everything that had happened to her, beginning with her loss of the kingdom. Weeping, her head bowed low, she told him everything. The king wiped her eyes with his own upper garment and said to her, "Daughter! Do not cry. Fate affects even the gods and the anti-gods."

'Just as the king was saying this, a god came into the court, spreading light like the rays of the sun. He folded his hands in reverence and said to Damayaṃtī, 'I am the thief Piṅgala who, following your advice, became a monk. In the course of my wanderings I went back to Tāvasapura. I meditated there in the cremation grounds. I was burnt by the flames of a funeral pyre, and intent on meditating on the doctrine, reciting to myself the prayer to the five who are worthy of honor, I confessed my sins and repented. I died and was reborn as a god. I knew my previous birth through my supernatural knowledge, and I have now come to see you, for you have helped me greatly by saving my life and making me renounce the world and become a monk. May you have much happiness." With those words the god caused seven crores of gold pieces to rain down on Damayaṃtī and then vanished. When King Riupanna saw how the god had given them direct proof of the rewards of good deeds, he became a firm believer in the Jain doctrine

'Now one day the brahmin Harimitta said to the king, "Lord, send Damayaṃtī back to her father's house." Candajasā agreed. And so King Riupanna sent Damayaṃtī off, accompanied by an army of elephants, horses, chariots and footsoldiers. When King Bhīma heard that she was coming, drawn to her by affection as surely as if he were being pulled by a cord, he and Queen Pupphadaṃtī went out to meet her. When Damayaṃtī saw her father and mother, she got off the chariot and fell at their feet in delight.

'At last after longing to see each other for so long, they were finally together. The water that fell from their eyes soaked the ground and turned it into mud.

'Damayaṃtī embraced her mother as the river Yamunā

embraces the Ganges; hanging on to her mother's neck, she cried in loud sobs.

'They washed their lotus-like faces in clean water and then proceeded to tell each other all their joys and sorrows.

'Pupphadaṃtī took Damayaṃtī onto her lap and said, "Daughter! Stay here with us, living happily in your own home. You will see your husband again; for a person eventually sees good fortune if he lives long enough."

'The king was delighted with Harimitta and gave him five hundred villages. He ordered that the gods and teachers should be worshipped for seven days with particular fervour in thanks for Damayaṃtī's return. On the eighth day he said to Damayaṃtī, "I will do something that will bring you together with Nala very soon."

'Now Nala, after he had abandoned Damayaṃtī, wandered in the forest. He saw smoke billowing out of a grove of trees. Black as a pack of bees, the smoke rose up in a solid column, like a mountain whose wings had been cut in days of old, when the king of the gods clipped the mountain's wings; the smoke could be seen climbing higher and higher in the sky. It was like a huge cloud, with flashes of lightning that crept along the surface of the earth as from that mass of smoke leapt terrifying flames. Then the entire forest seemed to catch on fire; there was a loud popping sound as bamboos split open, while the cries of savage beasts were terrifying to hear. That was when Nala heard these words, "O Nala! Sun that makes bloom the lotus that is the Ikkhāgu clan! Save me!" Since he was by nature compassionate, Nala ran in the direction of the voice. He saw a gargantuan snake in the middle of the forest. It was now shouting at him, "Stop! Stop!" Nala was astonished; he wondered, "How does this creature know my name and my clan name? And how can a snake speak with a human voice?" He threw down his upper garment in an effort to pull the snake towards him. The snake coiled its body around the cloth. Nala pulled the snake as one pulls a rope from a well; he dragged it to a place that was untouched by the forest fire. As he was about to let it go the snake bit him on the hand. Nala threw the snake on the ground and said, "I see how you repay a kind deed; I see how grateful you are to me. It is true what they say about your kind, that even if you feed a snake milk it will still bite you one day."

'Even as Nala spoke these words, the poison travelled through his body, which became bent like a living bow. Nala now looked like a demon with yellow hair; he looked like a camel with a protruding lip; he looked like a beggar with stubby hands and feet; like the elephant god Ganesa with his swollen belly. When Nala saw how hideous every part of his body had become he thought to himself, "What use is it for me to live if I look like this?. I will renounce the world and become a monk; at least that will do some good for me in my next birth."

'As Nala was preoccupied with this thought, the snake suddenly turned into a god, with hanging jewelled earrings, radiating light all around him. He said, "Do not despair. I am your father, Nisaha. I gave my throne to you and became a monk. I died and have become a god. With my supernatural knowledge I came to know what had happened to you. I magically turned myself into a snake and when you were already miserable enough, I caused your body to be deformed like this. It must have seemed to you as if I were just throwing salt on your wounds, but you must look on this as good for you, like drinking some bitter medicine. You had made all of the other kings into your servants; now when they see you deformed like this, they will never suspect that it is you and they will not cause you any harm. And you must not desire to renounce the world just yet. You must still rule over the earth. I will tell you when it is time for you to renounce the world. Now take this fruit and this jewel box and guard them with care. When you want to look like yourself again, break open the fruit. You will see garments of fine cloth inside it. Open the jewel box and there you will see some jewellery, pearl necklaces and other things. The instant you put on the fine clothes and the jewellery you will look like yourself again." Nala asked the god what had become of Damayaṃtī. He told Nala how her great chastity had saved her many times. The god said to Nala, "Why do you wander like this in the forest? I will take you wherever you want to go." Nala said, "Take me to the city of Suṃsumāra." The god did as he was asked and then went back to the world of the gods.

Nala prayed to Nemināha in the Jain temple in a garden just outside the city and then proceeded to the city gate. There he saw a mad elephant that had broken away from its post; the seat on its back was jostling to and fro as if struck by the wind; with its trunk it seemed to grab even the birds flying overhead as it trampled down a grove of trees. From the city wall King Dahivanna proclaimed, "I will give the person who can bring this elephant under his control whatever he asks of me." Hunchback Nala declared, "Show me that mad elephant so that I can subdue it." At that very moment the elephant appeared, trumpeting like a thundering cloud. The hunchback rushed toward the elephant. He brought the elephant under his control, skilfully parrying the thrusts of its trunk, dodging in front of it and then behind it and then to this side and that. Like a giant bird he leapt onto its back. He readjusted the ropes and swung his feet around and then struck the elephant on the temples with his fist. Then, using the elephant goad, the hunchback made the elephant go where he commanded. The people began to shout in praise of the hunchback's victory. The king gave him a chain made of gold. Nala, having subdued the elephant, guided him back to his post. He got off the elephant and without so much as a bow to King Dahivanna, he sat right down next to him.

'The king asked, "O hunchback! You clearly know how to deal with elephants. Do you know anything else?" The hunchback replied, "What shall I say? If you want to see how I can cook just with the heat of the sun, then I will show you." At that the king went into the palace and brought out beans, rice, vegetables and spices for the hunchback. The hunchback set the cooking pot in the sunlight and meditated on a magic formula to the sun; the dish was ready. The king and his retinue ate the tasty dish, that was like something that had come from the wishing trees in heaven. The king proclaimed, "That was a masterpiece! The taste was so delicate. It was so refined! It was truly a feast for all the senses! I thought only Nala knew how to cook like this. I haven't had food like this for a while, not since I last went to pay my humble respects to Nala. Are you Nala, then, O hunchback? But Nala was not ugly like this. And how could he have come this far along a road with so many obstacles, a distance of a hundred furlongs? And why would Nala, who rules over half of Bharaha, be alone?" The king in his delight gave the hunchback clothes and jewelery, a hundred thousand coins and five hundred villages. The hunchback accepted all of the gifts except the five hundred villages. The king asked him, "Shall I give you something else?" The hunchback replied, "If you want to do something more for me, then put an end to hunting and to drinking intoxicating drinks throughout your kingdom." The king respected his words and did as he asked.

'On another occasion the king asked the hunchback, "Who are you and where have you come from?" The hunchback replied, "My name is Huṃḍia. I was the cook of King Nala in Kosalā. It was from him that I learned the traditional arts like cooking and taming elephants. Nala was defeated by his brother Kūvara in a game of dice and lost his kingdom. He took Damayaṃtī with him and went into the forest. Nala died there. That was when I decided to come to you. I could not bear to stay with the wicked Kūvara, who was like a deep well filled with deceitful tricks."

'When King Dahivanna heard the news of Nala's death

he was so overwhelmed with grief that he could not utter a single word.

'One day King Dahivanna happened to send a messenger on some friendly errand to Damayaṃtī's father.

'Bhīma welcomed the messenger. As they were talking about one thing and another, the messenger just happened to say, "Nala's cook is staying with my master. Nala taught him how to cook in the sun." When she heard that, Damayaṃtī said to her father, "Father! Send a spy and let him see what this cook looks like. Nala is the only person who knows how to cook in the sun. The man might be Nala in disguise."

'The king sent a Brahmin named Kusala, "The Skilled One", who was indeed skilled in performing the tasks his master gave him. Kusala was to find out just what Dahivanna's cook looked like.

'He arrived in the city of Suṃsumāra, his zeal for his task doubled by the good omens that accompanied him. But when he saw that the cook was a hunchback, he sat down in total despair.

'Kusala thought to himself, 'What a difference there is between this hunchback and Nala, as great a difference as there is between mighty Mount Meru and a tiny mustard seed!'

'But something nagged at Kusala's mind and so he recited this verse:

'There is no one so cruel, so heartless, so cowardly as Nala, who abandoned his chaste wife Damayaṃtī as she slept in the forest at night.'

'When Nala heard the verse being sung over and over again, he remembered Damayaṃtī and began to cry, his tears falling to the ground. Kusala asked him, "Why are you crying?" The hunchback replied, "When I heard your sad verse I was roused to pity and so I began to cry." The hunchback then asked Kusala what lay behind the verse. Kusala told him everything, beginning with Nala's dice game and ending with Damayaṃtī's arrival in her birthplace, Vidabbha. The brahmin Kusala then said, "Hunchback! A messenger of Dahivanna said in front of King Bhīma that you know how to cook in the sun. Damayaṃtī, thinking that only Nala knows that secret, asked her father to send me to see you. But when I got here and saw you I thought to myself, 'What a difference there is between this hideous hunchback and Nala, whose every feature, every limb, radiated charm. What a difference there is between a heron that gobbles down schools of fish and the moon that brings delight to the eyes of everyone. As I was on my way here I saw many propitious omens; clearly they have not borne fruit, for you are not Nala.'" Overwhelmed by his love for Damayaṃtī, the hunchback took the messenger home with him. For it is said:

> Even a crow that has come from the direction in which the one you love dwells brings you joy; how much greater is the joy that comes from seeing a person your loved one has actually sent to you!

'The hunchback asked, "What can I do to welcome you to my home, you who have told me about the great man Nala and his extraordinary chaste wife?" With those words he served the messenger dinner and honored him with the customary hospitality. He even gave him the jewellery that Dahivanna had given him for subduing the elephant.

'Kusala then returned home safely to Kuṃdiṇapur. He told Bhīma all about the hunchback and how he had subdued the mad elephant. Damayaṃtī said, "Father! I am sure it is Nala. He has somehow become deformed, either through the fault of something that he ate or through his bad karma.

'"This skill in taming elephants, the ability to cook in the sun, and this great generosity, all of this could not belong to anyone else but Nala!

'"Father! Think of some way to bring he hunchback here so that I can see him for myself."

'Bhīma said, "Daughter! Let us pretend to organize a public ceremony for you to choose another husband. I will invite King Dahivanna. Dahivanna wanted to marry you before, but you chose Nala. When he hears that you will take a new husband he will surely come running. The hunchback will come with him. If he is really Nala then he will not stand your being given to another man. Besides, Nala knows the secret of horses. If the hunchback is Nala, then we will know from the way he drives the horses. If Nala drives the horses they will gallop with the speed of the wind. I will set the date soon. If the hunchback can come that quickly we will know he is Nala. Ordinary men cannot bear to see anyone take their wives, to say nothing of Nala!"

'Bhīma thus sent a messenger to Dahivanna. The messenger announced to him that Damayaṃtī would choose a new husband on the fifth day of the bright half of the month of April. Dahivanna thought to himself, "I want Damayaṃtī, but Vidabbhā is far away. The fifth is tomorrow. I can never get there by then. What can I do?" Dahivanna was agitated, like a fish tossing about in the shallows. The hunchback thought, "Damayaṃtī is the most chaste woman; she would never desire another man. And even if she did, what man could have her while I am still alive? I will see to it that Dahivanna gets there in twenty-four hours; he can watch the goings on, but I will also get to see for myself what is happening."

'The hunchback said to King Dahivanna, "What is bothering you?Tell me what is on your mind. A sick person cannot get treatment if he does not tell anyone what ails him." The king said,

"Nala has entered the city of the gods, and Damayaṃtī will now choose another husband. I want Damayaṃtī, but Vidabbhā is far away. There are only twenty-four hours left.

It took the messenger days to reach here. How can I get there in such a short time? This thought is driving me crazy; it leaves me no peace." The hunchback said, "Give me a chariot yoked with your finest horses and I will get you there by tomorrow morning." The king thought to himself, "Clearly this hunchback is no ordinary mortal; he must be some demi-god or god," and so he gave him the chariot he had asked for. King Dahivanna made the chariot ready and then told Nala to get on.

'Five men, the king, his betel-leaf carrier, his umbrella bearer and two chowry bearers mounted the chariot; the hunchback was the sixth.

'The hunchback tied the fruit and the jewel box in a corner of his waist cloth; then praying to the Jinas and the monks, he stirred the horses on.

'The chariot began to fly, its fine horses driven on by Nala, who knew the secret of horses; it was like a chariot of the gods, set in motion by the gods' mere thoughts.

'Dahivanna's scarf fell, blown about by the wind that the chariot raised, as if he had taken it off to make a gift of it to Nala in appreciation for his help.

Dahivanna told the hunchback that the scarf had fallen, but the hunchback only smiled and said in return, "O king! Where is your scarf? The chariot has already gone twenty five furlongs since your scarf dropped. In fact these horses are just average; if they had been the best, then we would have gone fifty furlongs in that space of time."

'Dahivanna pointed to a fig tree and boasted, "I call tell you the number of fruits on that tree without even counting them. On the way back I will show you." The hunchback said, "With me as your charioteer you do not have to worry about losing a few minutes. With one blow of my fist I can bring all of those fruits to the ground." The king said, "Then see for yourself what a marvellous skill I have. Bring the fruit down. There are eighteen thousand fruit on the tree." The hunchback made the fruits fall to the ground with one blow of his fist. Dahivanna counted them; there were exactly the number that he had said there would be. The hunchback was impressed and imparted to Dahivanna his secret knowledge of horses. In return Dahivanna gave him the secret knowledge of counting fruits. As dawn broke they reached the outskirts of the city Kuṃḍinapura: King Dahivanna was beaming with joy.

'At that very moment, in the last hours of the night, Damayaṃtī had a dream. She dutifully reported the dream to her father. "I saw the Goddess of Perfect Peace in the sky; she was bringing the garden of Kosalā right here. She told me to climb a mango tree that was laden with fruit and flowers and I did. The goddess gave me a beautiful lotus. There was a bird that had alighted on the tree before; it suddenly fell from the tree." Bhīma said, "Daughter! This is a propitious dream. The Goddess of Perfect Peace is the ripening of all your meritorious deeds. The garden of Kosalā is the acquisition of the kingdom of Kosalā. Climbing the mango tree is your union with Nala. The fall of the bird that had climbed the tree before is the fall of Kūvara from the throne. Since you saw this dream early this morning, it means that you will be reunited with Nala on this very day."

'Indeed at that very moment Dahivanna was at the city gate. The servant whose task it was to announce good news informed Bhīma of his arrival. Bhīma rushed to meet him and embraced him as a friend. He gave him excellent quarters in which to lodge. He then offered him the customary gestures of hospitality, a meal and so on. This done, Bhīma said to him, "I hear you have a cook who can cook in the heat of the sun. Show him to me." Dahivanna ordered the hunchback to make something for Bhīma. In the twinkling of an eye the dish was ready, as if it had come ready made from one of the wishing trees in heaven. At Dahivanna's urging King Bhīma and his retinue tasted the hunchback's cooking. Bhīma then sent a bowl filled with Nala's cooking to Damayamatī so that she could try it. As soon as she tasted it she knew for sure, that the hunchback was Nala. She said, "A monk who was a storehouse of knowledge once told me, 'In the entire continent of Bharaha there is no one besides Nala who knows how to cook in the sun.' This must be Nala. There must be some reason why he has become a hunchback. One test of Nala's identity is cooking, but there is another one. At his slightest touch, even just the touch of his finger tip, my whole body responds with joy. Let the hunchback touch me with his finger. Let us see if he passes this test, too." They asked the hunchback, "Are you Nala?" He replied, "Think of Nala with his handsome broad chest and look at me, a hunchback, ugly enough to make people's eyes smart when they see me!" But Damayaṃtī was insistent, and when the hunchback just brushed his finger against her chest, with just that slightest touch of his finger, Damayaṃtī's whole body trembled with joy. Damayaṃtī said to him, "My beloved, you abandoned me while I slept, but now you are mine. Where can you go now?" And with those words she led him into her room. She begged him, "Let me see you as you really are." Nala then took the clothes and jewels from the fruit and jewel box and turned back into himself. When Damayaṃtī saw him she was delighted; as a creeper clings to a tree, she wrapped herself around him in a tight embrace.

'Bhīma too realized the hunchback was Nala and he seated him on his own throne. He declared, "You are my master. I await your command," and stood before Nala with hands folded in reverence. Dahivanna then said to Nala, "Forgive me. I did not know that you were the king; forgive me for ordering you around in my ignorance." Damayaṃtī sent for King Riupanna along with Queen Candajasā. She also sent for Sirisehara, ruler of Tāvasapura. Bhīma welcomed them all with proper ceremony.

'One morning as they were all gathered in Bhīma's court, a god came to them, rays of light streaming from his body. He bowed his hands in reverence and said this to Damayaṃtī,

"I am the chief of the ascetics whom you awakened to the truth of the Jain doctrine. Through the great powers of the Jain doctrine when I died I was reborn as a god." He caused to rain down on Damayaṃtī a rain of seven crores of gold pieces and then went home. Together Bhīma, Dahivanna, Vasanta and the other rulers consecrated Nala as king. Nala commanded them to gather their armies. Surrounded by these fighting forces Nala reached the city Kosalā, with his mighty elephants trumpeting, the sky thick with the dust raised by the hooves of the horses, and the sounds of his chariot wheels ringing in the ears of his frightened enemies. He sent a messenger to Kūvara with these words, "Nala has come to see you. He is just outside the city of Aujjhā." When Kūvara heard that Nala had arrived, his body felt like it was burning up with fire.

'Nala spoke to Kūvara through the messenger, saying, "Fight with me now. Either you will have my royal glory or I will have yours."

'Kūvara, afraid to meet Nala in battle, proposed instead another game of dice. He lost everything to Nala, who had acquired much merit.

'Virtuous Nala knew that Kūvara was cruel, but he bore him no ill-will. Out of regard for the fact that Kuvāra was his younger brother, Nala appointed him as crown prince, as he might have appointed his own son.

'Having won back his kingdom, King Nala accompanied by Damayaṃtī eagerly went to pray in the Jain temples of Aujjhā.

'Nala ruled over half of Bharaha for many thousands of years; kings and princes bowed down at his feet and brought him gifts of tribute.

'One day the radiant and splendid God who had been Nisaha, Nala's father, saw that Nala was distracted by his many pursuits of the pleasures of the senses. He went to Nala and rebuked him:

'"Can you call yourself a man, worthy of that designation,

when you do not even protect yourself from being robbed of your wisdom by passion and the other vices, that are like so many thieves?

'"I promised you once that I would tell you when it was time for you to renounce the world. And so I tell you now, "Pick the fruit of the tree of having been born as a human being; become a monk."'

'Having said these words the god vanished. The Jain monk Jiṇabhadda arrived on the scene, a treasure house of jewels in the form of pure knowledge.

'Nala went with Damayaṃtī and paid his respects to the monk. He sat down in front of the monk, and then folding his hands in reverence, he asked him, "Blessed One! What did we do in a previous life that we enjoyed ruling over this kingdom, lost it and then regained it again?"

'The teacher said, "Listen, my son. Here on Jambūdvīpa, in the continent of Bharaha, near Mount Aṭṭhāvaya there is a city named Saṃgara, 'Battle', which has really never seen battle with an enemy army. There reigned King Mammaṇa, who had romanced all the Ladies of the Four Directions. He had a queen named Vīramaī. One day the king, who had set out to go hunting, happened to see a Jain monk who was travelling in the company of some traders. The monk was like religion incarnate; he was calm and tranquil, endowed with all of the virtues of a monk, contentment and the others. The king thought, 'This monk is a bad omen for me; he will bring me bad luck in the hunt.' He snatched the monk from the company of traders, as one might snatch an elephant from its herd. The king took him home with him. For a good twelve hours the monk was treated with contempt in the king's palace. Then the king and queen took pity on the monk and asked him, 'Where did you come from? Where are you going?' The monk said, 'I set out from the city Rohīḍaka with this caravan to worship the images of the Jinas that adorn Mount Aṭṭhāvaya.' As soon as they heard these words, the king and the queen were no longer angry; they were like poisonous snakes that lose their poison when the snake charmer recites his spell. Because the monk knew that they were destined for release, he taught them the Jain doctrine, which stresses compassion for all living beings. They had never heard the Jain doctrine before in their lives, and so their faith in it was still slight. They gave the monk food and water to break his fast. He stayed with them for some time, but eventually having imparted to them knowledge of the Jain doctrine, as one might give medicine to the sick, the monk left for Mount Aṭṭhāvaya.

"'The king and queen, having been awakened to the truth by contact with that monk, carried out their religious duties with the care that the miser lavishes on protecting his money. One day the Protecting Goddess of the Faith took Queen Vīramaī to Mount Aṭṭhāvaya in an effort to strengthen her faith. There she felt the greatest pleasure as she beheld the images of the Jinas that were worshipped by the gods and the anti-gods, and that were encrusted with various kinds of jewels, each image of a prescribed size and color. She worshipped the images and then returned to her city. Vīramaī was filled with faith after seeing this great holy place, and she undertook a series of twenty fasts in honor of each Jina.

"'Vīramaī then had an exquisite pair of images made for each of the twenty-four Jinas; they were all of gold and adorned with precious gems.

"'On another occasion she and her retinue went to Mount Aṭṭhāvaya and worshipped the Jina images, bathing them, smearing them with unguents and making offerings to them and performing other ritual acts.

"'With great faith in her heart she painted beauty marks on the foreheads of the Jina images; those marks shone like flowers on the tree of her merit.

"'She gave gifts to the monks who visited the holy place on special days and in this way helped support the ascetic community.

"'Then thinking that she had made her human birth

worthwhile and that she had made her wealth worth having and her life worth living, Vīramaī would return to her city.

"'Much time passed thus for the king and queen, who though two in body were one in mind, utterly devoted to the Jain religion.

"'Because all living things must die, in time they died a pious death of fasting and meditating. King Mammaṇa became a god. Queen Vīramaī followed him in death and became his wife in heaven, too. After all, how long does the moonlight last once the moon has set?

"'In time the soul of Mammaṇa fell from heaven and was born right here in Jambūdvīpa, in the city Poyaṇa, ornament of the land of Bahali. He was born as Dhanna,the son of the Ābhīra cowherd Dhammilāsa and his wife Reṇuya, and he was endowed with every fine virtue.

"'The soul of Vīramaī was reborn as his wife; her name was Dhūsarī. Dhanna would take his herd of buffaloes out to graze. One day in the rainy season it began to rain; Dhanna took an umbrella and went to put his buffaloes to pasture.

"'Dhanna went into a forest; there he saw a Jain monk, emaciated from all of his fasts, standing in meditation, as still and unmoving as a mountain.

"'Filled with faith, he held his umbrella over the head of the monk and thus prevented the rain from disturbing the ascetic.When the rain stopped, Dhanna bowed down to the monk and asked him, 'Where have you come from?'

The monk answered, 'Sir! I have come from the Paṃḍu country. I was on my way to the city Lankā to pay my respects to my teacher, who had gone to Lankā. It has been raining for seven days and seven nights, and so I have not been able to travel onward.'

"'Dhanna said, "Lord! The ground is now muddy and it is difficult to travel. Come now into the city; you may ride on one of my buffaloes."

"'The monk said, "Ascetics are not permitted to ride on

animals." The ascetic then went with Dhanna into the city. Dhanna said to him, "Wait here for a moment. I'll just get some milk from my house and be right back."

"'Dhanna hastened to his house and quickly returned with the milk. Filled with devotion, he gave the great ascetic milk to drink to break his fast.

"'Dhanna and his wife both formally accepted the duties of being lay Jains under the guidance of that monk. The monk stayed right there in the city of Poyana for the rest of the rainy season.

"'Later on Dhanna and his wife Dhūsarī both went to another place, where they lived for a long time. Having observed with care the duties incumbent upon lay Jains, they later renounced the world.

"'Dhanna was a Jain monk for seven years before he died with his wife. With their strong love for each other they were reborn together as twins on the distant continent Hemavaa.

"'They died and then the soul that was Mammaṇa was reborn as a god; his wife was reborn again as the same type of god as he.

"'When Dhanna fell from heaven that time, he was reborn as you, Nala, O lord of men! Dhūsarī was reborn as your beloved, Damayaṃtī.

"'Because in a previous life you made gifts to a Jain monk and accepted the duties of the Jain laity, in this life you were both handsome and a king over a kingdom. Damayaṃtī, as a result of the religious deeds she performed, has been reborn as your wife. No one could harm her because of the great power of her austerities and her worship of the Jina images, on which she once painted beauty marks.

"'But because you caused trouble to a Jain monk for twelve hours, you lost your throne for twelve years.'"

'When King Nala heard what the monk had said, he was seized by a feeling of disgust for worldly desires and gains. He installed his virtuous son Pukkhala on the throne and along with Damayaṃtī he renounced the world to become a monk under the guidance of this teacher.

'He studied the sacred texts, practiced austerities and endured the typical hardships a monk must endure: hunger, thirst, insects, cold and heat. But because karma works in such strange ways, and because passion is so difficult to overcome, the monk Nala again felt desire in his mind for Damayaṃtī.

'The elder monks rejected him, but his father came and awakened him to the truth. Unable to keep his vows, Nala renounced all food and undertook a fast to death.

'Damayaṃtī, ever devoted to Nala, died along with him. Nala was reborn as the god Kubera and Damayaṃtī was reborn as his wife.

'Because they did not strictly keep their monastic vows they were reborn as only minor gods. Both of them will eventually fall from that godly realm; they will destroy their karma and obtain Final Liberation.'

(from the *Kumārapālapratibodha* of Somaprabhasūri, p.47)

21

SIṂHIKĀ

Now when her time came the Queen Vicitramālā, wife of Sukośala, gave birth to a son. The delivery was smooth and the baby bore all of the auspicious marks. Since the mother had a complexion of gold while the child was still in her womb, they gave the handsome child the name "Hiraṇyagarbha", "Born from the Golden One". So virtuous was this King Hiraṇyagarbha that the Golden Age of old seemed to have returned, as if attracted by his good qualities. Hiraṇyagarbha married Amṛtavatī, daughter of Hari. He had many devoted friends and relatives and was learned in all the sciences. Glorious, he had inexhaustible wealth, like a mountain made of gold. Noble Hiraṇyagarbha enjoyed every pleasure of the senses until the day he noticed a grey hair amongst all of his dark hairs. Seeing that grey hair in the mirror, like a messenger sent by the god of Death to warn him, he was filled with sorrow. 'Alas!' he lamented, 'old age has taken hold of my body, intent upon destroying my strength and beauty. This body of mine, which is now like a sandalwood tree, will become like a heap of charcoal, burnt by the fire of old age. Old age will lie in wait, spying out where disease has made me weak, and then like a demoness, old age will attack my body. Next death, who has been waiting patiently like a tiger ready to pounce on his prey, will make haste to devour my body. Fortunate indeed are those stalwart bulls among men, who having been born in this land where it is possible to practice the true religion, grasp the raft of renunciation and cross the ocean of transmigratory existence.'

With these thoughts he installed Amṛtavatī's son Naghuṣa on the throne and became a monk under the tutelage of a pure and holy man. This Naghuṣa, 'Silence' was so called because when he was in the womb no one even said a word that was impure or unpropitious. Everyone bowed down to him, won over by his virtues. One day Naghuṣa left his wife Siṃhikā in the city and went North with his army to subdue the feudatories who were in rebellion. When the rulers of the South came to know that the king was absent from his capital city, they raised vast armies and proceeded to lay siege to Naghuṣa's capital Vinītā. The valorous Siṃhikā defeated them all in battle. She then appointed someone trustworthy to rule over their kingdoms. Siṃhikā was skilled and practiced in the use of various weapons; now she gathered the feudatories that she had already defeated and with them she marched deep into the South to subdue the rest of the rebellious kings. The queen conquered all of the rebellious vassals by her great valour and returned to celebrations of her victories in the capital.

In the meantime Naghuṣa had subdued the Northern region and returned to the city. He was in a rage when he heard about his wife's victories. He was convinced that no decent, self-respecting woman from a good family, faithful to her husband, could possibly be so bold. And so he turned against Siṃhikā. Although she was pure in character and stainless in her conduct, he removed her from her position as Chief Queen. She lived neglected and in poverty for some time.

One day the king was seized by a terrible fever that was beyond the reach of any of the medicines that the doctors could supply. When Siṃhikā heard that the king was so ill, she was filled with sorrow; she was also eager to prove to the world that she had been a chaste wife. She summoned all of their relatives and all of the vassals and the subjects. She took in her hands the water that the priest gave to her and she pronounced this oath: 'If it is true that no man but my husband has ever occupied my thoughts, then let the king be cured of his fever by the touch of this water.' As soon as he was sprinkled with the water from her hand, the king became so cold that his teeth began to chatter, as if he had been immersed in a bath of ice. The heavens resounded with the cry, 'Behold! How wonderful!' and a rain of flowers fell down from invisible hands.

Thus the king came to know that his wife had been faithful to him. He reinstalled her in the position of Chief Queen with great honor and respect. He enjoyed the pleasures of the senses with her for a long time and ruled without any trouble from rebellious vassals. Then, free of all desires for worldly pleasures, that king did what all his forebears had done. He installed his son born of Siṃhikā on the throne and followed in the footsteps of his father, becoming a monk.

(from the *Padmapurāṇa* of Raviṣeṇa, Ch.22)

22

ĀRYANANDILA

In the city of Padminīkhaṇḍa was a king named Padmaprabha. His wife was named Padmāvatī. In that very city also dwelt the merchant Padmadatta. His wife was named Padmayaśā. They had a son, who was named Padma. The travelling merchant Varadatta pledged his own daughter, who was named Vairoṭyā, to this son of theirs in marriage. And he married her in due time.

One day Varadatta, the father of Vairotyā, was on his way to foreign lands with all of his family, when they all perished in a forest fire. Vairoṭyā, though she served her mother-in-law faithfully and humbly, met with only contempt from the older woman who knew that she had lost her father. For what they say is true:

That women seem beautiful and possessed of hidden wealth, that women seem strong and spirited and

> enjoy their husband's favour, that women wield authority in their home, for sure all of this is nothing but the result of the status and power of their fathers, who are always there behind the scenes.

But though she was exceedingly pained by her mother-in-law's words, which burned like a raging fire as it consumes dry chaff, she cursed her own bad luck and never uttered a word against her mother-in-law. And she thought to herself:

'Everyone reaps the fruit of his own past actions. Another person is just the incidental cause of our misery or happiness, which we alone bring about through our very own deeds.'

One day Vairotyā had a dream in which the Snake King announced her impending pregnancy to her and she conceived a child. She began to crave sweet milk pudding. It was then that the Jain monk Āryanandila happened to stop in a nearby public garden; like Āryarakṣitasvāmin before him, he possessed knowledge of thirteen of the fourteen ancient texts. Now that mother-in-law proclaimed, 'This woman will give birth to a daughter, she will never produce a son.' The chaste and faithful Vairoṭyā, pained by the harsh words of her mother-in-law, which pierced her ears like a sharp sword, went to pay her respects to the Jain monk. She bowed down to the monk. She told him about her dreadful relationship with her mother-in-law. The monk said, 'This is the fault of some previous deed that you have done in another life. Do not let your anger grow. Do not let it grow, because it is the cause of rebirth and continued suffering. O daughter! In this birth, anger gives rise to such things as bodily harm, constant fighting and even undying hatred; and in the next world, it results in the most terrible suffering that comes from rebirth in hell and similar terrible misfortunes. I promise you, you will give birth to a son. I know that since you have become pregnant, you long to eat sweet milk pudding. I promise you that somehow your craving will be fulfilled.'

Delighted by these words of the monk, she went back home. And she thought to herself, 'What they say is true:

> No matter how long we wander this earth, which is girded by the four vast oceans, we will never meet a person of truly noble nature to whom we can tell the long-kept secrets of our many miseries or even joys, and thereby for a minute, or even for a half a minute, feel suddenly at rest and peace.

'But I have met such a person today in meeting this monk.'

One day, Padmayaśā, for her part, on the full moon night of the first month of spring, performed a ritual fast and was about to break her fast with appropriate ceremony. On that day it was the custom to give to the monks an ample portion of sweet milk pudding and to show particular generosity to all the lay members of the Jain faith. She did all of that. But because she hated her daughter-in-law, she gave her only coarse fare of cheap grain. Now the daughter-in-law secretly took some of the sweet milk pudding that was left over in a large cauldron and hastily poured it into a small pot, which she concealed under her clothes as she went out to the lake to fetch water. She set the pot down under a tree and went to wash her hands and feet.

Now it so happened that at this very moment in time there was a snake named Aliñjara, who lived in the underworld, and whose wife was also pregnant and longing to eat sweet milk pudding. She had come out from the nether regions and was now roaming the earth in search of some sweet milk pudding. That was how she came to see the pudding in the pot under that tree. And she ate it all. The snake lady then set out for her home by the very same path that she had taken to come up from the underworld.

When Vairoṭyā had finished washing up and got back to the tree, right away she saw that there was no sweet milk pudding left in the pot any more. But even so she did not get angry and she did not utter a single nasty word. Instead she spoke these words of blessing,

'May you find fulfilment of your wishes, whoever you are, who ate this pudding.'

Now Aliñjara's wife, concealed from view by the tree, heard her words of blessing. She returned home and told her husband what had happened. Vairoṭyā went home too. That night, the wife of the snake Aliñjara appeared to a neighbor of Vairoṭyā's in a dream and said, 'Fair lady! I am the wife of the snake Aliñjara. Vairoṭyā is my daughter. She is pregnant and longs to eat sweet milk pudding. You must fulfil her wish. And so I instruct you that you should say these words to her, 'Your father is gone. But I shall take care of you as your own father would have done. I shall cool the burning pain that you feel from the fire of your mother-in-law's wrath.'

The next morning Vairoṭyā's neighbour treated her to a meal of sweet milk pudding. Her pregnancy longing fulfilled, she gave birth to a son. As for the snake lady, she gave birth to a hundred sons. When the day came for Vairoṭyā's son's naming ceremony, the snake Aliñjara made a huge party for her. He had all the snakes in the underworld build a magnificent and beautifully appointed mansion on the spot where her father's house had stood. All the snakes gathered, with their troops and their elephants, their horses and their finest chariots. They filled her house with riches. And Aliñjara's wife, who now considered Vairoṭyā to be her adopted daughter, went there too, along with her husband and her many sons, and showered her with the most beautiful gifts of the finest clothes, silks, gold, and bracelets and necklaces all studded with precious gems. And Vairoṭyā began to visit Aliñjara's wife frequently after that. Vairoṭyā was treated with great respect by Aliñjara's wife and shown much honour. Her mother-in-law, seeing that Vairoṭyā's father's house now had returned, as it were, to its former wealth and splendour, began to treat Vairoṭyā with great deference, for it is true what they say: 'People show respect to someone whom others already honour.'

The snake lady sent her very own young sons to protect Vairoṭyā and watch over her. She put all those snakes into a pot. Now one day a servant girl chanced to put that pot on top of a metal pan that had just been heated on the stove. At once Vairoṭyā took it off. She sprinkled the snakes with water and revived them. But one baby snake had lost the tip of his tail. As she saw him slither and slip, having trouble without his tiny tail, she affectionately called out, 'Long live my clown of a tailless one, who'll show us all a trick or two before he's done.' And the snakes, who were bewitched by Vairoṭyā's charming son and loved him very much, all became like members of her own family and they gave her fine costly garments, gem stones and gold. And having made such a fine celebration for her son's naming day, eventually they all went back to their own homes. Vairoṭyā came to be the object of everyone's respect because of all the wonderful things the snakes did for her.

One day the snake Aliñjara noticed that one of his sons had lost his tail and he became furious. 'What wicked person has damaged my son's tail?' And when he knew through his supernatural powers that it was Vairoṭyā who was responsible for the loss of his son's tail, then, despite all the kind feelings he had cherished for her up until that moment, he became enraged at her now. And in his anger he went to her home in order to do her some harm in return. Aliñjara hid himself in her house. Now Vairoṭyā had come to have the habit that whenever she entered a dark room, she would call out a little blessing to that snake that she had inadvertently injured, in order to ward of any evil that might lurk there. She would say, 'Long live my little clown of a tailless one,' as she had called him that day. Now when he heard Vairoṭyā call out these words, the snake king was pleased with these words, 'My daughter, from this day on you must come regularly to us in the underworld and the snakes will come to you.' And Vairoṭyā through the power of this boon from the snake, did indeed come and go between the earth and underworld as she pleased. She called her son "Nāgadatta", "Gift of the Snakes".

At that time the Glorious monk Āryanandila told Padmadatta, Vairoṭyā's father-in-law, 'You must tell Vairoṭyā, "Go to the domain of the snakes and say to the snakes: you must help everyone in our world. You must never bite anyone."' Her father-in-law related these words of the monk to her and she told them to the snakes. She went down there and she told them in a loud and clear voice, 'Long live Aliñjara's wife. Long live Aliñjara. They restored my father to me even though he was dead by restoring the prestige of his house. They were my refuge when I had no refuge. Hear, hear, all you young snakes. The Great monk Āryanandila commands, "Do not trouble our world. Help every one of us."' Vairoṭyā then went back home. The monk composed a new hymn called "Praise to Vairoṭyā". Whoever recites this "Praise to Vairoṭyā" need not fear any harm from snakes.

Vairoṭyā brought all the snakes to the monk, who had become her teacher. He instructed them in the Jain faith. They all became calm and pure in mind. Vairoṭyā's son, who was called Nāgadatta, became a rich and prosperous man. Padmadatta became a Jain monk and his beloved wife became a Jain nun. He practiced austerities and went to heaven. And for her part Padmayaśā became his divine wife, according to his wishes, for he had achieved the power to bring into being anything that he desired. And Vairoṭyā died while meditating on the king of snakes and was reborn as the wife of the snake Dharaṇendra, a protector of the Jain faith. In that rebirth she kept the name Vairoṭyā.

(from the *Prabandhakośa* of Rājaśekharasūri, p.5)

23

THE GODDESS AMBIKĀ

Bowing down to the holy mountain of Ujjayanta and to the Jina Neminātha, I write the story of Kohaṇḍidevī as I have heard it from the elders.

There is in the territory of Surāṣṭra a city named Koḍīnagara bustling with rich people who have plenty of gold and money. In that city dwelt a wealthy brahmin named Soma, who was punctual in his performance of his religious duties and was knowledgeable in the Vedic scriptures. His wife Aṃbinī wore costly ornaments on her person, but her greatest treasure was her purity of conduct. As this couple enjoyed the pleasures that life can bring they produced two sons. The first was named Siddha and the second was called Buddha. Now it happened that the time had come to perform a ceremony on behalf of the family ancestors and the brahmin Soma invited many brahmins for a ritual meal to take place on the day of the memorial service. Some of the brahmins were engaged in reciting the Vedas; some made offerings to the ancestors; others performed sacrifices and made oblations into the sacred fires. Aṃbinī prepared many foods for the occasion; she made cakes of rice and lentils; she made spiced delicacies with the finest condiments, and even sweet milk pudding.

And then, when her mother-in-law went to take her bath, at that very moment a Jain monk came to their home looking for alms so that he might break his fast that had lasted one month. As soon as she saw him, Aṃbinī was filled with joy; as she rose to serve him she felt her body tingling with excitement. Her heart filled with devotion, she offered the Jain monk the first serving of the foods that she had prepared.

As soon as the monk accepted these alms, the mother-in-law reappeared on the scene, back in the kitchen after her bath. She could see that some of the food was gone. Furious, she kept asking her daughter-in-law what had happened. Aṃbinī told her exactly what had taken place, and her mother-in-law began to scream at her and abuse her. 'You slut! Now what have you done! You haven't even worshipped our family deity, you haven't yet served the brahmins, you haven't put out the offerings for the ancestors. How dare you give the first food to some Jain monk!' And the mother-in-law told the brahmin Soma what his wife had done. He was enraged and he threw her out of house, fearing that she would bring ill luck upon them all.

Despondent at this humiliation, Aṃbinī took Siddha by the hand and, carrying Buddha on her hip, she left the city. As she walked on, the children became oppressed by thirst and begged her for water. Her eyes filled with tears, but then, lo and behold, a dried-up lake that lay in their path became filled with water by the power of her pure conduct. She gave them both cool water to drink. Then the children grew hungry and begged her for something to eat. A mango tree on the road at once burst into fruit. She gave them ripe mangoes to eat. The children felt satisfied.

Now hear what happened while she was sitting down to rest in the shade of that mango tree. When she was still at home she had fed the children and she had then taken the leaves that they had eaten from and thrown them away outside. A guiding Goddess of the Jain faith took pity on her, moved by the great power of her purity. The goddess turned all those leaves into gold platters and dishes. And the drops of children's saliva that had fallen from the leaves onto the ground were turned into costly pearls. Even the food that Aṃbinī had given to the Jain monk was magically restored to the pot from which she had taken it. Her mother-in-law saw this miracle and told the brahmin Soma. And she also told him, 'Son, your wife will bring us good fortune and is a faithful and pure wife. You must bring her back, for she will be the support of this family.' Thus it was that the brahmin Soma, obeying his mother's command, and burning with the painful fires of remorse, went to bring his wife back home. But when she saw that best of brahmins coming after her Aṃbinī was terrified. She looked this way and that in search of rescue. And then she saw an old well right in front of her eyes. Her mind fixed on the best of Jinas, her heart rejoicing in the gift that she had made to the monk, she threw herself into the well. Giving up her life with her mind filled with lofty thoughts, she was reborn as the powerful Goddess Ambikā in the sphere of the Gods known as Kohaṇḍa, just four leagues from the heaven Sohamma. She is also known as Kohaṇṃi after the heavenly sphere in which she was reborn. For his part, the brahmin Soma, seeing that most faithful of wives jump into the well, threw himself in the well after her. He too died and became a god in the very same heavenly sphere. By the power of his magic he transformed himself into a lion and became her mount. Others say that Aṃbinī jumped off the summit of Mount Revaya and that the brahmin Soma followed her and died in the same way. They relate all the other details of the story in exactly the same way.

This Blessed Goddess holds the following attributes in her four arms: in her right arms she holds a sprout of mangoes and a noose and in her left arms she holds a child and an elephant goad. The colour of her skin is the soft and gentle glow of liquid gold. She lives on the peak of Mount Revaya as the protecting Goddess of the Jina Nemināha. Adorned with every kind of ornament on every part of her body, sporting a crown, earrings, a pearl necklace, jewelled bracelets and anklets, she grants all the wishes of faithful Jains and prevents any harm from coming to Jain believers. She shows to those who are devoted to Jainism all kinds of spells and magic diagrams, and displays before them many a wondrous power. Through her power no evil spirit, ghost, goblin or witch can work its magic on a devotee, and the faithful grow rich, become kings, and have fine wives and sons.

(from the *Vividhatīrthakalpa* of Jinaprabhasūri, No.61)

24

Rudradatta's Beloved

In a region in the territory of Lāṭa there was a city called Guḍakheḍaka, home to wise men, much money and a plentiful supply of grain. Jinadatta, a pious Jain layman, lived there with his wife Jinadattā, who was also devoted to the Jain faith. They had a daughter Jinamati, steeped in the Jain doctrine. She was skilled in all the arts and endowed with humility. In that same town lived the rich merchant Nāgadatta; he had a young and beautiful wife named Nāgadattā. They had a handsome son named Rudradatta. He was a delight to all of his family; he was virtuous and a faithful devotee of the god Rudra or Śīva.

Now one day Nāgadatta asked Jinadatta if he would give his daughter Jinamati in marriage to Rudradatta. When Jinadatta heard Nāgadatta's request, he replied, 'I am an extremely pious Jain and you are equally devoted to your god Śiva. There is no way that pious Jains can marry those who believe in Śiva; we feel that those who believe in Śiva are perverse and stupid in their beliefs.' When Rudradatta heard what Jinadatta said, he declared, 'Really all religions are one; there is no difference between them. Uncle, I will become a Jain right away!' With these words Rudradatta hastened to a Jain temple. With lust in his heart he approached the monk Samādhigupta and abandoning his devotion to Śiva he accepted the Jain religion. When Jinadatta learned that Rudradatta had become devoted to the Jain Faith, he gave his daughter Jinamati to him. Once he married the girl, the deceitful Rudradatta renounced the Jain Faith and once more began to follow the Śaiva way.

One day, after they had eaten and Jinamati was relaxing, Rudradatta saw his chance. He said to her, 'Lovely one, Śiva has proclaimed the ritual of consecration which puts an end to all suffering and is without flaw; it is of benefit even to miserable, sinful souls. This Śaiva consecration is not diminished in its efficacy even by millions of sins. Śiva, husband of the goddess Gaurī, has said that it is of benefit even to those who are filled with hatred. For it is said in one of the texts,

> This pure, flawless ritual of consecration destroys all sin. It has been proclaimed by Śiva expressly for the benefit of the most wretched souls.

'This rite of consecration sacred to Śiva is still effective even for those people who harbour hatred against their teacher and commit a hundred sins; thus Śiva himself proclaimed. Give up your Jain religion, which no important people believe in anyway, and accept the religion of Śiva, which grants the happiness of Final Release.'

When Jinamati heard her husband's words she said to him, 'My love, I have no intention of giving up my Jain faith. Why don't you give up your belief in Śiva, which is so dear to you, and fix firmly in your mind that Jain religion, which is dear to the wise?' Now hearing these words of his wife, Rudradatta replied, 'How can the doctrine of the Jinas be better than the Śaiva ritual of consecration?' At that Jinamati suggested, 'Why don't you just continue in your worship of Śiva and I will continue in my devotion to the Jina.' Her charming husband answered his captivating wife with these words, 'But I cannot allow you to practice your Jain religion.' Thus these two spent much of their time listening to each other discourse on religion, sometimes debating, sometimes quarrelling, often arguing.

One day Rudradatta said to his wife, who was always respectful and well-behaved, though she continued to be devoted to the doctrine of the Jinas, 'If I ever catch you going to the Jain temple again or giving alms to Jain monks, I will throw you out of this house. But if you go to the temple of Rudra and with faith in your heart give alms to the Śaiva ascetics, then I shall adore you, my lovely wife!' When she heard this Jinamati stood her ground, 'If you force me to do as you say, my master, then I shall die. Or let us try this: you stop going to the temple of Śiva and I will no longer go to the Jain temple to worship the image of the Jina.' Each one then rashly made a promise to the other, but there they were, living together in that house, each one practicing his own religion.

Just to the east of the city Guḍakheḍaka there was a dense forest with many trees. It was inhabited by barbaric people and tribals and was a favorite haunt of tigers, lions and other ferocious beasts. One day a wild horde came out of the forest and descended on the city, setting it ablaze. As the city was engulfed in flame, all the townsmen with their wives and children ran here and there, not knowing what to do. The sky was red with flames as far as the eye could see; gradually the blaze reached Rudradatta's house. Jinamati, her lotus-like face beaming, approached her beloved husband Rudradatta, who was devoted to Śiva. 'You have often sung the praises of your devotion to Śiva to me, but there was no place for Śiva in my heart, which was already given to the Jina. And I in turn often spoke to you about the religion of the Jina, which delights the wise, but you were not impressed. My lord! The god who rescues us from this danger, the god who spares us and our home, let that god be our refuge!'

When Rudradatta heard Jinamati's words he said, 'Lovely lady! Well put. What you have said is surely pleasing to the mind. Who can save living beings, if not Śiva, husband of Gaurī, the one who rides on a bull? How could the universe obey the will of any god other than that one, who brings delight to all the world? How could I even begin to describe the wondrous qualities of that god, who brings all living beings under his sway through his divine play?'

When Jinamati heard these words she said to her husband, who was deluded and devoted to Śiva, 'If your god has any power, then let him quench this fire, O love, without much further ado!' Hearing his wife's words, Rudradatta said to his wife, whose entire body shuddered with delight in her great faith in the Jina, 'O fair-hipped one, what do I care about this trivial fire, that will die out anyway? I have all I want, my firm faith in Śiva.' And having said this to his beloved, Rudradatta took a vessel for worship filled with things like curds and sacred grass. He stood there, muttering some sounds. Rudradatta prayed to Śiva. He faced north and poured the contents of the vessel on his own head. 'O protectors of the world! Hear my words!' proclaimed Rudradatta, intent on protecting his world. He went on, 'If the religion of devotion to Śiva is the correct way, and if Śiva is the highest god; if the world emerges from his heart at his will; if the consecration ritual leads to Final Release and is truly flawless and pure, then may that god Śiva protect me and all the world, and all my family, too.'

But as Rudradatta recited the name of Śiva the flames only blazed more brightly and fiercely around him, twice as fierce, three times as fierce. Then Jinamati said to

Rudradatta,who by now was quite thoroughly terrified, 'Collect yourself and call upon a different god this time.' Obedient to his wife's words, he began to call out the name of Brahmā, Skanda, Viṣṇu; of Agni, the sun, the moon, the planets, even Gaurī. But the fire went right on blazing, lighting up everything everywhere with its flames, fanned by a wind as fierce as the wind that blows at the end of time.

Rudradatta said to his beloved, 'My love, none of these gods whom the masses worship is really god, who can protect us from this fire as we call on him for aid. Worship your Jina, who like the moon gives light in the darkness, O lovely one! Make an offering to him so that we may be saved from this impending disaster.' Thus her husband and her children implored Jinamati. Jinamati first renounced desires for worldly things in thought and in deed. She then made this pronouncement: 'If there really are Noble Ones, who have reached Omniscience, who are free from all passions and beyond the range of all harm, devoid of lust and delusion; if there truly exists the doctrine of the Jinas, that one should never do violence to a living creature, the doctrine that teaches compassion to all living beings, that is the source of happiness in this world and the next and has been proclaimed by the noble ones; if moreover that doctrine is the true consecration that leads to Final Release and puts an end to all of transmigratory existence, then may it protect me and my husband and children.' These words of hers resounded throughout the world. She then made an offering to the Jina and stood silently in meditation. As she was standing there in meditation, her mind firm, the fire suddenly vanished along with the horde of barbarians, both terrified of her power. The terror that the blazing fire had struck in the hearts of the frightened people was also gone, as if it was itself in fear of Jinamati.

When he saw that miracle Rudradatta, calm in mind, renounced his faith in Śiva and became a Jain. Many were those who had been unwilling to express any opinion before, but who now also became pious lay Jains, firm in the right belief.

(from the *Bṛhatkathākośa* of Hariṣeṇa, No.54)

25

PADMALATĀ

A merchant asked Padmalatā, his fifth wife, the reason for her firm faith in the Jain doctrine. Padmalatā said to him, 'Listen while I tell you the reason for my firm faith in the Jain doctrine.

'There is a charming city called Campā in the country of Aṅga. There reigned the glorious king Dantivāhana. The king's chief queen was named Vinayaśokā; she was endowed with humility and virtuous conduct and the king loved her very much. Now in this same city there lived a rich merchant named Ṛṣabhadatta; his wife was named Padmāvatī. They were very much in love with each other. They had a daughter named Padmaśrī, who was endowed with firm faith in the Jain doctrine and was as lovely as a tender lotus blossom. There was another merchant in the city named Buddhadāsa, who was a committed Buddhist. His wife was named Buddhaśrī and she, too, was a devout Buddhist. They had a son Buddhasaṃgha, who brought joy to their eyes and hearts. He was endowed with faith in the Buddha, as well as being very handsome indeed.

'One day Buddhasaṃgha was making his rounds of the temples in the city and came in turn to the magnificent Jain temple. There he saw Padmaśrī worshipping the Jina with flowers. Buddhasaṃgha was immediately smitten with love. When he got home he refused to eat or sleep or do anything at all. He took to his bed in silence. When his mother saw her son lying there in his bed, not saying a word, suffering, his face looking like a withered lotus, she asked him, "Son, why do you spurn food, flowers, betel, your bath and fine fragrances, saffron and the like, to lie there so pathetically in bed?" When Buddhasaṃgha heard his mother's words, stung by the arrows of love, he sighed with deep hot breaths and said, "I swear that if and only if I can have Padmaśrī, the daughter of Ṛṣabhadatta, as my wife, will I live. If I do not get this woman who delights my eyes and heart, then I promise you, Mother, I will die tomorrow."

When his mother heard what he said, she feared that he might indeed die and she told his father all that had happened. Having heard his wife's words, the father told his son, 'Son! We are Buddhists; we even eat meat. Everyone knows that Padmaśrī's father is a devout Jain; how could he who reveres the Jina as his god give his daughter to the likes of us? But wait, I have an idea of how we can get him to give us his daughter. My child, take heart. You will renounce being a Buddhist.'

'Having decided together on this stratagem, the father and son happily went to see Yaśodhara, the best of Jain monks. They sat down near the monk and listened to him expound the Jain doctrine. Then the two of them accepted the duties of Jain laymen: not to harm living creatures, not to lie, not to steal, not to commit adultery and not to be overly attached to their possessions. Thus they pretended to become pious Jains and bowed down to the monk in mock devotion. They abandoned their practice of Buddhism and began to worship the Jina; they gave alms to the Jain monks time and time again and happily observed the Jain fast days.

'The merchant, Padmaśrī's father, saw their devotion to the Jain faith and the Jain community and began to feel real affection for them as fellow Jains. One day Buddhadāsa was fasting and praying in the Jain temple. Padmaśrī's father was pleased and invited him to his house to break his fast. When it was time to eat, he gave him a fragrant drink. Buddhadāsa, lowering his head in respect, said to him, 'O Ṛṣabhadatta! If you give your daughter Padmaśrī to my son in marriage, then I will eat this meal.' When he heard this, the merchant stood before him and replied, 'Everyone knows that we are pleased to give our daughters to pious Jains.' After he had indeed given his daughter to Buddhadāsa, the two men sat down to eat with proper ceremony.

'Ṛṣabhadatta worshipped the Jinas, who had conquered their enemies, with great fanfare, with flowers and incense and other things. He spared no expense in celebrating the marriage of his daughter to Buddhadāsa's son.The marriage was performed with all due ceremony, to the auspicious sounds of drums and conches. Having married Padmaśrī with all the proper rituals, the son undertook a fast. That done, both father and son considered that they had completed what they set out to do.

'Now one day a Buddhist monk expounded the Buddhist doctrine in all its details to Padmaśrī, but she was firm in her faith in Jainism and was not interested in becoming a Buddhist. The monk told her again and again how the Buddhist doctrine was beneficial to all living beings; how it was a doctrine of compassion for all beings and how it resulted in happiness. 'O Mother, I have knowledge of the three times, past, present and future. Buddhists gain such knowledge and are content in this world. With my excellent knowledge that is always correct, never wrong, I know everything, exactly as it exists. I know, for example, that your father foolishly practiced the religion of the Jinas and has been reborn as a deer in a dangerous and terrifying forest.' When Padmaśrī heard this, she said, 'I can imagine just what kind of knowledge you have, that lets you know without any doubt that my father has become a deer in a forest crowded with trees!'

'One day Padmaśrī invited all the Buddhist monks to her home and they all came with their shoes and umbrellas and took their proper places. The Buddhist monks, eaters of meat, carefully took off their shoes and put them in a corner of the room and then they sat down in the proper order. Padmaśrī quickly took one shoe from each pair and tore it up into tiny pieces. She made those pieces into tasty dishes for them to eat, fragrant, rich, with many different flavors. Padmaśrī then served them the dishes she had made and they ate heartily, savouring the food and snapping their fingers in delight. When they had finished eating and went to get their shoes, they were astonished to find only one shoe from each pair. They politely asked Padmaśrī, "Buddhist lay disciple! We put our shoes in this room, but now there is only one shoe from each pair. The second shoe of each pair is nowhere to be seen. Find our shoes for us so that we can go home." When Padmaśrī heard their question, she replied, "You all have knowledge that reveals all things in the universe. After all, you knew by that knowledge of yours that my father has become a deer in the forest. Use that knowledge now and find your own shoes." The Buddhist monks, who took refuge in the Buddha, were furious at her words, and told Buddhadāsa everything that had happened. "Your vicious daughter-in-law invited us and then cooked our shoes and fed us our own shoes to eat." When he heard that, Buddhadāsa's eyes blazed in anger. He gave the king plenty of money, which the king did not hesitate to take. The angry king then banished Padmaśrī and Buddhasaṃgha from his city.

'Having been banished from the city, Padmaśrī and

Buddhasaṃgha joined two merchants who were leading a caravan to some distant land. That night the two caravan leaders and their party ate some poisoned food, not knowing it was poisoned, and they all died. Buddhasaṃgha had also eaten the poisoned food. The poison spread throughout his limbs and he was on the verge of death. Buddhadāsa came to know of everything that had happened from his servants and, filled with sorrow, he hastened to the spot. When he saw his son on the verge of death, he cried to the people with him, "Surely, people, Padmaśrī has poisoned my son. And all these other people in the caravan have also been killed by that woman for no reason at all." Thus did Buddhadāsa in his deluded state make this accusation against Padmaśrī, although it was without a grain of truth. Having made this public accusation, Buddhadāsa took his son by the hand and threw him at the feet of Padmaśrī. When he did this, Padmaśrī declared, "Through the power of my observance of the Jain rule never to eat at night, may my husband stand up." As soon as she uttered these words, Buddhasaṃgha was free of the poison and stood up, hale and hearty.

'At that very moment the gods in the sky in their delight lavishly worshipped Padmaśrī. Amazed, the invisible gods worshipped Padmaśrī from heaven; again and again they proclaimed, "See how devout Padmaśrī is! See how she has carried out her vows as a Jain lay devotee! Look at her great faith in the Jina, her deep faith in the Jain doctrine!" When King Dantivāhana and his ministers saw the miracle that Padmaśrī had performed, they too were greatly astonished. They transferred the great burden of the kingdom to their sons; they were filled with disgust for the pleasures of worldly existence and their minds were now set on achieving Final Release. The King Dantivāhana, his ministers and his subjects all renounced their possessions and became monks under the guidance of the Jain monk Śrīdhara. Even Buddhadāsa, along with Padmaśrī, Buddhasaṃgha and some other merchants, abandoned their wrong beliefs and accepted the doctrine of the Jains.'

This was the story that Padmalatā told the merchant and his other wives. 'When I saw that miracle that Padmaśrī performed, I became firm in my faith in the Jain doctrine.'

(from the *Bṛhatkathākośa* of Hariṣeṇa, No.68)

26

MADANAKĪRTI

In Ujjain dwelt the Digambara Viśālakīrti. He had a disciple named Madanakīrti. Now this Madanakīrti, having defeated all his rivals in debate in the three directions, the East, West, and North, and having obtained the honorific title, "Crest Jewel among all the Philosophers," had come back to Ujjain, which was graced by the presence of his teacher, and there he had humbly submitted himself to Viśālakīrti. Madanakīrti had become famous everywhere, and everywhere people talked of him. He boasted to his teacher and his teacher was amused. Then after a few days Madanakīrti said to his teacher, 'O Blessed One! I want to defeat in debate the philosophers in the South. Please, let me go to the South.' The teacher said, 'My child! Do not go to the South. For that is the land of pleasures. No monk could go there and not be shaken from his vows, no matter how great an ascetic he might be.' Madanakīrti was puffed up with pride in his own learning and so he ignored these words of his teacher. And he set out with a host of disciples, carrying with him a net, spade and ladder, to seek out any possible rivals in the seas, on earth and in heaven. After he had first crushed all the philosophers in Mahārāshtra, Madanakīrti finally arrived in Karṇāṭak.

There in the city Vijayapura he sought an audience with the king. Fornally ushered into the royal assembly hall by the door-keeper, Madanakīrti saw the King Kuntibhoja seated amongst all his courtiers. Now this king was himself learned in the three Vedas and he was eager for the company of other learned men. Madanakīrti praised the king with these verses:

'Lord, how can we tell which one is the snake Śeṣa or which are the stars? How can we know which is the milk ocean and which is the moon; which is a jasmine blossom and which is a lump of camphor, what is a hailstone and what is mother-of-pearl? How can we find the Himalaya mountains, when everywhere is made shining white by your fame which shimmers like so many drops of molten mercury, heated to the boiling point by the blazing flames of your military prowess, which leap and sputter from your valiant and prideful strong arms!'

'Your fame, O Kaikaṭa, Kuntibhoja, plunges deep into the heavenly river, the Ganges; encircling the Guardians of the Quarters and making the earth into a blazing ball of light, it traverses the seven oceans, and as if to proclaim to all and sundry that it belongs like a faithful wife to you and you alone, it touches the world of Viṣṇu on high, and reaches below into the retherworld to stroke the many crests of the snake Śeṣa who supports the universe.'

The king was charmed with his words. The Digambara was given lodgings near the royal palace. The king commanded him, 'Write a book that tells of the deeds of my forebearers.' Madanakīrti said to the king, 'My Lord, I can compose five hundred verses in a day, but I cannot write them down that fast. Give me a scribe to assist me.' The king said, 'My daughter, whose name is Madanamañjarī, will sit behind a curtain hidden from your sight and write down your verses for you.'

The Digambara began to compose the work. The princess wrote down five hundred verses each day. And so passed a few days.

One day the princess heard Madanakīrti's voice, which was sweet like the voice of a warbler in springtime, and she thought, 'He must be as handsome as his voice is beautiful. But how can I see him from behind this curtain? I must think of something. I know, I shall have the cooks put too much salt into his food.' Now Madanakīrti also wanted to see the princess, who was so learned and who also had such a sweet voice. When he found his food too salty, the Digambara said, 'How this makes me shiver!' The princess replied, 'A cold wind blows no good!' And with their coquettish banter back and forth and their clever puns and jibes, both pushed back first the curtain of respectful distance demanded by convention that had kept them apart, and then the real curtain of cloth that divided them from each other. They beheld each other's divine beauty. At once the Digambara said:

'In vain does the lotus creeper spend its life, if it has never beheld the orb of the moon with its delicious cooling beams.'

And the princess, for her part, replied:

'And the moon, too, rises in vain, if it does not awaken the lotus creeper with its touch.'

And as the saying goes, "The many arrows of love strike fast and furious once lovers have enjoyed the first pleasurable glimpse of each other"; so these two gave up their virginity for passionate lovemaking.

People began to talk. The book was not progressing very fast. One evening the king took a look at the work. 'Why did you do so little today?' All the Digambara had written there were two or three verses of quite poor quality indeed. And then he said to the king, 'Lord! Long ago I made the solemn promise that I would never recite my work and have it written down by someone who was not learned. Now your daughter did not understand this section very well. And so it took some time. That is why the book is not progressing so fast.' The king thought to himself:

'This sounds like a sorry excuse to me. I shall have to take a good look and see just what those two are doing together.'

One day, as soon as the sun came up, the king went alone in disguise to the room where they were wont to work and hid behind one of the wall-partitions. At that very moment the Digambara said these words to the princess, words that a lover would say to his angry mistress:

'O you, with your lovely eyebrows! Since you became angry with me, I have stopped eating; I cannot bear even to mention a word about women and I have not touched my fine perfumes and vials of fragrant incense. O angry one, be angry no more. I throw myself at your feet. Have mercy on me now. Without you, my beloved, the world is a cold and joyless place for me!'

When he heard this poem, the king was sure that the two were behaving wantonly and he crept silently from that room. The Lord of the Earth returned to his assembly hall. Furious, he summoned the Digambara to him at once. When the Digambara got there, the king said to him, 'O scholar! What is this new verse I heard you recite, the one that starts off, "O lovely one"! Since you became angry with me, I have stopped eating?' The Digambara reflected, 'The king has definitely seen me. I have been caught red-handed. Never mind. I still must answer him in some way or another.' And he thought of all sorts of things and, finally, he said to the king, 'My Lord! For the last two days my eye has been hurting me terribly. I was addressing my eye with this verse, trying somehow to make it stop tormenting me.' And with those as opening words, that Digambara, undaunted, went on and on like this, explaining away his extraordinary behaviour. The king was secretly delighted by Madanakīrti's clever speech, but he was still furious over his unpardonable offence. And so raising one eyebrow in an expression of his fury, he called to his servants, 'Tie this fellow up! And kill him for his criminal acts.' Madanakīrti was bound by the king's men.

Having heard what had happened, the princess grabbed a knife and rushed into the assembly hall with thirty-two of her friends who were similarly armed. She stood right before the king and said,

'If you release my beloved, then all will be fine. If you do not release him, then you will be guilty of thirty-four murders. One will be the murder of the Digambara and the others will be the murder of these thirty-three young women.' At that point the king's ministers advised him:

'My Lord, you yourself brought these two together. And the presence of a woman for a young man is the springtime shower that makes the tree of love blossom in all its fullness. Who is to blame for what has happened? For what they say is true:

> The glances of women, even in a painting, rob the minds of those who see them; what chance does a man have before the throbbing glances of a live woman, with all her amorous games?

'Show mercy and release the Digambara. And give your daughter to him.' He listened to their words, released the Digambara and made his daughter the Digambara's wife. And the Digambara was given a share of the kingdom. He gave over to his father-in-law whatever riches he acquired in conquest. Abandoning his religious vows, he enjoyed worldly pleasures.

From Ujjain, his teacher Viśālakīrti heard all these things

that had happened to Madanakīrti. And he thought, 'How mighty is the power of wealth, youth, and the company of bad friends; for through these things even a man like Madanakīrti, faithful to his monastic vows, learned, a fine philosopher, and adept in spiritual exercises, has stumbled onto a false road that can lead only to the most terrible rebirths in the next life. Alas, alas! The mind is beset by some strange distortion, rife with all the many delusions that arise upon the destruction of right discrimination; unknowable, never even experienced before in any other birth, this strange process at once is like ice to the warmth of wisdom within and causes terrible burning pain.'

Thinking such things, he sent four of his most skilled disciples in order to bring Madanakīrti back to his senses. When they got there they said to him: 'O wise one! Turn away from the momentary pleasure of the company of a woman, a pleasure that will soon vanish. Seek the company of the damsels Compassion, Wisdom, and Friendliness. For in hell no firm breasts adorned with pearl necklaces will save you, nor any woman's thighs with jangling girdle bring you solace.

'Your teacher recalls you to your senses with words like these. Accept his instruction. Do not be deluded.'

Shameless, Madanakīrti wrote down some verses for his teacher on a piece of paper and told them to deliver them. They went back there. The teacher read the verses:

'Logic can be twisted to prove anything you want. The scriptures are all different. There is no teacher whose words can be accepted as the absolute truth. They say that the real truth is hidden in a secret place. The true path is that one followed by every man.'

'Seeing my beloved is the only divine sight I need. You may call your philosophy divine sight, but who needs it, when even the man with lust and sin can feel such bliss from the sight of the woman he loves.

'The man who has passionately and forcibly kissed his

angry mistress, while she was biting her tender sprout-like lips in rage and furiously shaking her fingers at him, while her eyebrows danced up and down as she shouted, "Let go of me, you good-for-nothing! Let go of me!" and her eyes were clouded from the steam of her own breaths that escaped, despite everything, from the passion of the moment, such a man has truly tasted the nectar of immortality. Seeking this divine drink, the Gods were silly, indeed, to have gone to such fuss to churn the ocean.'

When he read these verses and others similar to them, the teacher was silent. As for Madanakīrti, he had a very good time for himself indeed.

(from the *Prabandhakośa* of Rājaśekharasūri, p.64)

27

REVATI

Now there was in the land of the Pāṇḍyas a city called South Mathurā. It was rich in grain and money and adorned with many Jain temples. There reigned King Pāṇḍu, intent upon protecting his subjects; he had charmed everyone in the world by his many excellent virtues. His wife was named Sumati, "The Clever", and indeed she was thought to be quite smart. She was chaste, beautiful and soft-spoken, and her fame reached the very corners of the world. An ascetic, a teacher named Munigupta, also lived there. He was a veritable ocean of virtue and knew all of the sacred texts; he possessed supernatural knowledge and practiced severe austerities.

One day some Vidyādhara prince endowed with magical powers came to the city South Mathurā; his name was Manovega, "Swift as Thought", and indeed he dashed to the city with uncustomary speed. Filled with devotion, he circumambulated the most excellent Jain temple three times and said a prayer to the Jina; such prayer puts an end to all suffering. He worshipped the ascetic Munigupta with all the devotion due one's guru, and then bowed down to the other ascetics. Finally he sat down near Munigupta. The wise Manovega was silent for a few moments, listening to the discourse on the Jain doctrine; then he bowed his head in reverence and said to Munigupta, 'Blessed One! I wish to go to the city of Śrāvastī to pay respects to the Jina; tell me what I may do for you when I get to the sacred city.' When he heard Manovega's words, Munigupta spoke to him, with a voice so deep that it made the peacocks think the clouds were rumbling and set them dancing. 'If, O lay disciple, you go to the lovely city of Śrāvastī to worship the Jinas, who are worthy of being worshipped by hosts of gods, then you must carefully convey my words of blessing to the lay disciple, the lady Revatī, whose mind it totally permeated with thoughts of the Jain doctrine.' Having heard those words of the ascetic, that lay disciple was surprised. Not understanding the monk's intention, he thought to himself, 'This monk takes special care to send his blessings to the lay disciple, the lady Revatī, but does not have any special words of reverence for the monks nor for the male lay disciples.' So he thought to himself for awhile, and then, desirous of testing the ascetic, he said to him again, 'I will go to the city of Śrāvastī.' The ascetic heard what the lay disciple said; he told Manovega, who had a crooked mind and was definitely operating under false impressions, 'If you are going to that city to worship the Jinas, then you must convey my blessings to the lay disciple, the lady named Revatī.' Manovega was even more surprised and angry, too. He asked, 'Blessed One! Tell me, what makes that lady Revatī so special that even when I asked you three times you still sent your blessings all three times to her and not to any of the male lay disciples? Furthermore, in that city there is a great Jain ascetic named Bhavyasena, who practices severe austerities; he knows from memory the eleven texts and is a leader of the four-fold Jain community, the monks, nuns, and lay disciples, male and female. He is the best of the monks and removes all doubts concerning the verities of the Jain doctrine, the soul and other entities. Why did you not send your respects to a noble ascetic like him?'

When he heard these words of the Vidyādhara, the lord of ascetics replied with a voice so deep that it made all of the world echo with the sound. 'That Bhavyasena of whom you spoke is deluded and does not believe in the existence of earth-souls. Not to believe in the categories as they have been expounded is an example of false belief, and the soul that is sullied by false belief wanders endlessly in the cycle of rebirths. That is why I did not exchange respectful greetings with him, O Vidyādhara, nor did I send him any friendly words. And as for what you have asked me, why I would send words of blessing to the lady Revatī and not to any of the male lay disciples, listen to me as I explain why that is so. Revatī is endowed with right belief; she adheres to the doctrine propounded by the Jinas, and her mind is repulsed by the actions of heretics and those who are monks but adhere to wrong doctrines. She accepts only the Jina as God and the renunciation of all possessions as the path to release; she believes that the highest religious action is non-violence and that true asceticism is control of the senses. She accepts as her teachers only those steadfast ones who follow the correct code of conduct and observe total chastity, those ascetics whose bodies are adorned by the virtue of forbearance. It is for this reason that I send my blessings to Revatī and not to the others, whose souls are sullied by false belief.'

When the Vidyādhara heard these words of Munigupta, that were destined ultimately to result in happiness, he raised his eyebrows and thought to himself, 'See how even monks can be afflicted by passion; otherwise why would he say that a lay woman is the best of all, pure in her right belief, and that a monk who knows all the sacred texts and is a great ascetic has succumbed to false belief? What use is it to argue with him like this? I will go to that city, and as soon as I get there I will make my own test to determine the truth.'

Manovega bowed down to the Jina and to that ascetic and then angrily rushed away. In an instant he reached the city of Śrāvasti. With his magic powers he made himself appear as the Hindu god Brahmā in the east; the fine likeness of Brahmā was seated on a royal swan and holding a water pot; he had four faces. With his magic powers he took on the form of Viṣṇu appearing in the south; Viṣṇu was seated on the bird Gāruḍa and held the conch and club and wheel. With his own magic powers he took the form of Rudra, appearing in the west; Rudra held the skull club and the snake Vāsuki was in his hair; he was mounted on his bull. With his magic powers he quickly made a very handsome likeness of the Buddha appear in the north; the Buddha was seated in meditation and was calm in appearance. The devotees of each of these were delighted when they saw the gods, Rudra and the others. The foolish Jain lay disciples, men and women, also went to see what was going on; only Revatī stayed home. Then Manovega used his magic powers to make twenty-five Jinas appear in the middle of the city, along with the eight wondrous signs that accompany them, which include things like haloes, the sound of drums, and a rain of divine flowers. Bhavyasena, the leader of the Jain monks, when he heard that the twenty-five Jinas had appeared, went to see them along with the nuns, the male lay disciples and the female lay disciples.

A group of women then said to the lay disciple Revatī, 'See, twenty-five Jinas have all come to the center of the city. The monks and nuns, the male lay disciples and the female lay disciples, filled with devotion, have all gone to see them, bearing flowers in their hands for worship. Let us take flowers and rice grains, fruits and incense, sandalwood and lovely lamps and go quickly, my friend, to worship them, too.' The lay disciple Revatī then said to the pious women, who were contentedly gazing on her lotus-face, 'I am busy here in the house and cannot go now.' Her friends, filled with affection, replied, 'This city alone of all cities is blessed with the protection of the gods like Brahmā; you do not belive in the religions devoted to these gods and so it was right that you did not go to see them. But if you do not go when the Jinas have come down here, too busy with tasks that only occasion sin, you will surely go to hell!' With those words, her friends made ready to go. Revatī told them, 'The lords of the monks clearly told me that there are only twenty-four Jinas, including those of the past, the present and the future. There is no twenty-fifth Jina, there never has been and there never will be. I know that this is some magician's trick. Don't bother me; go home.' When they heard these words of Revatī, the women were utterly taken aback. They left Revatī's house and went about their business.

Bhavyasena with great devotion bowed down to the twenty-five Jinas and then with the other Jains went back to his residence. Manovega saw the entire Jinas community there, but he did not see Revatī. Then he abandoned the form of the Jina and took on the guise of a novice monk. Afflicted by fake pains, he fell on the road. He vomited and had diarrhea and groaned; shouting out the name of the lay disciple Revatī, he rolled on the ground. Some woman went to Revatī's house and told her, 'Friend! There is a young monk lying on the road who is calling out your name.' When she heard this, Revatī asked, 'Where is he?' The other woman replied, 'He is lying on the main road.' Revatī then went to the monk. She took him by the hand and brought him home with her.

When the monk got to Revati's house, he said to her, 'I am starving. Hurry, give me something to eat.' Revatī first made sure the monk was seated comfortably and then she joyfully offered him some food, for she considered any monk to be a worthy recipient of her gift. No sooner had she brought him some tasty beans to eat, than with his magic power he devoured them all. No sooner had Revatī brought him some rich butter, than that one who used magic powers gobbled that up too, in one swallow, with his tricks. No sooner had she brought him plump sweetmeats than he swallowed them whole, not even bothering to sprinkle them with sugar. No sooner had she brought him tasty seasoned dishes, than he grabbed them from her and belted them down in a single mouthful, before she even properly offered them to him. No sooner had she brought him sweets in a sauce of curds, than that magician gulped them down, not even bothering with the sauce. No sooner did she bring him cakes and sweetened milk, than he drank all the milk, leaving the cakes untouched. Whatever tasty food she gave him to eat, he snatched from her hands and with his magic devoured whole. When he had eaten all that she gave him and was still not sated, he boldly said to Revatī, who was undaunted, 'Mother! When I heard how famous you are for your firm belief in the Jain doctrine, I came to see you, tormented though I was by hunger and thirst. But the food you have given me has left me still hungry; I have to say that I am not satisfied with what you have served me. Bring me tasty food and lots of it. See to it that I am satisfied at last!'

When she heard these words of the novice monk, Revatī was taken aback. But she did not let herself be discouraged and hastened to give him more food. She made all kinds of things to eat, sweets, sweetmeats, cakes with ghee, dumplings, and delicacies, fried snacks, sweet and savoury. She made him heaping mounds of candies and sweetmeats and she offered them all to him with respect and devotion. And he gobbled everything up. He drank hundreds and thousands of pots of water that she brought for him, gulping them down in a split second. Then that sorcerer began to have diarrhea and to vomit up everything that he had eaten and drunk, not once, but again and again. Revatī cleaned his stinking vomit and faeces with her own hands and threw it all outside. When he saw Revatī's humility and how she took care of him so carefully and single-mindedly, the Vidyādhara Manovega dropped his appearance as a novice monk and revealed to her his true form as a Vidyādhara. When Revatī saw his divine form, with his gold earrings; when she saw how the many light rays that streamed from his shining teeth whitened the very sky itself, she asked him, 'Who are you? Why have you come here?' In answer to Revatī's questions, the Vidyādhara replied, 'Know me to be a Vidyādhara named Manovega, O lovely lady! I came here to test you, using my magic to create the gods Brahmā and the others, and then to turn myself into a novice monk. The monk Munigupta told me that seeing you was even more auspicious than seeing the ascetic Bhavyasena, and now I have seen for myself that what he said was true. O Revatī, the monk Munigupta, who guards his thoughts, words and deeds, sends to you his blessings.' Noble Revatī took five steps towards the Vidyādhara and then gently bowed her head at his feet. Having explained himself to her and having told her how he had come to test her, Manovega, his mind at ease, then vanished.

The Vidyādhara Manovega circumambulated the lofty temple to the Jinas; he praised the Jina and the excellent monk Bhavyasena, leader of the monastic community. He then sat down to listen to Bhayvasena's discourse along with other lay disciples, who had mastered the meanings of all the sacred texts and who accepted the Jina as their deity. When the discourse was over, Bhavyasena went outside with the speedy Manovega to move his bowels. The Vidyādhara, with his magic, made these three things disappear from the vicinity: ashes, potshards and bricks. When Bhavyasena had finished, he ordered the lay disciple, 'Quick, quick. Go find some ash or brick or potshards.' Instead, the lay disciple brought a good-sized clod of earth. Curious to see what would happen, he showed it to the monk. 'I could not find any one of the three things you asked for, O monk! So take this pure piece of earth I have brought you; it has no living creatures on it.' The king of monks looked carefully at the clod of earth and then took it in his hand; since he doubted the existence of earth-souls, he then said to the lay disciple, 'Some teachers say that without exception all the elements like earth contain living souls, but Manovega, I do not accept that.' With those words, the monk, who did not believe in the existence of earth-souls, took the clod of earth and used it to clean his hands.

Manovega now knew that the lay disciple Revatī was adorned with the true right belief and that the monk indeed did doubt the existence of earth-souls. He went back to the monk Munigupta and bowed down before him again and again. He then told him everything that had happened. That done, he went home.

One should never praise a monk who is not a true Jain monk; praising false monks destroys true faith in the Jain doctrine. After all, poison and the nectar of the gods will never be the same. There are six things that are worthy of respect: knowledge, an ascetic possessed of knowledge, those who have attained release, a Jain temple, proper conduct and an ascetic possessed of such conduct. Other than these things that lead frightened souls to turn to religion, there is nothing worthy of devotion. Revatī loved to bow down at the lotus feet of the Jain ascetics, as a bee yearns for the taste of lotus pollen. She was not deluded by the magic tricks of the Vidyādhara.

(from the *Bṛhatkathākośa* of Hariṣeṇa, No.7)

28

ĀRĀMASOHĀ

Here on the island continent of Jambudīva, which is located in the middle of many continents and oceans, is the famous land called Bharaha, divided into six parts. In the middle of Bharaha is the best of countries called Kusaṭṭa, rich in cows and bulls, the abode of every good quality that a country should possess. In the country of Kusaṭṭa is the grand village named Thalāsayam, and if you want to know what it is like, you must know how to play with words, making each combination of words refer at once to the village and to something else. This village is like the chest of men and women, wearied from physical exertion; for their chests are filled with their heaving breaths, while the village is filled with much grain; it is like a great sage, who exercises many restraints, while the village is well protected; it is like the coiffure of a lovely woman, which sports a fine part, while the village boasts well-defined and cared-for borders.

The village is charming with its hundreds of happy villagers; it is inaccessible to thieves and wicked kings; it is the home of self-control, compassion and generosity. But strange to say, the village seemed to be peculiarly totally devoid of plant life. One might say: on all four sides of the village, to a distance of a furlong, there was no plant life at all except some grass.

Now there lived in this village a brahmin named Aggisomma, skilled in reciting the Ṛg and other Vedas. He had a wife, a brahmin lady named Jalanasihā. As they enjoyed together the pleasures of the senses, a daughter was born to them. They named her Vijjupahā. She was endowed with a host of excellent qualities, among them, great beauty. One might say:

She surpassed the women of the gods in her beauty and put to shame the most excellent swans by her soft murmuring speech and her languid gait; she seemed a veritable moonbeam dripping the nectar of immortality; like the goddess Pārvatī she was resplendent in her loveliness.

She was clever and modest, respectful to her elders; she was master of all the arts that are praised in a woman; the virtues of truthfulness, purity and chastity were her natural adornments; she was totally honest by nature, incapable of a crooked thought or deed.

Now when this girl was eight years old her mother was snatched by the jaws of death, which has as its terrible fangs the torments of sickness and old age. Thus it was that the young girl took over all of the work in the house. It was this way:

She would get up at daybreak and milk the cows; then she would smear the courtyard with cowdung and sweep the house and do everything else that was to be done.

And then she would go out to keep watch over the cows as they grazed until midday, when she would bring the cows back and milk them once more.

She would cook for her father and serve him his meal,

and only then would this young girl eat; having finished her meal, she would go out once more to look after the cows.

In the evening there were still more chores, so many that she could not sleep; thus was this young girl overwhelmed by the household responsibilities, day after day.

Then one day, feeling totally oppressed and exhausted, the young girl boldly told her father, 'Father, you must do something to get a mother for me, for I am totally exhausted doing the housework.' Her father thought to himself, 'That is a good idea,' and he found some woman somewhere. But she only threw added burdens onto the shoulders of the young girl, for all she was interested in was bathing herself and rubbing her skin with fine unguents and then donning fancy clothes and jewels. This made Vijjupahā think, 'I brought this on myself; trying to lessen my burden, I have made my suffering twice as heavy.' And so it was that once more she would have to go out at dawn and now she would not even come back until mealtime was well over; she would eat whatever was left and go out again, not to return until nightfall. Thus passed twelve years.

One day while she was watching the cows as they grazed she lay down to sleep in the grass, for there was no shade anywhere. It just so happened that a snake made its way to the same clump of grass. Furthermore:

He was large and black with red eyes and a forked tongue that darted hither and thither; he raised his hood and slithered quickly towards her, terrified by something.

A demi-god, the prince of snakes, had possessed his body and so this snake could converse in the language of humans; he woke her up with gentle words.

When he saw that she was fully awake, the snake spoke to her, 'Child! I have come to you because I am afraid. Wicked snake-charmers pursue me. I am terrified that they will capture me and stuff my body into their basket, where I will suffer no end of misery.

'Therefore, young girl, I beg of you, wrap me in a corner of your garment. Protect me, for I am terrified. O daughter, make haste!

'I am possessed by a demi-god, the prince of snakes, and I cannot disobey the commands of the deity that controls the magic formula of the snake-charmers.

'Do not be afraid; do not hesitate, just do as I say.'

And the girl did as the snake asked her and concealed him in a corner of her garment.

At that moment the snake-charmers rushed upon them, holding bunches of magic herbs in their hands. They asked the young girl, 'My child, have you seen a large snake pass by this way?' She replied, 'I have been sleeping here with my eyes covered. It's no use asking me about anything.' At this they said, 'She is but a child. If she had seen a large snake surely she would have run away in fear. She must not have seen it. Let's go on up ahead and look there.' And so they looked everywhere for the snake, ahead along the road and back where they had come from. When they did not see him they sighed, 'How can it have disappeared right from under our very own eyes?' With those same eyes wide open in surprise, the snake-charmers gave up and went home.

When they had gone, the girl said to the snake, 'You can come out. The men have gone.' The snake crawled out. The demi-god, the snake prince that had inhabited the snake's body, revealed himself to her; abandoning his form as a snake he allowed her to see his divine form. He told her, 'Child! I am pleased by the incomparably brave deed you performed just to help another living being in distress. Choose a boon for me to grant you.'

When the girl saw the god with glittering earrings and shimmering jewels, she replied, 'If you are truly pleased with me, then make some shade for me so that I can look after the cows as they graze without suffering so. There is no shade now and the heat makes me feel so terribly sick.'

The god thought to himself, 'Is this all she asks of me as a boon, the silly, poor girl? Never mind, I will do something wonderful for her.' And so he created above her a beautiful garden. Here is what the garden was like:

It had many species of the finest trees; flowers of every season were in bloom there, while all around the garden wafted the scent of pollen from the many blossoms and the sound of drunken bees resounded far and wide.

The rays of the sun could not penetrate its lushness; delightful to the mind and adorned by wonderful fragrances and colors, such was the garden that the god made for her.

The god told her, 'Child! Through my power this garden will follow you wherever you may go. When you go home, at your command it will follow you and remain there, spread out over your head. If you are ever in trouble or in need, call upon me.' With those words the god disappeared. The girl stayed there until nightfall, her thirst and hunger appeased by the taste of the divine fruit. Then she took her cows and went home. The garden went with her and spread itself out over the house. When her step mother said, 'Eat!' she answered, 'I'm not hungry.' In the last watch of the night she gathered the cows and went into the wilderness. Several more years passed, in this very same routine.

One day as she was sleeping happily in the wilderness under the shelter of her garden, the king of Pāḍaliputtapura, named Jiasattu, was returning from his victorious campaign. He saw the garden and said to his minister, 'Make camp here in this delightful garden.' The minister at once assented and placed the king's throne under a magnificent mango tree. The king sat down on the throne. Then:

The excited horses were tied to strong trees with the best of ropes, while their saddles and reins were hung high on the trees' branches.

The elephants, wild in rut, were tied fast to the strong trunks of the trees while the camels and other animals were stationed at proper spots.

The young girl woke up when she heard the sounds coming from the king's camp. She saw that her cows had fled out of fear of the huge elephants and other beasts. As the minister watched, she ran to get the cows back. As she ran, the entire garden, horses, army camp and all, went after her. The king and all his retinue stood up at once, their eyes wide open in astonishment. 'What 's happening, what's happening!' they cried. The king asked the minister, 'Is this some magician's show?' The minister replied, 'My lord! There was a young girl asleep here. She woke up and rubbed her eyes, which were wide open in fear, and then she ran away. This garden, too, ran off behind her. She must have some magic power. I can tell that she cannot be a goddess by the way that she rubbed her eyes, this much I can swear to.' With those words the minister dashed off after the young girl, calling out to her. 'What did you say?' she replied, and she stopped in her tracks along with her garden. He called out to her, 'Come back here.' She answered, 'My cows have run off.' The minister promised, 'We'll bring them back for you,' and true to his words he dispatched some riders after the cows. They brought the cows back. The girl returned and stood by the king. The garden stood there, too. The king first marvelled at her unusual gift; then he began to look her up and down. He saw that she was just a young maid and he fell in love with her on the spot. He glanced over at his minister, who divined the king's state of mind and said to the young girl, Vijjupahā:

'Lovely lady! Accept as your most excellent husband, your lord, this man, who is lord over all the earth. Many are the princes who bow down at his lotus-like feet in humble submission.'

She replied, 'I am not master of myself.' 'The minister asked, 'Then who is your master?' She said, 'My mother and father.' The minister asked, 'Who is your father ? Where does he live? What is his name?' She answered, 'He is the brahmin Aggisomma, living right here in this village.'

When he heard this the king commanded his minister, 'Go at once to ask for her hand.' And so the minister went into the village, straight to the brahmin's house. The brahmin saw the minister coming and respectfully rose to greet him. He offered him a seat and said, 'Tell me,what I can do for you?' The minister said, 'Tell me, do you have a daughter?' 'Yes,' replied the brahmin.' In that case, give her to the king in marriage,' said the minister. The brahmin replied, 'Consider it done. My very life belongs to the king; why should not my daughter, too, be his?'

The minister said,'Come, let us go to the king.' And so Aggisomma went to the king. After offering the king his blessing, the brahmin sat down near the king. The minister explained what had taken place. The king, unable to wait a moment longer, took the girl without benefit of proper ceremony. He changed her name. It was like this:

Since there shone above her a garden, resplendent with many trees, he called her Ārāmasohā, "The Girl who is Adorned with a Garden".

The king realized that the poor brahmin would now tell every one that he was the king's father-in law; embarrassed at the thought of having a pauper for his father-in-law, he gave the brahmin twelve excellent villages and prepared for a hasty departure. He sat Ārāmasohā on a fine elephant. The garden still stayed right above her. The king was absolutely delighted. One might say:

The king was convinced that his life's goal was achieved when he obtained that girl; after all, who would not be satisfied at getting a most excellent jewel?

All the way home the king could not keep his eyes off her face; then again, is it any wonder that the eye, once it alights on something beautiful, is reluctant to move on?

Why should we be surprised if the king was infatuated

with her? She was, after all, extremely lovely, and to top it off, she had been given magic powers by a demi-god!

When they arrived at Pāḍaliputta the king commanded:

'Decorate the marketplace! Raise high the flags! Let the entire city be decked out with stages and seats for the spectators!

'What more need I say? Let everything me made ready so that I may enter the city with my queen with all due pomp and splendor.'

When all the king's commands had been carried out by the townspeople, the king entered the city, at each step honored by appropriate ceremonies and good wishes.

After the king had entered the city, all the people poured out of their homes, eager to see the king and his queen.

The men praised the king, while the women were amazed by the queen. One young man remarked, 'Fortunate indeed is the king to have obtained a woman like this. She surpasses all the women of the gods and has moreover great magical powers; she is truly the source of all of life's pleasures.'

Some old man added, 'This is clearly the result of previously earned merits. We must also do such good deeds so that in another life we too may be so fortunate.'

Some child, seeing the marvellous fruit hanging over the elephant, piped up, 'Oh my! How can I obtain such wonderful fruit for myself?'

Among the women one chimed in, 'Look! Look at this great wonder!', and to her a second woman replied, 'Surely all of this is due to the power of some god.'

A third remarked, 'Just look at how beautiful she is,' while another cheekily retorted, 'Who wouldn't be beautiful with clothes and jewels like that!'

Still another said, 'Glorious indeed is she among living beings, who shares the throne of the king!' while someone else replied,

'O lovely lady, why do you praise her in this way? She's

a bit too bold for me. See, she isn't even embarrassed to parade herself with the king in front of all and sundry!'

Still another said, 'Aren't you amazed? An entire garden, so lovely, hovers above that best of elephants!'

Someone else replied, 'What's so surprising about that? The powers of the gods can do all sorts of things like this!'

The king passed through the crowd, abuzz with remarks like these. He alighted from the elephant in front of his own grand palace.

While the king and queen entered the palace, the divine garden hovered over the palace through the power of that demi-god.

As the king enjoyed the pleasures of the senses with her, like some god in heaven, he did not even notice time going by.

Now in the meantime Ārāmasohā's step-mother had given birth to a daughter. This girl was now of age. The stepmother thought to herself, 'If somehow this Ārāmasohā could be got rid of, then the king would surely fall in love with this daughter of mine and marry her. I must figure out some means to get rid of Ārāmasohā.' She asked her husband, 'Why don't I send something delicious for Ārāmasohā to eat?' He told her, 'Beloved! What would she want with anything we might send? She already has everything she could possibly want.' She replied, 'You are right. She does have everything she could possibly want, but still I'd like to send her something.' Her husband realized that she was adamant and so he said, 'In that case, make something.' Her eyes popping with joy, the woman made some fancy candies. She put a good dose of drugs inside the candies and then coated them with honey. She then put the candies into a pot. She instructed her husband, 'Take these candies to her yourself. Don't let anyone take them from you along the way.' Her husband was a simple and honest fellow; he had no idea of her evil intentions. As he was about to set off by himself with the carefully sealed and labelled pot on his head, his wife told him again, 'You must give these candies to Ārāmasohā and to no one else. You must tell her, "Daughter, please eat these candies by yourself. Do not give them to anyone else. We wouldn't want everyone at the court to make fun of my cooking!"'

Her husband agreed to do as he was told, and set out on his journey. Morning, noon and night he watched over his charge, making sure it remained sealed, and at night when he slept he placed it carefully under his pillow; thus he made his way to his destination, Pāḍaliputta. There, on the outskirts of the city, exhausted, he fell asleep under a huge fig tree. Because of the strange ways of karma, the tree under which he fell asleep turned out to be the very tree in which the snake prince that had befriended Ārāmasohā had made its nest. The snake prince thought, 'Someone is sleeping under my tree, totally exhausted from a long journey. Who can it be?' He used his supernatural knowledge and saw that it was none other than Ārāmasohā's father. He asked himself, 'What does he want coming to Pāḍaliputta. and what has he brought with him?' and no sooner did these questions come to him, then he saw the poisoned candies. As soon as he saw the poisoned candies, he further thought to himself, 'What a wicked stepmother! But I will never let that girl die as long as I am alive!' And so he spirited away those poison candies and put candies with the nectar of immortality in their place.

A few moments later the father woke up and went into the city. He reached the gate of the king's palace and said to the doorkeeper, 'Sir, tell the king, "Ārāmasohā's father has come from afar and wishes to see the king."' The doorkeeper informed the king, who ordered, 'Bring him in at once.' The brahmin then approached the king with words of blessing. He presented the gift to Ārāmasohā, who was with the king. He said, 'Lord! My daughter's mother says,' "I have made these with the love that is in a mother's heart. They are for my daughter and no one else. What more is there for me to say? You must be sure that you do not make me a laughing stock in the king's court."' At that the king looked over at his wife. She gave the candies to her servant and had her bring them to her quarters. The brahmin was honored with gifts of jewels, fine ornaments and clothes. The queen retired to her quarters. When his formal duties were over in the court, the king joined her in her quarters. When he was seated comfortably, the queen said,

'My Lord, grant me your favor. Give the order for this box to be opened.' Hearing her words, the king replied,

'My queen! Do not hesitate. You are in command here. Do as you like. Open the box yourself.'

Now when the queen opened the box, suddenly a divine fragrance filled the room, such as was difficult to encounter in the world of mortals.

The king was overcome by the fragrance for a moment; when he came to, he looked inside the box and saw there large, divine sweets, like fruits of the gods, containing the nectar of immortality.

The king was amazed and showed the candies to everyone who was around. Then he proceeded to eat them, even more amazed by their taste.

The king said to his queen, 'Queen! These are marvellous. I have never tasted anything like them. Send one to each of your sisters.' She did as she was told. Everyone sang her mother's praise, and it was said far and wide, 'Surely no one knows how to make candies the way she does!'

Aggisoma wanted permission to take Ārāmasohā home with him for a while. He asked the king, 'Lord, let my daughter come with me for a short time.' The king replied, 'Brahmin! The king's wives are not allowed to be touched by the rays of the sun. They cannot go outside.' Knowing that the king's answer was firm, the brahmin went home. He told his wife all that had happened. She thought to herself, 'Can it be that my efforts were in vain? I'll fix things. This time I will make even finer sweets for her.' And so a few days later she gave her husband a box of even better candies and sent him on his way. As before, he eventually came to that very same fig tree. The demi-god saw him and again took away the poison. Once more his wife's cooking was praised far and wide. The third time, when the stepmother heard that Ārāmasohā was pregnant, she gave to her husband a box of cakes, each carefully wrapped in palm leaves, and sent him off with these instructions, 'This time you must be sure to fix it so that your daughter comes home with you and gives birth here. If the king refuses to send her, use your power as a brahmin to convince him!' Her husband agreed and off he went. When he got to the tree, once more the god took away the poison. Everything else happened just as before; then the brahmin again asked the king:

'Lord! Now let my daughter come home with me so that she may give birth in her own home.'

But the king still refused, saying, 'That is impossible.' At this the brahmin started to stab himself in the stomach. He told the king, 'If you do not let my daughter come with me, then my death, the death of a brahmin, is on your head.' This convinced the king that the brahmin was determined and would stop at nothing. He conferred with his minister and finally gave permission for Ārāmasohā to go, accompanied by the appropriate retinue and gifts.

When the stepmother heard that Ārāmasohā was on her way home, she ordered a huge well to be dug behind their house. She also hid her own daughter in an underground chamber.

Ārāmasohā arrived with her escort of soldiers. She was given the proper welcome. When her time came, she gave birth to a son, who was like a god. Now one day when it just so happened that all her maidservants were somewhere else and only her stepmother was near her, Ārāmasohā needed to go outside to urinate. Her stepmother had to help her. She took Ārāmasohā to the back door. When Ārāmasohā saw the well, she asked her step-mother, 'Mother, when was this well dug?' She replied, 'Daughter! When I heard that you were coming I had it dug right away. I was afraid someone might attempt to poison you, so I decided that we needed to have our own well, right here near our house.' Ārāmasohā was curious about the well, but when she went right up to it to have a look down, her cruel stepmother pushed her into the well and she fell head first. As she fell she remembered the agreement she had made with the demi-god and she called out, 'Father! I need your help now!' At once the snake-prince caught her in his hands. He made an underground palace for her in the well and placed her there, where she could stay in all comfort. Even her garden followed her down into the well. Now the demi-god was angry with the stepmother. Ārāmasohā calmed him down, saying that after all the woman had been like a mother to her.

The stepmother dressed her own daughter in clothes suitable for a woman who has just given birth, and settled her on the bed that Ārāmasohā had been occupying. It was not long before Ārāmasohā's maidservants came back. They saw this woman:

She wasn't very attractive and her complexion was sallow; her eyes were a bit sunken in, but still, the woman they saw there lying on the bed did bear some resemblance to their mistress.

They asked her, 'Mistress! How is it that you look so different?' She replied, 'I don't know. I just don't feel very well, that's all, I guess.'

The maidservants were frightened and asked the stepmother, 'What has happened to her?' The mother beat her breast and cried:

'Alas, alas, I am ruined, daughter! I am indeed an unfortunate creature! Alas, my daughter, your beauty has faded.

'Could someone have put the evil eye on you? Have you

got the wind? Or have you some affliction, some child-bed fever?'

While she went on lamenting in this way, the maidservants said, 'Don't cry. Just do whatever you have to do right away!'

At that the stepmother proceeded to perform all sorts of strange rituals, but none of them produced any change in the state of the girl's body.

The maidservants became despondent, for they were terrified at what the king would do to them. Not long after that the king's messenger arrived. He announced, 'The king has commanded me to bring the queen and the prince back at once.' They made everything ready for Ārāmasohā's departure. As the party was about to depart, Ārāmasohā's servants asked, 'Where is your garden? Why is it not coming today?' The girl replied, 'I let it go to the well at the back of the house to have a drink of water. It'll come later. Let's go.' The party started off. In time they reached Pāḍaliputta.

The king was informed of the good news. Delighted, he had the marketplace decorated to welcome them. He declared a holiday. The king himself went out to receive his queen and son. When he saw what the queen looked like he asked, 'Queen! Why do you look so different?' The maidservants told him, 'Lord, after she gave birth she must have been afflicted by the evil eye, or a disturbance of wind, or possibly by child-bed fever that has caused this change in her bodily appearance. We're not quite sure.' When he heard this the king looked crestfallen at the news of the queen's troubles, despite his joy at the birth of his son. Nonetheless, he controlled himself and they all entered the city. He asked her, 'Where is the garden?' She answered, 'I left it behind so it could drink some water. It will come as soon as I call it.' But whenever the king looked at her body he could not help wondering, 'Is this really she or is it some other woman?' One day the king told her, 'Bring the garden.' She answered, 'Oh, I'll bring it when I need it.' When the king saw her vacant expression, he became even more suspicious. He thought, 'This is not my queen. It must be someone else.' This doubt began to preoccupy him more and more.

In the meantime, Ārāmasohā told the snake prince, 'I miss my child very much. You must do something so that I may see him.' He replied, 'In that case, my daughter, I can give you the power to go there, but you must not dally; as soon as you have seen your child you must come back at once.' She agreed. The snake prince warned her, 'If you stay there until the sun rises, you will never see me again. I will give you a sign if we are never to meet again; I will make it so that you will see a dead snake falling from your hair.' She said, 'So be it. I must see my son.' And so the snake prince let her go. By his power she reached Pāḍaliputta in an instant. She opened the gate and walked right into the innermost room of the palace. What was it like? Well, like this:

Jewelled lamps were ablaze there, and gemstones, pearls and jewels were in such abundance as to amaze those who entered; there were flowers everywhere and a pleasant fragrance from clouds of incense filled the room.

The finest betel nuts and leaves had been placed amongst a heap of fragrant precious substances, like camphor and aloe.

There was food to eat and refreshing drinks; there were mechanical birds all around. And in the midst of that splendour she saw a bed on which slept the king and her very own sister!

When she saw them there she felt a twinge of desire as she remembered her former lovemaking with the king; she felt a pang of jealousy at seeing her sister there embracing the man that she loved; she felt rage as she recalled how her own stepmother had pushed her into the well; and then feelings of affection washed over her as she remembered her son; tears of joy filled her eyes when she saw all her retinue. She lingered a moment, overcome by all of these different feelings, and then hastened to where her son slept on a golden bed that was encrusted with jewels, his nursemaid and the other servants now also fast asleep. She picked up the prince and gently touched his body. Before she left him she scattered all around him fruit and blossoms from her garden.

When morning came the nursemaid hastened to tell the king, 'Lord! It seems that last night someone worshipped the prince with so many flowers and fruits.' When the king heard that, he went to have a look for himself. He saw all the fruit and flowers. He asked the woman living as his wife, 'What is the meaning of this?' She answered, 'Oh, I fetched my garden. Then I put these fruits and flowers here.' The king said, "Why don't you bring the garden right now?" She said, 'I can't bring it during the day.' When the king saw her vacant expression and pale face, he thought, 'Surely there is something wrong here.' The next day the same thing happened. On the third day, while the woman slept, the king took his mighty sword and hid in a shadow. Not long afterwards Ārāmasohā arrived. As soon as he saw her the king thought to himself, 'This is my beloved wife. That other woman is someone else. But still I don't quite understand what is going on here!'

As he stood there steeped in thought, Ārāmasohā did exactly as she had done on the other nights and vanished. The king went back to sleep, mulling over in his mind all sorts of possibilities. When morning came he said to the woman, 'Today you have to bring the garden.' When she heard that she turned even paler. On the fourth night when Ārāmasohā had finished doing what she was doing, the king grabbed her hand and said, 'Beloved! Why do you deceive me in this way, although I have only the truest love for you!' She replied, 'Master! I am not trying to deceive you. But there is a reason for my behavior.' The king said, 'What could that possibly be?' She replied, 'I will tell you tomorrow. Now you must let me go.' The king said, 'Even a foolish child would not give up the nectar of immortality once he had it in his possession.' She warned him, 'Master! If you keep me here, you will surely regret what you have done.' He said, 'In that case you must at least tell me what lies behind all of this.' But as she started to tell him all of the wicked things her stepmother had done, from beginning to end, the sun began to rise. As she tried to arrange her hair that had become a mess, she saw a dead snake fall from her tresses. When she saw that dead snake she cried out, 'O Father!' and fell to the ground in a faint. The king fanned her until she came to. He asked, 'Beloved! Why do you grieve so?' She replied, 'Master! The snake prince who had granted me a boon and protected me by his presence warned me, "If you stay away beyond sunrise without my permission then you will never see me again. I will send you a sign confirming that. You will see a dead snake." Now all of this has happened because you would not let me go.'

Ārāmasohā did not bother to go back again to her parents home. She stayed there in the palace. That morning the king in his anger had the other woman tied up. When he grabbed a whip and prepared to beat her, Ārāmasohā fell at his feet and begged him:

'King! If you care about me, then release my sister. Look on her as you did before, as an act of compassion to me.'

The king replied, 'Queen, you ought not to spare this wicked girl after what she has done. Nonetheless, I will obey your words.'

Ārāmasohā took the girl,once the king had her released, and treated her like a sister, showing all the world the difference between a good person and a wicked one.

The king then summoned his men and commanded them, 'Take back the twelve villages that I gave the brahmin and quickly expel him from my realm. Cut off his wife's nose, lips and ears and banish her from my kingdom.' When she heard those words, once more Ārāmasohā threw herself at the feet of the king and implored him in these words:

'O King! When a dog bites you, do you bite him back? Let my parents go.

'O King! Do not do that which in the end will only cause us pain in our hearts. Do not go ahead with this punishment of my parents.'

When he heard her words the king said, 'Beloved, I will not do anything that causes you pain, even if I do consider it my utmost duty to do it!'

Time then passed as those two enjoyed together the delights of the senses. One day as the king and the queen were discussing some issues concerning religion they had this conversation:

The queen said, 'Master! I went through a period of intense misery and now I have become supremely happy once more. What karma did I have that produced these results? I must ask, if we should be so fortunate as to meet someone with supernatural knowledge who can give me an answer.'

The king said, 'In that case I shall instruct all those who watch over my gardens to inform us if any wise man should come here.'

And just as the king and queen were having this conversation, one of the gardeners approached them beaming with joy.

After bowing down to them, touching his head to the ground, the gardener announced, 'Someone with supernatural knowledge has come to the Sandalwood Garden.

'He can see right before his eyes everything that has happened, will happen and is happening in all the three worlds, heaven, earth and the netherworld. He sees these things as clearly as he can see a fruit resting in the palm of his hands.

'His name is Varicanda and he has come with five other monks. He is the best of Jain monks; men, Vidyādharas and even gods bow down at his feet.'

When the king heard this, in his great faith, he felt waves

of joy course through his body. He told the queen, 'Beloved! Your wish has come true already!

'Get up quickly, my love. Let us get ready to go and pay our respects to that monk. Let us ask him the question that is in your mind.'

As soon as she heard the king's words, the queen made herself ready. In an instant she and the king were at the garden.

They saw the monk, surrounded by a group of all sorts of people; he was teaching the doctrine of the Jinas, which brings happiness to all living beings.

The king and queen bowed down to the monk and then sat down on a level piece of ground, not too close to where the monk was sitting.

The monk increased the intensity of his discourse. He told them all, 'Wandering from birth to birth in this cycle of births that is without beginning, through the force of their karma souls somehow attain birth as human beings. There they enjoy various pleasures, brought about by their practice of good deeds. Birth in a high caste and a family of some status, health, wealth, happiness, enjoyments, good looks, strength, and even fame are all brought about by the performance of good deeds.

'Being together with those we love, having a retinue of servants to obey our commands, indeed every pleasure that one can think of, all of this comes from the performance of good deeds.

'The company of heavenly damsels and the enjoyment of the most excellent pleasures, even Final Release from all pain, these too come about through the practice of good deeds.'

At this point Ārāmasohā, her hands folded in reverence in front of her forehead, asked, 'Blessed One! If everything is the result of past good deeds, then what did I do in a past life to earn this reward?'

The Blessed One began to explain, in a voice as deep as

the rumbling of a newly formed rain cloud that was filled with rain:

'Here on the continent of Jambudīva, in the land of Bharaha, is a city named Campanayarī. There was in this city a most excellent merchant named Kulaṃdhara, who had as much wealth as Kuvera, the god of wealth. He had a wife named Kulānaṇḍā, who was endowed with beauty and virtue. As he enjoyed various pleasures with her, they had seven marvellous daughters, all endowed with every good quality, including beauty. Here are their names: Kamalasirī, Kamalavaī, Kamalā, Lacchī, Sirī, Jasoevī, and Piyakāriṇī. They all made good marriages, marrying into the best of families, and enjoyed incomparable pleasures. Now after a time an eighth daughter was born. Her father and her mother were not exactly pleased by her birth; in fact they were disgusted and did not even bother to give the poor girl a name. Neglected and unloved, she grew up, a source of pain to her mother and father, despite the fact that she was a great beauty. Others called her "Unlucky One". All she had to do to make her mother and father miserable was to come into their sight. One day people began to ask the merchant, "Why don't you find a husband for this daughter of yours? Everyone is saying how it is wrong of you not to marry her off."

'When the merchant heard what the people were saying he became even more depressed. And because he had no intention of doing as they said, he began to worry and worry about the whole business. One day as the merchant sat in his shop, absorbed in thought, a traveller happened by. He was covered in dust and was exhausted from his long journey. He had come into the merchant's stall just to rest for a bit. The merchant asked him, "Young man! Where have you come from?" He replied, "I come from the land of the Coḍas, from across the ocean." "Who are you? What is your caste? What is your name? Why have you come here?" The traveller replied, "I am Nandaṇa, the son of the merchant Nanda from Kosalā and his wife Somā. Driven by poverty I went to the country of the Coḍas in search of wealth. There too I was afflicted by poverty and I was too proud to go home. I served others and earned my living there. I have now been sent here with a letter by the merchant Vasantadeva, who has some business here. I am to deliver the letter to the merchant Siridatta. Show me his house so that I may go now and deliver the letter."

'Kulaṃdhara thought to himself, "He would make a perfect husband for my daughter. He is from an average family and is poor and a foreigner. If he takes my daughter back with him he will never come here again. For one, he has no money, and besides he seems to be a proud type." Having thought all of this to himself, he now said aloud, "Son, come to my house. In fact your father and I are great friends." The young man replied, "First I must carry out the task for which I was sent here. After that, Father, I will surely come to your house."

'The merchant sent one of his own men with the newcomer, instructing him, After you have delivered the letter be sure to bring him to my house. The merchant's servant then took the newcomer to the home of the merchant Siridatta, where they delivered the letter and explained the situation. Nandaṇa himself told Sridatta, "My father has a friend here, the merchant Kulamdhara. When he saw me he sent his own servant with me to make sure I would come back to his house. I must go with him now, but I will come back to see you some other time." The newcomer, Nandaṇa, then went to Kulaṃdhara's house with the servant. The merchant arranged for him to have a bath and gave him fresh clothes. He served him a meal and then said, "Son, marry my daughter!" Nandaṇa answered, "But I have to return to the Coḍa country today." Kulaṃdhara said, "You can take her with you. I will give whatever you need for the journey." When the young man agreed the merchant married his daughter to the fellow.

'On the wedding day Siridatta told Nandaṇa, "If you are going to stay here, then I will send someone else. My business cannot wait." Nandaṇa replied, "Don't worry. I will go for you. Just let me take my leave of the merchant Kulaṃdhara and then I will come back and talk to you." The next day Nandaṇa told the merchant, "Father. I must go. I have important business in the land of the Coḍas." When the merchant heard these words, which were exactly what he wanted to hear, he said, "If you are determined to go, my son, then go. But take your wife with you to the country of the Coḍas. I will send your goods after you." Nandaṇa then reported back to Siridatta, "I am ready to go. Tell me now whatever it is that you need to tell me." Siridatta then entrusted him with a letter and gave him some verbal instructions as well. When all was ready Nandaṇa departed, taking his wife along with him.

'They went alone, taking with them only those provisions that they needed for the trip, and travelling without a stop they reached the city of Ujjain. There Nandaṇa thought to himself, "We have not come very far, but our provisions are almost used up and I am exhausted from the journey. I will wait until she falls asleep, and then I will leave her here and go where I want." This was what he thought, but here is what he said, "Beloved! Our provisions are nearly finished. What should I do now? I will soon be reduced to begging. Will you go begging with me?" She replied, "Master! Listen to what I say. Even begging in the streets with you will be a source of pleasure to me." With that they both went to sleep for the night in a hostel for the poor and for travellers that was just outside the city.

'Nandaṇa got up in the night and took the bag of food. He stealthily crept out of the place, heading in a different direction. He was ashamed to have to beg and so he abandoned his wife and slunk away. When the sun rose the young woman did not see her husband there. She did see that their bag of food was gone and she realized that he had abandoned her. She thought to herself, "My husband has surely not behaved properly. He took me from my house only to abandon me alone here. Alas, alas! O shameless one! O cruel one! Having abandoned me here, a young woman in her prime, O you barbarian, how will you dare show your face anywhere! I am a young woman, after all, O cruel man! If someone else should take me, then the stain will fall on your entire family. Alas, what use is all this lamenting? I can protect my own virtue, as long as I can find some merchant who will take me in and be like a father to me. Unfortunate creature that I am, no one treated me with any kindness in my own house. I shall stay here and find some menial work to support myself." With these thoughts she plucked up her courage.

'She went into the city and looked around everywhere. At one of the houses she spotted a man who looked kind and decent. She threw herself at his feet and implored him, "Father! Be my refuge. I am without anyone to protect me, miserable and frightened. Women alone are always under suspicion. Help me, I beg of you! I am the daughter of the merchant Kulaṃdhara from the city of Caṃpā. I was travelling with my husband in a caravan to the land of the Coḍas and somehow got separated from the group. Be a father to me now in my time of misery and affliction!" The man, a merchant named Māṇibhadda, was touched by her words and her modest behavior. He said to her, "Child! You are my daughter. Come, live in my house as if in your own father's house. I will take care of everything. I will find the caravan." With those words, Māṇibhadda dispatched some of his own servants, but they found no trace of any caravan; no one had even heard of the travelling party. When he learned this, the merchant began to wonder. He thought to himself, "I must find out if she told the truth or if she lied to me." At that he dispatched one of his men to Campā city, to find out from the merchant Kulaṃdhara himself what the truth was.

'The servant went there at once and asked Kulaṃdhara, "Do you have a daughter? Is she married and where does she live? Tell me. Māṇibhadda has sent me here because he wishes to be united with you through the bonds of a marriage between your children." Kulaṃdhara answered, "I have eight daughters. Seven of them are married to men from here and live here now. The eighth one too is married, but she has gone with her husband to the country of the Coḍas. I have no more daughters. How can our families be joined together in this way? You must go and tell Māṇibhadda all that I have said."

'The servant returned and told Māṇibhadda everything. Knowing the truth, Māṇibhadda treated the girl with even greater deference. The young girl stayed there in his house, as happy to be there as if she were his own daughter, and everyone in the family was charmed by her humility and her other virtues.

'Now this Māṇibhadda was a pious follower of the doctrine taught by the Jina. He had a lofty temple built for the Jina. With faith in her heart, the young girl cleaned the temple and smeared cow dung on the floor; she did this every day, possessed of great faith in the doctrine of the Jina. She was often in the company of Jain monks and nuns, and she became an exemplary pious lay Jain like the laywoman Sulasa, incomparable in her devotion. What more need I say? Whenever the merchant gave her anything special to eat, she would save it and donate it to the temple of the Lord of Jinas. The merchant became doubly and triply pleased with her and gave her even more. She had a beautiful jewelled triple umbrella fashioned for the Jina image. This is what it was like:

'The umbrella was adorned with various jewels and had garlands of gold that hung from it; it was decorated with hanging pendants of fine pearls.

'It was covered with fine cloth that looked like the skin

sloughed off by the king of serpents. Its excellent pole was made of fine gold studded with precious stones.

'Such was the umbrella that she had made. She donated it to the temple of the Jina with great fanfare. She did other virtuous deeds, giving alms to the poor and performing austerities herself, whatever was appropriate at the time.

'She was always worshipping and serving the monks and nuns and her fellow Jains. She made extra effort to study and learn the Jain doctrine.

'Now one day she saw that merchant sunk in worry. With the greatest deference she asked him:

'"Father! Why do you appear to be afflicted by the demonness of worry?"

He answered, "Daughter! Listen to the cause of my worry. The garden of the temple to the Jina, once filled with fruit and flowers and extremely lovely, has suddenly withered. No matter what I do I can not restore it to its former beauty. That is why I am so upset." "Do not trouble yourself about this," replied the young girl. "I vow that if I cannot restore its beauty by the power of my good conduct, then I will renounce all food and drink." Although the merchant tried to dissuade her, she remained firm in her resolve. She went to the temple to meditate upon the superintending goddess who protects the Faith. On the night of the third day the goddess suddenly appeared before her and said, "Do not worry. In the morning you will see that the garden is restored to its former state; by your power it will be released from the clutches of the evil spirit that had caused it to dry up." With these words the goddess returned to her place. The sun, enemy of the darkness, suddenly appeared, chasing the night away.

'When the girl told the merchant everything that had happened that night, his eyes opened wide in delight. He hastened to the garden of the Jain temple. When he saw how the garden was resplendent with marvellous fruit and flowers and foliage, a deep green like the color of a cloud heavy with water, the merchant rushed back to the girl. "Daughter!" he said, "my wish has come true through your miraculous power. Come, get up and come home and break your fast, O lady of excellent virtue!" With these words, the merchant, accompanied by all the monks and nuns, escorted the girl back home as drums resounded and crowds of people looked on. They shouted, "Behold the power of this girl's virtue! She how the garden that was dried up has been restored to its former state in a twinkling of an eye! Great must be her merit; fortunate indeed is she! Her life is truly fruitful, for the gods wait upon her and through her work such miracles! Indeed, this merchant Māṇibhadda is no less blessed, for this young girl, like a magic wishing jewel, resides in his house." As the people all praised her with words like these, the girl reached the house. She first offered food to the monks, nuns, and pious lay men and women and then she broke her fast herself.

'Now one night in the last watch she woke up from her sleep and began to think about all of the things that had happened to her. She concluded, "They are truly fortunate in this world who give up all the pleasures of the senses, and free from attachments renounce the world and devote themselves to the practice of austerities and restraints. But I am a miserable creature indeed, stuck here, hankering after pleasures of the senses. Indeed, I am so wicked that I do not even get what I long for. My only good fortune is that I have obtained the doctrine of the Lords of the Jinas, which is beyond compare, a boat to cross the ocean of transmigratory existence. Now that I have obtained that doctrine it is only right for me to renounce completely all worldly pleasures and possessions and become a nun. But I am afraid that I am unable to do that. Instead I will practice intense austerities right here at home." This was what she thought, and when morning came she began to carry it all out. Her body became emaciated from her austerities and in the end she renounced all food. Following the proper rituals, she died the pious death of a devout Jain. She was reborn as a god in heaven, and when she fell from there she was reborn as you, the daughter of a brahmin, named Vijjupahā, whose lot contained some measure of suffering.

'The merchant Māṇibhadda also became a god and then was reborn as a human being, and then as the snake prince. The sins that you committed while still in your father's house, when you were deluded by a false religion, resulted in the suffering that you had to endure. The good deeds that you did while in Māṇibhadda's house resulted in the incomparable happiness that you enjoyed. Because you brought back to life the garden of the Jain temple, the snake prince gave you this garden, which follows you wherever you go. Because you had such strong faith in the doctrine of the Jinas you have been given this kingdom, which yields every possible worldly pleasure. Because you gave that beautiful triple umbrella to the Lord of the Jinas, you always walk in shade, as if under an umbrella. Because you gave things like betel to the temple, you always have these things to enjoy. All of this is the fruit of faith in the Jina: highest happiness as a god and, now here, the pleasures of a kingdom. In time you will even attain Final Release.'

When Ārāmasohā heard these words, she fell into a faint and collapsed on the ground, right before the eyes of all the onlookers. Her servants fanned her and she soon came to. She bowed down at the feet of the monk and humbly said, 'I have remembered my past births and have now seen for myself everything that you told me through your supernatural knowledge. Having heard your words and seen my own deeds for myself, O master! I am now thoroughly disenchanted with worldly life. I will go take my leave of the king and then I wish to renounce the world at your feet, for only renunciation can put an end to the sufferings of countless rebirths.'

When the king heard these words of the queen, he said, 'O Blessed One! Once a person knows all of this to be true, how can he continue to take delight in worldly existence? I will install our son Malayasundara on the throne and then I too will become a monk under your guidance.' The Blessed One next spoke, 'Sir, sir, do not lose a minute, for things in this world of the living are as evanescent as a drop of water on the tip of a blade of grass.' 'We will return at once,' replied the king and queen, and they installed the prince as king to rule over his own home and over the kingdom. Having crowned the prince, both the king and the queen along with many of their retinue renounced the world at the feet of that monk in a lavish ceremony. The former king and queen followed the laws for renunciates, and in time became quite learned. The monk appointed both of them to positions of authority. They awakened to the truth many who were ready to accept the Jain doctrine, and in time they performed the ritual fast to death. Both were reborn in heaven. In time they will fall from there and be reborn as humans, and then as gods, and eventually they will obtain Final Release. Such is the incomparable fruit of faith in the Jina.

(from the *Mūlaśuddhiprakaraṇa* of Pradyumnasūri, pp. 22-34)

29

DEVADHARA

There is on our very own continent of Jambudvīpa, in the land of Bharaha, in the territory of Kaliṅga, a city named Kancaṇapura, which surpasses the city of the Gods in its loveliness and all of its other wonderful qualities. There reigned King Bhāmaṇḍala, who with his great valour had conquered all of his enemies. He was greatly loved by all, and he surpassed even Indra, the king of the gods, with his handsomeness and other fine qualities. And his chief queen was Kittimaī, who was as obedient to his every wish as is the shadow that follows a man.

Now in this same city dwelt the merchant Sundara, chief amongst all of its wealthy inhabitants. His wife was Sundarī. Now all of the children that were born to her died. Though she did everything that she could, not a single one lived. Greatly saddened, she then thought:

'Oh what good is my life, when I have not a single living

child? My life is full of suffering; surely I must have accumulated not an ounce of merit, for not a single one of my children survives.

'Surely I must have stolen great jewels from someone in a past life, and so my children die now, seemingly without cause.

'Evil deeds that people so happily commit turn out to bear fruits like this, so terrible to endure.'

And while she was pained by such sad thoughts, her beloved friend Piyamaī, the wife of the feudatory prince Sūrapāla, who was now away in his home territory, came to see her. She said, 'My goodness! Why do you seem so dejected?' Sundarī said:

'The secret that cannot be told even to a father mother, sister or brother, not even to a husband or a son, can always be told to a friend.

'And so, my sister, I tell you. The cause of my distress is the death of my children.' Piyamaī said:

'You must have done some harm to some living creature in a past life. That is why, no doubt, my beloved friend, you must suffer like this in this life.

'But do not grieve. My dear husband has gone to his home territory, leaving me behind. I am pregnant. When my child is born I promise that I shall give it to you.'

Sundarī said, 'In that case then come and stay in my house. I too am pregnant. And if by some lucky quirk we should both deliver at the same time, then that would be ideal. But we must not tell this to anyone.' And her friend agreed to it all and stayed there with her in her house. And the deeds that they had each done in their past lives determined things in such a way that they both gave birth at the same time. They exchanged the dead baby for the live one. Now a few days later Piyamaī died of childbed fever. And at the appropriate time Sundarī, summoning all the merchants and other people, named the baby Devadhara. He grew up and soon turned eight years old.

Now when he had mastered all the seventy-two arts, because of some bad deed he had committed in a previous life both his mother and his father died. His entire family line was wiped out and all of their considerable wealth was lost. He suddenly found himself alone, in the grip of dire poverty. With no other way open to him to support himself, he began to work as a servant in the home of the merchant Dhaṇaseṭṭhi. He was given his meals there as well. Because he was well brought up and because he was a pious Jain, he went to worship in the Jain temples every day. He worshipped the Jain images and he went to the monasteries and nunneries to bow down to the monks and nuns. And so time went on until one day on some occasion or another, Saṃpayā, the wife of the merchant, gave him particularly fine food to eat. Now at that very moment a pair of the most excellent Jain monks arrived there. They had abandoned all attachments; they had mortified their bodies with many strict ascetic practices; they had studied all the eleven Jain texts; they had conquered that most difficult of enemies, the God of Love.

They were protected by the three protectors, watchful of mind, speech and body; they practiced the five acts of attentiveness in everything that they did, in walking, in speaking, in eating, in receiving, in excreting, so as to avoid any harm to any living creature; they were possessed of moral courage, and they regarded everyone as equal, friend and enemy alike.

And when he saw them, Devadhara, his body rippling with joy, thought, 'Oh! Today I have acquired the means to do good, something that is not easily acquired.

'The recipient is pure, the gift is pure, and the mind of the giver is pure. All three are propitious, because of some good act that I have done in the past. I shall make my life fruitful by giving this food to these monks.'

With this thought he went and bowed his lotus-like head

at the feet of the monks and proclaimed, 'Blessed Ones! Show favour to me by accepting this gift.'

And the monks realized the strong faith that motivated him and said, 'You give us too little, layman!' And they held back their begging bowls.

And as the monks kept saying, 'More, more,' he became agitated and put all that he had into their bowls.

Thinking, 'Today I have fulfilled all my desires,' he sat down right there, placing his plate in front of him.

At that moment the merchant, who had gone inside to worship before he took his meals, saw Devadhara there. He said to his wife Saṃpayā, 'Give something to Devadhara.' She said, 'I gave him all sorts of wonderful things, but he has given all he had to some monks.' The merchant said, 'He is lucky to have done something like that. Give him some more.' She said, 'I don't know what you are talking about.' The merchant said, 'Do not grumble and complain where you ought to rejoice and encourage a good deed. For by rejoicing in a pious deed a person can share in the merit it brings. For it is said:

> Both the person who himself does what is good and the one who rejoices in the good deeds that others do obtain a good result. Consider the story you know so well of the deer who rejoiced in the gift made by the carpenter to the monk Baladeva, and who died right then and there with the monk and the carpenter and achieved the same great result as they did, a long life in heaven.

'Let us both share in the fruit of his good deed by rejoicing in what he has done. Give him something else to eat right away.' And with these words he went in to worship the gods. Saṃpayā got busy and had not yet had the chance to serve Devadhara, when he finally got mad and began to think:

'How painful is poverty, which causes good men who should command respect and pull great weight, as a mountain stands mighty and firm, to be treated in this world as if they were of no more substance than the lightest blade of grass or cotton fluff.

'What use is the life of those men who are pained by the burning fires of poverty and who must ever endure contempt and scorn from others who are scarcely their equal?

'It is wealth alone of all the ends of man that in this world is paramount. For with it even men who are full of faults become greatly honored in this world.

'Fortunate indeed are those who have put a lasting end to all humiliation; those men are honored in the triple world, heaven, earth and the world below, who have become monks and are freed from all sin.

'But I am truly wretched. I cannot become a monk and I must therefore endure this terrible pain of being humiliated.'

While he was thinking in this way the merchant came out. And he saw him sitting there, still with an empty plate. The merchant said to him, 'Get up, my child! Come and eat with me.' And so Devadhara got up and he ate the very best of foods with the merchant. And the time passed for Devadhara, who would acquire the wealth of a great kingdom in this very life through the power of the gift that he had given to those monks; who was devoted to honoring the Jinas and the Jain monks and nuns, and who had yet to live out the fruit of the actions that he had done in a past life and which necessitated that he yet suffer some unhappiness in this life.

Now there also lived in that city a merchant named Rayaṇasāra. His wife was Mahalacchī. And as they enjoyed together the delights of love Mahalacchī became pregnant. Now when the child was just six months in the womb the merchant passed away. And when her time came, Mahalacchī gave birth to a daughter who surpassed even the women of the gods in beauty and was endowed with every auspicious mark. But the king took away all of her husband's wealth, leaving only a meagre amount for the support of the daughter, on the grounds that the merchant had no male offspring. When the time came Mahalacchī named the girl Rāyasirī. As she grew up, her mother used the money that the king had released for her use to have her educated in all of the arts.

In time, greatly pained by the death of her husband and the loss of her wealth and much troubled, Mahalacchī died. Rāyasirī was taken by her maternal aunt whose name was Lacchī. Lacchī went out to work in the homes of the wealthy so that she might support Rāyasirī. Now Rāyasirī was a pious Jain and she worshipped the Jina images every day and honored the Jain nuns and monks. She also constantly upbraided herself because she was unable to practice such pious acts as giving to others.

'Alas, alas! What use is this life of mine which is totally worthless and which leads to no good result either in this world or in the next! It is no better than the useless breast that hangs from the neck of a goat.

'In this life so bereft of merit am I that I am eating alive my very own aunt, who is like a mother to me, making her slave for me and do such harsh tasks.

'I cannot bear to eat without being able to give some food to some worthy person; my food eaten alone lacks all savour, but I have no wealth or goods that allow me to give.'

And then one day her aunt received four choice sweetmeats as a gift for the work that she had done in the home of a wealthy merchant.

She said to Rāyasirī, 'Sit down, my daughter, and eat. Today I brought you some fine cakes.'

Now the young girl sat down and as she took the sweets, she glanced at the door. She was thinking, 'Oh, if only someone would come, how fine that would be!

'If I could only give these delicious things which my aunt

has brought me today to some worthy person, I could fulfill all of my deepest desires and make my life one worth living.'

And at that very moment fate decreed that some Jain nuns came there in search of alms. They were endowed with every virtue and had taken upon themselves that most difficult vow of chastity. Their bodies were thin from the ravages of their strict ascetic practices.

They cared the same for grass or pearls or jewels and their eyes and thoughts were concentrated only on the small space of ground before them.

And that young girl, her body rippling with joy at being given the chance to fulfill her deepest desire, her steps made unsure by her eagerness and haste, served those nuns with a gift of pure food in which the mind of the giver, the thing given, and the recipients were all pure and good. And as she did so, tears of joy flowed from her lotus-like eyes.

And by that gift in which the recipients were so pure and the mind of the giver so pure, she earned merit which ensured that she would have many enjoyments right in this very life. And that good deed was even further increased by the delight that she took in it, as she said to herself again and again, 'Lucky am I! Lucky am I, for I have done such a righteous act.' And her aunt too praised her, saying, 'Lucky indeed is she, for though but a child she has done such a righteous act.'

Now time passed and Lacchī found that she could no longer support the girl and so she gave her to the Jain nun Suvvayā, with these words, 'Blessed One! I can no longer support this child. If it pleases you, then accept her for the faith.' The nun agreed. And so Lacchī left the child behind and went back home. When it came time to eat the nun said to the girl, 'Daughter! Eat.' She answered, 'Blessed One! How can I, still a householder, eat this food that the nuns have brought with so much pain? For it is winter and they must be bitterly stung by the harsh cold winds as they go on their begging rounds.' The nun said, 'Daughter! When the right time comes I shall ordain you as a nun. Now you must eat. And so Rāyasirī ate. And when the nun saw how devoted Rāyasirī was to serving them, she asked the demi-goddess Kaṇṇapisāiyā, whom she commanded by means of a magic spell, 'Is this girl worthy to be a nun or not?' The demi-goddess said, 'Do not ordain her yet.'

The nun, thinking that she would ask the demi-goddess again some time later, remained silent until the hot season had come upon them. Then one day Rāyasirī saw the nuns coming back from their begging rounds. They were roasted by the fierce rays of the sun; sweat was dripping from all over their bodies; they were suffering from hunger and thirst and they were burdened with their bowls of food and drink. And when she saw them Rāyasirī began to say, 'Blessed One! I fear that I do our faith great dishonor if I, still a householder, were to partake of the food and drink that these noble nuns have brought with such great pain. Please ordain me at once.' The nun then said, 'Be patient. For your propitious moment will come as soon as the rainy season starts, on the eleventh day of the bright fortnight of the month Phālguna.' And only after she promised this did she then ask the demi-goddess. The demi-goddess told her, 'She still has many fruits of her deeds to enjoy, which all entail that she should experience great pleasures.'

The nun, thinking, 'She will show great devotion to the images of the Jinas and the Jain monks and nuns,' remained silent until the rainy season was upon them. The rains began to fall. Knowing that Rāyasirī had not had any change of heart, she then asked the demi-goddess once more, 'What is the extent of her good deeds in the past that now entail that she must enjoy sensual pleasures?' The demi-goddess said, 'She will be the chief queen of five hundred and five queens. And she will enjoy great sensual pleasures for five hundred years.' Thinking, 'One day the demi-goddess will give me permission to ordain her,' the nun then did nothing.

Now one day Rāyasirī was seen by Devadhara who had

come to the nunnery to pay his respects to the nuns. And he asked the nun, 'Why have you not yet ordained this girl?' The nun answered, 'She is not fit to be ordained.' 'In that case, then why do you feed and support someone who is a lay person?' She replied, 'Because she will bring great honour to our faith and do much to further its cause.' He asked, 'In what way?' She said, 'I cannot tell you any more.' And so Devadhara made the vow to give up eating and die by starvation if the nun would not tell him all that she knew. And so the nun did tell him. And Devadhara thought to himself, 'Oh! What wondrous things can happen from a person's own actions! This girl, born in a family of merchants, is to become such a magnificent, rich queen and have such royal splendour! Having enjoyed that royal splendour, I have no doubt that she will then suffer some terrible rebirth. I shall marry her so that she will neither obtain royal splendour nor be forced to suffer a bad rebirth.' And with this in mind he said to the nun, 'Blessed One! Why don't I marry her?' And she put her hands over both her ears, 'Devotee! Why do you ask such a thing, as if you knew no better? We must not even speak of such things.' Devadhara said, 'Forgive me, I forgot myself. I meant no harm.'

But then he went to see Lacchī. Very politely, he said, 'Mother, give Rāyasirī to me.' She said, 'Son! I have already given her to the nuns.' He told her, 'But they will not ordain her as a nun.' She asked, 'And how do you know that?' He said, 'They told me themselves.' Laachī said, 'In that case, then, I shall ask them myself.' He said, 'Go ahead, but you must not then give her to anyone else.' And so Lacchī asked the nun, 'It it true that you are not going to ordain Rāyasirī?' The nun said, 'It is true.' And then Lacchī thought, 'Although he comes from a poor family Devadhara is a good young man. He is a believer in the Jain faith and the son of a pious man. No wealthy man is going to take this girl from me, a simple servant who earns her keep by working in the homes of other people. And he does seem to want her very much.' And with this in mind she gave Rāyasirī to Devadhara. And the deeds that they had done in the past determined that the day for their wedding was fixed as the eleventh day of the bright half of the month of Phālguna. But as the wedding preparations began, Rāyasirī had her own thoughts.

'If I had not done some bad deed in the past which now obstructed my way, if I were not so without merit, then, today my relatives and other devoted Jains would be getting ready all my clothes so that, with resolve firm, I might begin to undertake a life of difficult restraints.' So she thought and was anxious and impatient as they began to ready her wardrobe.

And on the very day of the wedding, as they bathed her and anointed her body with fragrant substances, she thought, 'Today they would be celebrating in honour of my going forth from the life of a householder to become a nun.

'Surrounded by all of my relatives, adorned with beautiful ornaments, I could be standing now in the temple of the Jinas, as drums resound, marking the auspicious occasion.'

And sitting in the temple devoted to the goddess, she thought, 'Having circumambulated the images of the Jinas, I would then bow down to the Jinas with my teacher.

'And in the presence of all the Jain community, my teachers would give my robes to me, and my dust-brush, and all the other things that a nun must carry.'

And as they painted her hands with auspicious designs, she thought, 'Ah, my soul! This is the moment when you, following the words of their teachers, should be taking your holy vows.'

As she walked around the wedding pavilion she reflected, 'And this would be the moment when I would circle round the entire gathering in reverence, while the community of the faithful sprinkled powder on me.

'And then, having been honoured by all present, I would

listen in respect, deeply moved, to the religious instructions delivered by my teachers.

'Alas, my soul, unfortunate soul! Why is that strong desire of yours to grasp firmly the treasure of restraining the senses thwarted by some obstructing past deed, now showing its might, as if by some terrible invisible goblin?'

And as she thought these things she was joined to Devadhara in marriage with all the proper ceremony. Devadhara then told the merchant, 'Father! Please give us some place to live.' And so the merchant gave him a small grass hut within the boundaries of his compound. Devadhara then took Rāyasirī there. She was totally devoted to her husband and deeply in love with him.

Now while Devadhara was enjoying the pleasures of love there with her, the merchant thought to himself, 'This Devadhara is like a son to me; he is a noble man; a faithful Jain; he is courageous and high-minded and has so many fine qualities. I should allow him to carry out some trade. I shall see how clever he is. If he proves himself worthy, well then, I shall do what I see fit.' And with this in mind he said to Devadhara, 'Son! Take some goods from me and carry on some trade with vegetables and plants.' Devadhara did exactly as he was told. He earned his keep, at least, until the rainy season came upon them.

And then he said to his wife, 'Get me some bricks from somewhere so I can cover this veranda which is about to collapse. I don't want the roof to fall down on anyone sleeping here.' She did exactly as she was told. As he was fixing the roof and removing some of the old crumbling bricks, he discovered five hundred gold coins. Without showing them to his wife he hid them in a pot. And when he was done with his task he went alone to the market, and with one of the coins he bought her some clothes and jewellery. She said, 'My beloved! How could you have afforded this?' He said, 'I borrowed one hundred coins from some good man.' She said, 'In that case, then, I don't need any presents.' He said, 'Do not be afraid. My friend is a wealthy man and very kind. It was a trifling sum for him.' And so she accepted the gifts. And he continued to carry on his business and in no time at all became lord of a thousand gold pieces.

Now one day Rāyasirī said to him, 'Jains are not allowed to dig dirt in the rainy season. Bring me some kind of a shovel so that I can gather some earth.' But he brought a heavy spade from the merchant's house. She said, 'I can't dig with this.' He told her, 'When no one is around, just at dawn, I shall do the digging myself. You bring a sack and a basket so that I can fill the sack with earth. I too am embarrassed to be seen carrying dirt.' And she did exactly as she was told. As soon as he struck the earth with the spade and broke ground he beheld a treasure of jewels worth hundreds of thousands of rupees. He said, 'Beloved! Quick! Let's get away from this place.' And when she asked, 'But why?' he said, 'My love, this will be the end of us!' She said, 'This is not the end for us. This is not the God of Death. It is the Goddess of Fortune herself, come to us on account of the many wonderful great deeds that you have done in the past.' He said, 'But should the king come to know of it we will get into serious trouble, for all buried treasure belongs to the king.' Now Rāyasirī though, 'Clearly he does not trust me,' and so she said, 'No one will hear of if from me. Go now, take what your own good fortune has brought you. Hurry, before someone comes.' And so, breaking open with the spade the seal of the casket in which the jewels lay, he quickly stuffed the jewels and riches into his sack. He put the sack inside the basket and then carefully placed dirt on top of it. The two of them then went back home. They hid the treasure in a corner of their hut. But one day Rāyasirī told her husband, 'These jewels are no better than stones.

'Oh my best beloved! Wealth that is not used for making images of the Jinas, for making temples, for worshipping the images, bathing them and carrying out festivals, is no better than worthless stones.

'Wealth that is not given to Jain monks and nuns for food, begging bowls, robes, beds, seats, housing, medicines and other basic needs, is no better than worthless stones.

'Beloved! Wealth that is not used to give food, betel, seats and clothes to our fellow Jains, to me, is no better than clumps of earth.

'My Lord! Wealth that is not used for its owner's personal delight, nor to help his friends, nor to aid those who are poor and in need, why that is no better then dust.

'And so I ask you, why do we wrongly hang on to this wealth?' He said, 'What else can we do under the circumstances?' She said, 'Marry the merchant's daughter, Kamalasirī. And then everything will be as we wish. He hastily interjected, 'But I don't need anyone but you.' She said, 'My Lord! You must consider what will lead to a good end.' He said, 'Well, in that case, if you insist, then tell me, how shall I win her over?' Rāyasirī said, 'You already know her. Now you must win her over with gifts of fruits and such. I shall do the same by giving her jewellery. For it is said:

> One should win the heart of a child with food and drink, of a young maiden with jewelry, of a whore with constant attendance, and of an old lady with abject servitude.

'Now she is both somewhat of a child and somewhat of a young maiden. And so she can be won over in this way.' Devadhara then gave his consent. 'You are surely right,' he said, and from that day on he began to give Kamalasirī fruits and things every day. And she began to follow Devadhara around and followed him right back into his home. Rāyasirī then gave her some jewellery to wear every day. Now when she got back to her own home her mother asked her, 'Who gave you these fruits? Who gave you this jewellery to wear?' She said, 'Devadhara gave me the fruits and Rāyasirī put the jewellery on me.' At this her mother asked her once more, 'Who is Devadhara? Who is that woman?' She said, 'Devadhara is the man who comes to our house everyday and the woman is his wife.'

Now one day the mother saw her daughter following Devadhara all around and laughed at her. 'My child! See how you stick to him, like glue! What, are you going to get yourself hitched to him for life?' Kamalasirī said, 'But did you doubt that? If you give me to anyone else then I will kill myself.' The mother quickly retorted, 'Foolish girl! He already has a wife.' Kamalasirī said, 'She is like my elder sister. I don't want any other husband, not even the richest man in the world.' Seeing that her daughter was madly in love with Devadhara, Saṃpayā told the merchant exactly what had happened. He said, 'My beloved! If our child is so insistent, then let her marry him. For Devadhara is both handsome and virtuous. And I can help him to get rid of his poverty. But first I must win over his wife.' And for her part Saṃpayā simply agreed with what her husband had said. And so the merchant instructed Devadhara, 'My son! Let me see your wife.' Devadhara, humbly assenting, summoned Rāyasirī. She came out and fell at the feet of the merchant. The merchant took her on his lap, blessing her with the words, 'May you never be a widow.' And when he saw her beauty and her loveliness, which far surpassed the beauty and the loveliness of any other woman, the merchant Dhaṇa thought: 'Why would this man who shares the embrace of a woman of such beauty, a woman who is so devoted to him and so in love with him, want my daughter?

'How could this Devadhara, who can always make love to this woman, who is like a flowing river of the divine nectar of womanly beauty, take pleasure in my daughter, pretty though she is?

'And if this woman should turn against her, how could my daughter ever be happy? Ah, my daughter is foolish to desire this man for her husband.

'But what can I do? I must first try to see what they really feel. Then I will do what I think is necessary.' And with this in mind he said to Rāyasirī, 'My child! My daughter Kamalasirī is deeply in love with your husband. If you have no objection, then I shall give her to him.' Rāyasirī said, 'Father! I am delighted. Dear father, fulfil my little sister's wishes.' The merchant said, 'My daughter! In that case then I give Kamalasirī into your care. From now on you must look after her.' Rāyasirī quickly said, 'Father! I am honored.' And then he turned to Devadhara. "My son! Take in marriage Kamalasirī, who loves you very deeply." Devadhara humbly assented, 'Father! As you command me, so shall I do.' And so the merchant made a wedding with all due pomp and splendour. He gave to Rāyasirī and Kamalasirī exactly the same jewellery. He set his son-in-law up in business and Devadhara earned much money. He used the wealth he had found earlier to build Jain temples and to perform other pious acts.

Now Kamalasirī had a friend named Paumasirī, who was the daughter of the king's minister Maisāgara. She had come to the wedding and when she saw Devadhara she immediately vowed before all her own girl friends:

'If that Devadhara by some act of fate can be brought to marry me, then and then alone will I enjoy worldly pleasures. Otherwise I renounce the world right here and now, in this very birth.'

And when her friends heard that vow of hers they told her mother Piyangasundarī at once. And she told the minister Maisāgara. He in turn summoned the merchant and respectfully gave Paumasirī to Devadhara. Devadhara married her with great ceremony. And the minister gave to all three women exactly the same jewellry.

From then on the minister often brought Devadhara to

the king to pay his respects. The king showed him great honour and offered him the finest seats to sit upon. And one day, while the king was himself being charmed by Devadhara's good looks and his many virtues, the queen Kittimaī, realizing that Devadhara was a good match for their own daughter Devasirī, dressed Devasirī up in all her finery and her jewels and sent her to bow down to the feet of her father. The king lifted her onto his lap. And as he looked her over it suddenly came to him that she had reached the age for marriage. And no sooner had he turned his thoughts to finding a suitable husband for her, than he noticed how Devasirī was looking again and again at Devadhara out of the corner of her eyes, with a glance that revealed that she had fallen in love with him, her bright pupils darting back and forth. At this the king thought, 'Oh! She seems indeed to be smitten with this fellow. And he is both handsome and virtuous. Let her enjoy the pleasures of wedded bliss with him.' He then said to Maisāgara, 'I give our very own Devasirī to your son-in-law. As the ocean is filled with jewels, so is she filled with virtues.' The minister replied, 'I am honored.' And so the king made a splendid wedding, sparing no expense. He gave to all four women exactly the same jewellery. And he gave to Devadhara the large territory that bordered the domains of his vassal Narakesari, and which was the most important of all the territories. And Devadhara lived indeed like a god, enjoying the pleasures of love with Rāyasirī and his other four wives, ensconced in a seven-storied palace that was filled with all sorts of costly things that the king had given him.

Now King Narakesari came to hear that the territory bordering his own had been given by the king to his own son-in-law, a mere merchant. And so, burning with such rage that the very flames of anger seemed to leap from his mouth as he spoke, he told his own servants, 'See with what contempt King Bhāmaṇḍala treats us! He has given the task of protecting our flanks to a veritable barbarian. Let us raid his territory and teach the king a lesson so that he will never do anything like that again. And as soon as he spoke they raided Devadhara's territory and sent word to King Bhāmaṇḍala that they had done so.' And no sooner did he get the news than, furious with this insult delivered him, the king caused the drums to beat to announce the departure of his own army. And so the king's army set out,

Swift as the wind, swift as the mind, gold ornaments flashing like bursts of lightning, rut dripping like rain from their temples, the elephants went forward like new-formed rain clouds.

Filling the world with their neighing, kicking up heaps of dust as their sharp hooves dug into the earth, making terrifying noises from their mouths, gums drawn back, the horses went forward.

Having proved their prowess many a time by slaying their proud and wicked enemies, sauntering, shouting, the foot soldiers went forward.

The very heavens seemed rent asunder with the trumpeting of the elephants, the clanking of the chariots, the neighing of the horses, the shouts of the warriors and the beasts of all the war drums.

And when he heard this terrible noise, like the roar of the turbulent mighty ocean, Devadhara asked his chamberlain,

'Are the very heavens being rent asunder? Has the earth split open? Are the mountains tumbling down? Or is this the very end of the world? Tell me sir, what is that noise?'

And the chamberlain, who knew exactly what was going on, told him in great detail about everything that had happened. At once Devadhara spoke up. And as he spoke his lips quivered in anger at the insult he had been dealt; his forehead was marked by three fierce lines of a frown, and his hand reached again and again for his sword. 'Hurry, make ready my elephant so that I my follow my father-in-law into battle.' And his men did exactly as he commanded.

Devadhara mounted his war elephant and rode to the king. He was freshly bathed and his body had been anointed with fragrant substances; he was adorned with garlands of white flowers and wearing his most costly clothes; his crown was surrounded by lotuses with fine long stalks; and he carried with him his sharp sword that was like the tongue of the God of Death. When the king saw him coming he thought to himself, 'Lucky am I to have such a fine son-in-law. Or perhaps it is the good fortune of Devasirī that she has found such a fine husband.' And as the King was thinking this, Devadhara threw himself at the King's feet and proclaimed, 'King! Lions do not attack jackals, forgetting about maddened elephants that are their more worthy foes. And so I beg you, command me so that I may pacify this disobedient vassal Narakesari. Besides, it was because he thought of me as a mere merchant that he dared to attack my territory. And so, O King, it seems only fitting that it is I who should go there.' The king, his body rippling with joy, said to him, 'My son! Do not ask that of me. Truly I shall not feel satisfied if I do not go out against Narakesari myself.' And Devadhara, realizing how the king felt, was silent. But a few moments later he asked again for permission to proceed, 'O King! Command me!' The king replied, Ask for what you wish.' He said, 'In that case I wish to proceed in the vanguard against Narakesari.' The king said, 'My son, I do not like what you ask. I cannot bear the thought of being without you even for a short time and we are yet hundreds of miles away from Narakesari.' Devadhara told him, 'Each day I shall come back by some swift conveyance and bow down to the king's feet.' And when he realized that Devadhara was not to be dissuaded, the King gave him permission to go. Devadhara left at once and soon reached the border of Narakesari's territory.

His enemy, having learnt form spies that he had arrived, bellowed, 'Seize that barbarian who does not know how powerful I am!' And as soon as King Narakesari had uttered these words his army stood armed and ready. And it was a mighty army indeed that went forth from Narakesari's domains. And when they saw it coming Devadhara's soldiers armed themselves at once. And there ensued a terrible battle.

Here men's heads lay cut off by sharp swords; there the headless corpses of warriors, jerking violently, put on a dancing show;

Here lay pearls fallen from the temples of elephants that had been torn open with sharp lances; there heaps of chariots that had been smashed to smithereens with strong maces lay clanking against each other;

Here she-goblins danced, drunk on blood; there jackals howled like ghouls, feeding on human entrails and flesh;

Here the sky was covered with streams of sharp arrows shot from taut bow-strings; there sparks shot out as weapons clashed and clanged together;

Here horses, elephants, and chariots roamed aimlessly, no longer carrying riders; there hosts of gods showered flowers, pleased by the warriors' brave acts;

Here ghosts laughed and hooted, each more terrible in form than the next; there terrifying demons brandished sharp cutting tools in their busy hands;

And as this terrible battle raged Devadhara, the prince, mounted on his elephant, shouted, 'Lead my elephant towards Narakesari's elephant.'

And taking up the command, the skillful elephant driver led Devadhara's elephant so close to Narakesari's mount that the two beasts could touch each other with their tusks.

And then Devadhara jumped onto the back of Narakesari's elephant and taunted him, 'Here I am, King, your barbarian! Stand tall now!

'Take hold of your weapon now! You will see what prowess even a merchant's son can have!' And the king, thinking that such a lowly foe was beneath him, yet had no choice and took hold of his magnificent sword.

And each blow that the impatient king levelled Devadhara

skilfully warded off. And he seized the king and he was filled with pride at his own act.

Devadhara's ministers sent word with a swift messenger to King Bhāmaṇḍala to inform him that Devadhara had met the enemy army. And he quickly rode out with his best soldiers. The prince Devadhara handed Narakesari over to him. Filled with joy, the king embraced the prince and then released Narakesari from his bonds. He honored him as was his due and then told him, 'You should continue to rule your own lands as a servant of this prince.' And Narakesari, giving to the prince his own daughter Mittasirī, too full of pride to serve under the prince, abandoned his kingdom and became a monk under the guidance of a good teacher. The king and the prince Devadhara crowned Narakesari's son as king and then went back to their own city.

The king, realizing that the moment had come, then said to all his sons, 'My sons! If you agree then I will crown your brother-in-law as king.' They all said, 'Do so. Whatever you wish is also our desire.' And so he informed all his ministers and chief councillors and on an auspicious moment the prince Devadhara was made king of both kingdoms, his own and the kingdom of Bhāmaṇḍala. And King Bhāmaṇḍala became a Jain monk and looked after the matter of his own spiritual welfare.

Now Narakesari's loyal retainers gave to King Devadhara their own daughters, two hundred and fifty of them, and many precious gifts. And his other vassal kings did the same. And so he came to have five hundred and five queens and he made Rāyasirī the chief queen amongst them all. She enjoyed great wealth and splendour. And Devadhara the king became a great king, lord over a vast territory, his commands honored by all.

One day, recalling their previous poverty, the king and the queen began to carry out pious acts to further the Jain faith. They had Jain temples built; they had Jain images consecrated; they had the images bathed, anointed and properly worshipped; they sponsored great religious festivals; they proclaimed that no one in their kingdom should ever take the life of any creature; they had the chariots belonging to the temples led around the city with the sacred images in them; they gave to the poor and miserable, gifts of compassion; they did honour to fellow Jains; they gave great gifts to the Jain nuns and monks, gifts of food and other necessities; they had books copied and properly worshipped; they listened to the words of the Jinas; they themselves observed the required daily duties of pious Jains; they fasted on the fast days; what more need I say? They spent their time doing just about everything conceivable that would further the cause of the Jain faith.

Now one day there came the Blessed Jasabhaddasūri, who was so wise he was almost omniscient. The king and his queen went to pay their respects to the monk. They bowed down to him, full of true devotion. They sat down on the ground, making sure that there were no living creatures there that they would crush. The Blessed One began his discourse:

'Wealth is by nature fickle; this miserable body is ever subject to the ravages of old age and sickness. Love is like a dream. And so I say put your efforts into the practice of religion.

'And in their best of teaching the Jinas have likened the difference between the life of a householder and the life of a monk to the difference between a mountain of gold and a mustard seed.

'The happiness that monks know, having renounced all pleasures of the senses, and being free from having to carry out the orders of others, cannot be experienced even by the emperor of the entire world.

'This religious practice which so many monks follow is like a thunder bolt to cleave the rock that is the accumulated effects of all of a person's past deeds, evil, heavy, accumulated over many a lifetime.

'Someone who has been a monk even for just one day

is honoured by kings and queens alike. Behold the power of the religious life, O King!

'A soul having been a monk even for a day, intently devoted to the monastic life, may not get absolute release, it is true, but for sure he becomes a god in heaven.

'Practicing austerities brings even greater merit than building the most magnificent of temples, with thousands of pillars, all of gold, silver and gemstones.

'And so, O King, abandon the householder's life, which is the abode of all suffering. Follow the course that monks follow, the one that destroys the cycle of rebirths.'

And when he heard these words the king Devadhara indeed felt a desire to renounce the world. He said, 'Blessed One! As soon as I crown Rāyasirī's son Guṇahara as king I shall accept the course that you describe. But I have one small request. Tell me, why did I and my queen have to suffer the loss of our parents when we were just children? Why were we oppressed by such terrible poverty?' The Blessed One said, 'Listen, great king.

'Just one birth ago you were born to a good family in the village of Nandivaddhaṇa. Your name was Kulavaddhaṇa. And your queen was then also your wife; her name was Santimaī. By nature both of you had few faults, were little given to anger and other evil passions, and were devoted to giving to others. Now one day two Jain monks in the course of their wanderings chanced to come to your house. Seeing them you said to your wife, "Beloved! Just look at these monks. They never give anything to anyone and have abandoned their duties to take care of their immediate family, their friends and their other relatives. What use are any of the religious austerities they do anyway, since they ignore their own people?" Santimiaī said, "My lord! What you say is absolutely true. There can be no doubt that what you say is just so." That is the deed that you both did that led later to your own loss of your relatives.'

'Now there was also in that village a rich Jain temple. A certain wealth Jain layman, Jinadeva by name, was in charge of looking after the properties of the temple. Now one day you lost a quarrel with Jinadeva, which prompted the angry Santimaī to say, "Lord! That temple servant is blinded with all that wealth that belongs to the temple as sure as if he was drunk with wine. And he disregards everyone and everything. As far as I am concerned, we'd all be better off if all the wealth belonging to the temple just disappeared." And you said, "Beloved! That would suit me just fine." And with those bad thoughts you both insured that you would suffer poverty. And you died without repenting your bad deeds and were reborn as you now are.'

When they heard this account they both remembered their former births. And they said, 'Your account is absolutely true. We remember everything now with the power to recollect our past lives. But what deed did we do then that enabled us to acquire this kingdom?' The Blessed One said, 'That you gave food with reverence to Jain monks and nuns in this birth of yours resulted in your enjoying the kingdom right in this very same life. As the sacred texts say,

> Some deeds done in this birth give their fruit in this very same birth; some deeds done in this birth give their fruit in a future rebirth. Some deeds done in a different birth give their fruit in this birth; some deeds done in a different birth give their fruit in that very birth.

And so you must always endeavour to do good deeds.' The king and his wife, agreeing, went back to their palace. Installing the prince on the throne, with great splendour the king and the queen renounced this world. They fulfilled the rest of their ordered days by living a pure life, and fasting to death they attained rebirth as gods. When they fall from heaven they will be reborn in the land of Mahāvideha where they will achieve final liberation.

(from the *Mūlaśuddhiprakaraṇa* of Pradyumnasūri, p. 160)

30

DEVADIṆṆA

There is on our very own continent of Jambuddīve, in the land of Bhāraha, a city named Tihuyaṇapura, "The City of the Triple World", which was indeed an ornament to the triple world of heaven, earth and the nether world. There reigned King Tihuyaṇasehara, "The Best in the Triple World," who was a veritable sun to chase away the deep darkness of his stalwart enemies. And foremost amongst the women in his harem was Tihuyaṇā, his queen. From her womb came forth the prince Tihuṇahadatta, "Gift to the Triple World".

Now in this very city there also lived a merchant named Sumaī, "The Clever," who was the leader of all the eighteen minor and major guilds of merchants, who had fathomed the meaning of that best of all religious doctrines, the Jain doctrine, which teaches such things as the distinction between living beings and insentient matter. And this merchant was greatly honored by the king. He had a wife named Candapahā, "Moonlight," who by her beauty surpassed all of the heavenly damsels. She and the queen Tihuyaṇā were devoted friends. One day the prince Tihuyaṇadatta, along with his retinue, went to see Candapahā, whom he called "auntie." She bathed him tenderly, massaged him with fragrant ointments, adorned him with jewels and then sat him on her lap. She placed her lips to his head and breathed in gently, and as she did this she thought:

'How fortunate is my friend and what good deeds she must have once done! Her life is fulfilled, she has accomplished her goal in having such a wonderful son!

'Many are the women who have fulfilled themselves in this world, bantering softly to their handsome children, the fruit of their very own wombs. And sitting there on their laps, the children coo back to them, showering them with playful words of love.

'But I am the most miserable of women, for I do not have even one child.

And as this thought ran through her mind, she let out a deep sigh and sent the prince back to his own home.

Now when the prince got home the queen asked, 'Who put all these jewels on the prince?' His servants told her, 'Your friend. But you must quickly sprinkle the prince with salt and say the right prayers so that no harm will come to him, for she let out a deep sigh right over the prince.' The queen said, 'Don't talk such nonsense. Her sigh will be like a blessing for the prince.' At this the servants fell silent. And the queen thought, 'Now why did she let out a sigh when she saw the prince? Oh, I know. She has no child, poor thing. Now what kind of friend would I be if I did not give her my own child and fulfill her deepest wish?' As she was steeped in this thought, the king entered. He asked, 'Queen, how is it that you seem to be disturbed by something?' And so she told him everything that had happened. He said, 'If that is the case, then do not be distressed. I shall find some means by which your friend will get a child.' The queen said, 'My Lord, your favour is great.'

The next day the king told the merchant, 'You have no son. You must propitiate my clan deity, the Goddess Tihuyaṇadevī, in order to gain a child. She has great powers and when worshipped grants whatever she is asked.' The merchant then said, 'King! What good is it if my son is then taken away as a result of some bad deed that I have committed in a previous life?' The king replied, 'Never mind, even if that is so you must do as I insist.' Considering in his mind that this was tantamount to an order from the king, the merchant went back home. He told Candapahā what had happened. She said, 'My lord! If you do that you will insult the true faith, for we are Jains.' Sumaī said, 'Beloved! If I do it as an order of the king, then there can be no insult to my faith.' And so the very next day the merchant, taking with him all the things that he needed to worship the goddess, went to the temple of Tihuyaṇadevī along with his wife. There they had the image of the Goddess bathed, anointed and worshipped, and when that was done the merchant addressed the Goddess, 'O Blessed One! The king said that I should ask you for a son. So, give me a son.' At this the Goddess thought, 'He surely does not seem very enthusiastic about all this! But for the sake of my own reputation I cannot afford not to show myself to him.' With this the Goddess said, 'Sir! You will have a son.' He said, 'How do I know?' And thinking, 'I shall cause that unenthusiastic fellow a bit of trouble,' the Goddess said again, 'When your child enters your wife's womb she will see this dream: she will go to a Jain temple to worship and she will behold the temple falling.' The merchant, thinking, 'Some harm is about to be befall the Jain faith,' was indeed troubled in mind as he went home that day.

Then one day his wife did see that dream that the Goddess

had foretold. When she woke up she said to her husband, 'Lord, I saw that dream, but it was a little different. When I had taken all the things for my worship and was entering the Jain temple I did see it falling, and as I feared that it would fall right on top of me I kept my eyes fixed upward as I worshipped the Jina. But then once I got outside the temple I could see that it was exactly as it had always been, only where there had been but one flag there were now five splendid flags. And I was filled with joy as I woke up. Tell me, what do you think?' He said, 'Beloved! This dream indicates that at first there will be some difficulty, but that in the end everything will turn out just fine. And so I think that you will have a son. For a time he will suffer misfortune, but afterwards he will acquire great wealth.' And she too agreed that such was to be the case and she wore the necessary amulets. All her desires fulfilled, when her time came she gave birth to a son who was handsome, his every limb just perfect. The merchant was given this great news by her maidservant named Suhankarā, "The Bringer of Joy". He gave the maidservant a handsome gift and made a great party in honour of his son's birth. And there:

The drums beat with a great thundering sound. Courtesans danced, wealth was distributed to all, with no one left out, and the leading citizens came to offer their congratulations.

All manner of rites and rituals were carried out to perfection and the relatives were all feted and honored. Prisoners were freed from their chains and the most excellent Jain monks were offered the proper alms.

The Jain images were worshipped, all the relatives were respectfully treated. In truth, how can I describe this party? Why, even the king and his harem showed up!

And so the party was held. When the baby was twelve days old they named him Devadiṇṇa, "Gift of the Gods." He grew up, and when he turned eight they handed him over to a teacher to learn the many arts. And he did grasp all of the arts.

Now one day when he did not have any lessons, he sat down where someone was discoursing on religion. At that very moment the subject of the discourse was the duty of giving. Here is what was said.

'By a gift you can bring people under your control. With a gift even hostility can be brought to nought. Even an enemy becomes a friend with a gift. A gift destroys all of a person's troubles.

'By giving a man becomes an emperor. By giving a man becomes king of the gods. By giving a man attains great glory. In time giving leads a person to great peace.'

And when he heard these words he thought, 'This person says that the act of giving alone is capable of warding off all harm in this world and granting peace and happiness. I should put all my efforts there.' And so he gave food and other necessities to the hungry. And as he got older he began to take things from the storehouse and give them to beggars and supplicants. He worshipped the Jina images, and with great faith in his heart he give food, clothing and begging bowls to the Jain monks and nuns. He did honour to his fellow Jains. Now one day the keeper of the storehouse, Taṇhābhibhūya, "Overcome by Greed", seeing that so much wealth was disappearing from the stores, told the merchant, 'Master! Devadiṇṇa is overcome by the vice of excessive giving and is destroying a vast amount of wealth.' The merchant said, 'Do not stop him. Let him give what he wants. Just be sure to replace what he takes out.' The other one replied, 'How shall I know how much he takes?' The merchant said, 'First do your measuring, then get ready what he needs and let him give it.' And he did just this. As for Devadiṇṇa, he gave away everything and anything that came into his mind. And so time passed.

Now it happened that Taṇhābhibhūya had an exceptionally pretty daughter named Bālā "Child," from his wife Muddhā, "Charming". Because she was so clever people called her Bālapaṇḍiyā, "Child-genius". One day while she was roaming about, Devadiṇṇa happened to see her. And as soon as he saw her he thought:

'Surely this maiden was made by God with a beauty that is not to be touched. For I have never known such loveliness in any woman that I have embraced.

'I think that the creator must have taken all the loveliness from every woman to make her body. In no other way is her beauty to be explained!

'Wherever this young maiden goes, herself unmoved, the young men are all astir with passion.

'What else can I say? Maybe she, radiant with a fiery beauty, was even made by the God of Love himself out of his own power, like a magic herb to conquer all men.

'He alone is fortunate, he alone is happy, he alone fulfils his life who kisses her beautiful face, as a bee drinks the nectar of a lotus.

'What good is the life of a man who does not toss to and fro amongst her broad breasts, like a snake struck by a stick, wriggling and writhing all the while.

'What else can I say? Lucky is the man who like a swan nestles in her, for she is like a divine river whose waters are the honeyed pleasure of love.'

And being thus struck with desire for her he thought, 'How can I get her to be mine? I know. I shall win her father over with gifts and things. For it is said:

> Whomever you wish to seize, seize first with a lure.
> And then greedy for more, he will do whatever you wish, good deed or bad.

'If I do not get her then I will leave this place. I must be clever and somehow make this known to her and to her father.'

And so the next day he gave Taṇhābhibhūya a fine

necklace. He said, 'Master! What is the meaning of giving me this necklace?' The young man answered with a riddle that involved a play on the word for necklace. In one sense he merely said, 'I am giving it to you; you are my servant and must accept it. Now take it and do with it what you wish.' But Devadiṇṇa really had another meaning in mind; for as he gave it to Taṇhābhibhūya he announced his intention to give himself up to the girl as a thief might do to a guard and he proclaimed that his fate was in her hands. But Taṇhābhibhūya did not understand that meaning. Still he did as he was told and took the necklace. He gave it to Bālapaṇḍiyā. She asked, 'Father, where did you get this necklace?' He said, 'Devadiṇṇa gave it to me.' Now she too had been in the throes of great passion ever since she had seen the young man. She had also noticed his intentions, and so to find out exactly what lay behind all of this she asked, 'Father! And did he say anything at all to you?' He repeated exactly what Devadiṇṇa had said. At once she understood its true meaning and so she recited this verse, playing upon a like set of double meanings:

> The thief is not sent away from the palace for his act of thievery, and the necklace does not go far from the treasury, occasioning a loss of wealth. Indeed I bear this necklace on my breasts and so shall he rest there too, ever so contentedly.

The word "treasury" here can also mean "the surrounding walls of the castle". The word "necklace" means the "young man". "Not taken far" means "not cast aside, not sent away in exile", because he has stolen the wealth. Rather she will bear the "necklace," or the "young man", in her heart, and he can live there happily. This was what she really meant to imply as an answer to his words.

The father, who did not understand any of this, said nothing. She thought, 'My goal can be accomplished if I am clever enough,' and so one day she said to her mother, 'Mother! Give me to Devadiṇṇa.' Her mother said, 'My child, you are always so smart. Why do you say something so foolish, as if you did not know a thing? Your father is his servant. How can you marry him? Choose someone of your own station.' She said 'Mother! At least try. Otherwise I swear that I shall take to my bed.' And she did just so. Now Muddhā saw how deeply in love she was and so she told Candapahā what had happened. And she in turn told her husband. He said, 'It is true that her father is our common servant. But I too have heard from our son's friends that he is also deeply in love with her. Let me see what our son feels and then I shall do what is right.' And so the merchant just happened to recite this verse within earshot of his son, 'A person should never abandon his father and friends. He should never trust his wife nor take her money, and he should never lust after one of his own servant girls.'

Immediately realizing his father's intentions, the young man spoke up, 'Father! If a weak wall is about to fall, is it better if it falls inward or towards the outside?' The merchant said, 'If it falls towards the inside then none of the bricks will be destroyed. And so I suppose that is to be preferred.' The young man said, 'If that is the case, then why did you say what you did?' The merchant, having understood his son's feelings, made him a wedding with all due pomp and splendour. And while the happy couple were shamelessly enjoying the delights of sex and falling deeper and deeper in love with each other, one day it so happened that Bālapaṇḍiyā went out for something. A woman, seeing her, remarked to her own companion:

'My friend! Surely this woman is the foremost of lucky women who have accumulated merit through many past lives, for she has been taken as a bride into a house that is so rich and wealthy.'

The other one said,

'Oh, my friend! Don't speak so fast. To me that woman

is blessed who, marrying a man whose wealth is gone, brings him great wealth and fortune.'

Now when she heard these words Bālapaṇḍiyā thought, 'Truly she has spoken words which require some thought. And when you think about them they do indeed seem to be true. I must send my own husband somewhere to earn money, while I remain at home devoted to pious acts, so that he many increase his great wealth.' And with this thought she went home. There she saw her husband, sunk as it were, in an ocean of worry.

When she saw him like that she asked, 'My Lord! Why do you seem to be so distressed?' He said, 'Beloved! I have good reason to be distressed. Today, dressed up in all my finery, surrounded by all my friends, I was seen by two men. One of them said:

'"Here is one who always seems to enjoy great wealth. And he is forever giving away things, as an elephant drips juice from its temples when in rut."

'"At that the second one said,

'"Sir! Why do you praise him? All he does is enjoy what his father acquired, like a son enjoying his own mother!"

'"He who can do all that this one does with wealth that he has acquired through the strength of his own arms is the one I would consider to be valiant. Anyone else is a coward."

'And so, beloved, as long as I do not go abroad and acquire wealth with the strength of my own two arms, I shall find no peace of mind.'

At the she was filled with joy and she said, 'My Lord! What a fine idea! For:

> He alone is fortunate, he alone is wise, he alone is learned, who wins fame through the wealth that he has acquired by the strength of his own two arms.

'My Lord! May your every wish be fulfilled. Do as you

desire.' And he thought, 'No wife would ever say such a thing when her husband expressed a desire to go abroad. For:

> All the joys of life are gone for a woman when her husband is abroad; women enjoy the pleasures of life when their beloveds are at their beck and call.

'But she says all of this with a straight face. For sure she must have a lover. What do I care, for at least she has not tried to stop me.' Determined to go, he went to his father and informed him:

'Father! Grant me leave to go. I wish to journey abroad in order to acquire wealth. I shall do many brave and valiant deeds.'

His father said:

'My child! We already have so much wealth in our family that is at your disposal for whatever you wish, for giving away, for enjoying and even for frittering away if that is what you choose.

'Use that wealth and stay here, free from care, for I could not bear to endure being separated from you.'

Devadiṇṇa said:

'What decent man would not shudder at the thought of living off the money that his ancestors had earned?

'And so I beg of you, out of your love for me, to grant me leave so that I may justly earn my fame with the wealth that I have acquired through the strength of my own two arms.'

When they realized that his decision to go was so firm, his mother and father both gave him their blessings and dismissed him from their presence. When all the preparations were finally under way for his departure, his parents feared that their daughter-in-law might prevent her husband from going, and so they said to her, 'Your husband seems eager to make a journey abroad.' She said. 'Father! And what can be unusual in my noble husband's resolve? For he has been born to parents like you two and is merely following in the footsteps of his honored ancestors who have gone before him. For it is said:

> These creatures leave their place of birth: lions, noble men, and elephants. And these creatures die where they were born: crows, cowardly men and deer.'

When they heard these words they had the same reaction as had their son, and so they remained silent. Now when the young man was ready, the merchant assigned eighty-four traders to accompany him, giving them each goods for trade. On an auspicious day, then, the young man appeared, mounted on an elephant. He distributed great wealth to those assembled and stood ready in a special pavilion erected to bless his departure. And Bālapaṇḍiyā too, was mounted on a magnificent elephant. She was dressed in her most splendid finery and her lotus-like face was aglow with happiness. She went forward to bow down to her husband. An instant later she announced, 'My Lord! Command me as you wish!' And the young man, in keeping with established custom, offered her a flavoured betel leaf with some flowers. As she put the betel into her mouth she proclaimed, 'My master! May I enjoy many a betel leaf that you yourself place between my lips!' With these words she bound her hair into a tight braid, and her heart overflowing with joy, she returned to her own rooms. As they observed her behaviour, all the townspeople were struck with doubt as they returned to the city.

The young man, too, had his thoughts. 'Strange indeed are the ways of women! No one can ever know what they are really thinking.' Turning this over in his mind, he proceeded on his journey. In time he reached the harbour named Gambhīraya, "Deep", as is its description here with its many embedded and hidden meanings, puns and word plays. For there he saw the ocean, and the ocean was like a magnificent elephant, like a grand palace, like a great jewel, like an excellent ascetic and like a lord of men. And what was their similarity? It was that they could all be described by just one adjective, if you are careful enough to turn the adjective this way and that. And when you do you see that the adjective means many things: the ocean was teeming with large sea creatures, while the elephant drips with ichor when in rut, the palace is abustle with pleasures, the jewel is ever desired, the ascetic is without passion and the king is forever proud. Again, it was like a cremation ground and like the Samkhyā school of philosophy, for they each can be described by the same adjective, read anew each time. The sea was filled with many types of shells; the cremation ground holds great terrors; and the Samkhyā school is made up of many great men who adhere to its tenets. In the same way it was like an excellent chariot, the sea having birds with the word "wheel" in their name, and the chariot having real wheels. It was like a temple which has a platform on which the image stands, in having a firm floor which is called by the same name. It was like an army marked by forbearance, in having many fish named by the same word that can indeed mean "forbearance." It seemed to rise up to greet him with its great waves that reached upward; it seemed to want to embrace him with its arms made up of garlands of waves. The ocean seemed to call out to him with the thunderous roar that the creatures in its depths made as they were churned hither and thither. And it seemed to smile and laugh with the white froth of its waves, which were like the dazzling teeth in a person's mouth when he smiles and laughs. It even seemed to chatter away at him with the clatter made by the birds there. He prayed to the ocean and then began to examine the boats that were there. And from them he chose to rent one particular boat that was like the teachings of the Jinas. It was unblemished and possessed of all the best qualities. It was covered with fine cloths that could be called by the same term used to designate the robes of the Jain monks. It had an excellent sail of white cloth, while the Jain doctrine has excellent monks who wear white garments. It was to be the cause of great success for him, as the Jain doctrine leads to the highest goal for men. Like the Jain doctrine, too, it rewarded those who trusted in it, and was capable of saving and bringing to shore those who were drowning, and it was protected by Gods of great strength. He loaded all of his goods onto this boat.

He gathered grains, water and sticks and performed a ceremony to worship his teachers and the Gods. He gave away great wealth, and then with his followers he got onto the boat. The boat was dragged to the shore; all the things necessary for carrying out religious rituals were brought there; flags were hoisted, the anchors were raised, the sails were hoisted, the helmsman and the first mates, the second mates and deckhands were stationed at their posts, and the boat cast off from the harbour. And as the wind was favorable, in just a few days they traveled over thousands of miles of ocean.

In the meantime, Bālapaṇḍiyā gave up bathing, anointing her body with fragrant ointments and wearing her jewels. She devoted herself to observing religious fasts, and for the most part she stayed in a nunnery with Jain nuns, praying and dedicating herself to the faith. Finally she won over everyone who saw her, and the nuns, her mother and father, her mother-in-law and father-in-law, in short everyone, said to her, 'Child! Your body is so delicate. Do not perform such strenuous asceticism.' She said:

'Elders! Do not be troubled. I shall carry out these penances for only six months. After that I shall fast to death if my husband has not come back with all his wishes fulfilled. I swear to this today, right before all of you.'

They said, 'Daughter! Your husband has gone far, far away. He cannot come back here in just six months. You must not make a vow like this.' She said, 'But I have made it already. Do not say another word about it.' And because they realized that she was firm in her resolve, they all kept silent.

One night, when the cold season had already begun to make itself felt, she was meditating without any cloak in a section of the nunnery that was exposed to the elements. There came by chance the demi-god Raisehara, "Best Lover of All", who was a complete non-believer. And he saw her. His mind was overcome by her great beauty, and he made himself visible to her and said:

'O young lady! Take me as your lover. For I am charmed by your fair qualities. O my beauty! Know that I am Raisehara, the God.

'But though I am a God, I am your most humble servant from this day forward, my love! So give yourself to me. You will not find one like me so easily again, nor will you always have such a body.

'For this body is formed by chance when the five physical elements come together. There is no such thing as morality, no such thing as the next world, and no such thing as spiritual liberation.'

And when she did not answer him as he was going on in this way, that wicked one began to try to enjoy her by force. And when he could not break down her resistance, for she had great power from her religious practices, then his mood changed and he became angry. He thought, 'I shall kill the husband of this useless woman to whom she is so faithful, so that she will die of grief at his death, burnt up by the raging fires of her pain.' Now he knew through his supernatural knowledge that Devadiṇṇa was in the middle of the ocean; he sped there and, delighted, jumped onto his boat. Taking on a terrifying form, he shouted, 'Hey you! Pray to your favorite God. For I shall sink this boat of yours right here in the middle of the ocean.' Devadiṇṇa said, 'What have I done wrong that you should act this way?' The God replied, 'This is the fault of that wicked wife yours.' 'Surely what I suspected before has come to pass, for even a God says such a thing about my wife.' With this thought, the young man again spoke up, 'If she has been false in her heart then, God, why do you not chastise her directly?' He said, 'I cannot do anything to her because of the great power of her religious austerities.'

With this the young man realized, 'This is some terribly wicked being who has no religious belief. He failed to tempt my beloved wife from the true path of virtue and from her true faith. And so he has come here in anger. He might well do what he says to us.' As Devadiṇṇa was about to recite to himself simple words of praise to the holy men of the Jain faith, that demi-god cast the boat into the sea and then returned whence he had come. All of the merchants were saved over the course of time by clinging to pieces of wood from the broken ship and they reached various islands.

Devadiṇṇa also got hold of a plank. And as he was intently reciting words of praise to the Jinas and those who had sought and found liberation in the Jain faith, he was carried safely ashore. In accordance with what his past deeds had determined for him in this life, he was seen there by the superintending deity of the salt ocean, Suṭṭhia, "Well-established", who recognized him as a fellow Jain, and delighted, said to him, 'Sir! I am the ocean. I am pleased by the faith you had in the words of praise to the Jinas. Go, my friend, to the demi-god Maṇoraha, "Wishes", who dwells in the midst of a jungle near the city Rayaṇapura, "Jewel City", which is five hundred miles from here. If I tell him to do it, he will give you whatever you ask.' Devadiṇṇa said, 'Blessed One! How can I travel such a long distance?' At this Suṭṭhia gave him a fruit that was filled with a magic nectar and said to him, 'Eat the seeds of this fruit as you go. Because of their magic power you will feel no hunger, no thirst, and you will not be tired. You will reach there in no time at all.'

Devadiṇṇa replied, 'As you command.' With these words

he set out. And indeed he did reach that jungle in just a few days. He saw the abode of the demi-god Maṇoraha, made of all sorts of jewels, redolent with the deep fragrances that came from burning incense sticks of aloe and camphor and other aromatic woods. The temple was presided over by a large jewelled image of the demi-god, and in it the demi-god's followers had carried out ceremonies in his worship. No sooner had he entered the temple than the demi-god Maṇoraha appeared to him in person and said, 'Sir, have you been sent here by the ocean?' And when he replied, 'That is so,' the demi-god said, 'In that case go at once to the city Rayaṇapura, not far from here. The king there is named Sakka, just like the King of the Gods. Whatever you desire in your heart he will give to you four-fold.'

And so he went and he saw that absolutely everyone there was absorbed in enjoying all the pleasures of all of the senses; no one did a stitch of work, not trade, not farming, not clerical work, not soldiering. They all seemed to be doing noting but playing. And looking at so many things that amazed him, he reached the royal palace itself. There he saw the king, like Indra, the King of the Gods, enjoying himself with every imaginable pleasure, and giving to people four times what they had wanted. He asked one man:

'No one in this city does anything to make money, not trade nor any of the other usual occupations, and yet where do they get all the money they clearly enjoy without the least little effort?'

He said to him, 'Have you come up from the nether world or fallen from the heavens? Or have you come from across the ocean that you ask such a question?'

Devadiṇṇa said, 'Do not be angry, for it is true that I have come from across the ocean and have been shipwrecked here. Please tell me exactly what goes on in this place.'

The man told him, 'In that case, listen. This king of ours

goes every day to the nearby jungle and there, by his great courage, he pleases the powerful demi-god Maṇoráha. The demi-god, satisfied, grants him a very great boon. Through the power of that boon the king gives to every person four times what he desires.'

When he heard this Devadiṇṇa thought, 'In that case why should I bother humbling myself before the king? I shall win over the demi-god himself. But I must see what the king does to please the demi-god.' He then went to the temple of the demi-god and, concealing himself behind a tree, he hid there until after the first watch of the night, when the king appeared all alone, with only his own sword to guard him. The king worshipped the demi-god and proclaimed:

'O, O, great demi-god! You who are possessed of such great power and unthinkable magnanimity! You who rescue all living creatures who display their faith in you through acts of courage! Appear now in person to me!'

And with these words King Sakka threw himself into a fire pit from which terrifying flames leapt.

The demi-god lifted him up with his lance and sprinkled him with water from his water pot. The king was as good as new. The demi-god said, 'Great Being! Choose a boon.' He said, 'In that case may I be able to give every man four times what he wishes through your powers.' 'So be it.' When the demi-god had replied, the king bowed down to him and then went back to his palace.

On the very next day it was Devadiṇṇa who spoke in this way to the demi-god and who jumped into the burning fire pit. In the very same way the demi-god came to grant him a boon. Devadiṇṇa said, 'Keep it in trust for me,' and with that he jumped into the fire pit yet a second time. The demi-god gave him a second boon. This repeated itself yet a third time. The fourth time, as he was about to jump into the fire pit, the demi-god grabbed him by the arm and said, 'Sir! Indra has given me this lance which has three prongs.

Through the power of this lance I can grant three boons and no more. Now ask for what you want.' Devadiṇṇa said, 'In that case, then, for my first boon give me the power that you give to the king every time he asks for a boon, but let me have that power for the rest of my life. As the second boon I ask that as long as I am alive, you do not give that power to anyone else. I shall hold the third in reserve.' The demi-god agreed to this and Devadiṇṇa stayed there in his temple, concealed from the sight of anyone else.

The king soon arrived at the temple but the demi-god barred him from entering. The king asked, 'Why do you keep me out?' The demi-god said, 'I have already given three boons to some great being.' At that the king returned to his palace, greatly troubled in mind. He lay down on his bed. The king spent the entire night tossing and turning in his bed like a fish thrown up onto hot sand, like a snake struck by a stick, like a deer caught in a trap. When morning came Devadiṇṇa went to see the king. He saw everyone in the palace overcome by grief. He asked someone, 'Why is it that everyone in the palace seems to be overcome with grief? He was told, 'Sir! For some reason our king has declared that today he will immolate himself. That is why everyone in the palace is overcome with grief.' Devadiṇṇa said, 'In that case, take heart. I shall see that nothing bad happens and everything returns to normal.' With these words of comfort he went directly into the presence of the king. He said, 'King! Why do you act like some common person?'

The king said, 'Sir! What is it to you?' He said, 'King! I have a reason for my question. Please, just answer me, my lord!' Realizing that Devadiṇṇa would not give up, the lord of men said, 'Sir! I am addicted to giving away my wealth. All this time I have been able to fulfil my desire to give through the power of a demi-god. But today I am without his favour and I cannot give like I used to. Anyway, what use is my life without the favour of that demi-god? That is why I am so upset and have decided to kill myself.' He said, 'If this is all, then, through my magic power which will last as long as I live, you can continue to give away great wealth. You do not need to propitiate the demi-god from now on.' The king was amazed by all of this, but he eagerly agreed to do as Devadiṇṇa suggested.

Devadiṇṇa then went back to the jungle. There, as he was getting out of a lake where he had been bathing, some middle-aged woman called out to him, 'O Noble One! Where have you come from and what are you doing here?' He said, 'I have come from across the ocean. The presiding god of the sea, Suṭṭhia, was pleased with me and sent me to the demi-god Maṇoraha.' At this the woman was just delighted. She said, 'In that case, come sit here under this tree so that I can tell you a secret.' He did just as she said. She too then sat there and began to tell him her tale.

'There is a wonderful mountain named Veyaḍḍha, with so many high peaks that reach up to touch the top of heaven's vault. It is home to all of the Vijjāharas, who have supernatural powers, and is adorned with many Jain temples made entirely of precious stones. There is a city on that mountain called Gayaṇavallaha. It is protected by King Candasehara, who is the crest-jewel of all the kings of the Vijjāharas. He has five chief queens, all foremost in his harem, and their names are Sirikantā, Kaṇagamālā, Vījjumālā, Mehamālā, and Sutārā. And they each have a daughter who is skilled in all the arts and who surpasses in beauty the women of the Gods. Their names are Kaṇagappahā, Tārappahā, Candapahā, Sūrappahā, and Telukkadevī. Their father Candasehara consulted an astrologer about them. "Who will be their husband?" The astrologer said: "Your younger brother Sūrasehara on his death became the demi-god Maṇoraha. He still bears you great affection. If your daughters stay with him they will surely get the right husband for themselves."

'And so their father gave the girls to Maṇoraha to take care of. Maṇoraha hid them all in an underground structure near his temple, and he gave them all such a fiery complexion that no ordinary man could look at them. Each girl he made more blindingly bright than her sister, with Telukkadevī the brightest. If you want you could ask for the girls. I am their former nursemaid named Vegavaī and, won over by your good qualities and handsome looks, I have told you all of this.'

Devadiṇṇa then said, 'I shall do as you command.' With that he went back to see the demi-god. He told him, 'Blessed One! For my third boon that I left in trust with you, give me those maidens who are here in their underground chambers.' The demi-god at once thought, 'Now surely those girls have been struck with desire for this man and have shown themselves to him. How else could he even know that they exist?' He said to Devadiṇṇa, 'There are girls here, but they are so fiery bright that no one can look at them.' He said, 'That doesn't matter. Just give them to me.' At that the demi-god showed him four of the girls, all except Telukkadevī. And as soon as they got near Devadiṇṇa, the fiery brilliance that the demi-god had given them disappeared. Then he asked, 'Why did you not show me the fifth girl?' The demi-god said, 'She is three times brighter than even these girls and you would never be able to look at her.' Devadiṇṇa said, 'Never mind. Just show her to me.' With that there appeared a girl who was as hard to look upon as the orb of the sun. But she too at once assumed her normal appearance when she got close to Devadiṇṇa. All of them as soon as they saw him fell deeply in love with him. The demi-god was amazed at this and thought to himself, 'Surely they belong to him.' He said, 'Children! Do you want this man for your husband?' They said, 'Father, it would be a great honour for us.' Maṇohara told them, 'He already has a wife who is the abode of so many good qualities. And even as your husband he will still always be devoted to her.' They all said, 'And what could be wrong with his being devoted to his senior wife?' At that the demi-god gave him the girls. He summoned King Candasehara and with much pomp and splendour they celebrated their wedding. The demi-god gave great wealth to all the girls. Then Telukkadevī said. 'Father! Will you not also give something for our elder co-wife, who is like our sister?' At this the demi-god gave her a jewelled signet ring. She said, 'What kind of a gift is this?' He said, 'My daughter! This is a magic jewel that grants all wishes.' Delighted, she accepted the ring. Candasehara took his leave of the demi-god and went home. And the girls through their magic powers made a magic castle for them all to live in. Devadiṇṇa stayed there with them, enjoying pleasure after pleasure.

Then one day, wondering what her elder co-wife was doing, Telukkadevī used her supernatural knowledge and saw that Bālapaṇḍiyā was intent on beginning her fast to death. The six-month period had lapsed and her husband had not yet returned. Clothed in the stained robes of a nun, she was sitting deep in meditation. Realizing, 'Surely this noble lady will fast to death tomorrow morning if her husband has not returned,' Telukkadevī went to the demi-god. She told him exactly what was happening. He too believed that what she said was going to happen and he said, 'My child! Go quickly, for the night is almost up. And he sent with her his servant, the demi-god named Dharaṇīdhara. And that one made a magic chariot which he filled with jewels, precious stones, pearls, coral, gold and other valuables. They put Devadiṇṇa in the chariot, fast asleep. Then the girls and their servants got in. Dharaṇīdhara held the chariot on the tip of his finger and hurtled it upwards. It sped onward with great speed and Devadiṇṇa was suddenly awakened by the jingling of the bells that hung along its sides. He asked Telukkadevī, 'What is going on?' And she told him everything.

As they watched the earth speed by them with its cities, towns and villages, in the twinkling of an instant they arrived at their destination. They saw Bālapaṇḍiyā in meditation at the nunnery. And when she saw her, Telukkadevī threw a garment of fine silk over her. Distracted, Bālapaṇḍiyā quickly uttered a few words of praise to the Jinas and came out of her meditation. She looked up to see what was happening. When she saw the chariot, she was frightened and went inside. She asked the other nuns, 'What is happening?' They told her, 'It must be that some God has come here, drawn by the power of your austerities.' And no sooner had they said this than the chariot came down from the sky and stopped right there in front of them.

The sun came up. They all got out of the chariot, and having uttered the traditional words renouncing mundane concerns, they entered the holy precincts. They bowed down to the nuns. Bālapaṇḍiyā, seeing her husband, in a flurry rose to greet him. She fell at his feet. When they heard that Devadiṇṇa was back, the king and all the townspeople, his father and all his relatives, came to see him. Devadiṇṇa sent Dharaṇīdhara back, and taking all the valuables from the chariot, with great pomp and splendour he returned home. A huge celebration was held in his honour.

Now his friends began to ask Devadiṇṇa what had happened to the other merchants who had gone with him. When she saw that Devadiṇṇa did not answer, Telukkadevī with her magic powers realized what was on his mind and she thought, 'Nothing should spoil a happy moment like this.' That was why she said, 'My noble lord has come swiftly on this magic chariot. The others all tarried a bit, doing various services for the local ruler and receiving in turn much honour. They will surely arrive soon.' Devadiṇṇa was delighted and thought, 'How clever my beloved is with words.'

But when people began to ask about the other merchants every day, then Devadiṇṇa remembered the demi-god. And through the power of the magic wish-granting jewel that the demi-god had given for Bālapaṇḍiyā, at that very instant the demi-god came to him. He asked, 'For what reason have you summoned me?' Devadiṇṇa said, 'Because I cannot make what your daughter said come true.' The demi-god said, 'If that is all, then I shall do everything that is necessary. I'll be right back.' Devadiṇṇa said, 'Please.' And the demi-god did do all that he had promised. Devadiṇṇa then spent many happy years like this, all of his wishes fulfilled by the power of the magic wish-granting jewel that he had obtained as a result of his acts of giving away wealth, acts that bore their fruit right here in this world. He was devoted to worshipping the Jinas and the Jain monks; he gave away wealth to the poor and the unfortunate; he fulfilled every wish that he had ever had, and he enjoyed to the fullest every conceivable pleasure of the five senses. He had many sons who were worthy of him.

Now one day in the course of his monastic tour the Jain monk Sīlasāgara came there. Devadiṇṇa and his wives went out to greet the monk and they bowed down to him with their hearts filled with faith. Receiving his blessings, they all sat down on a clean spot of ground from which all living creatures had been gently removed. The monk began to give a discourse on the Jain faith. He began, 'When a man has been fortunate to have been born as a human being and in a country where the true religion is taught, then he should spend his efforts in religious pursuits. Listen:

'All you noble souls! It is not such an easy thing to have been born as a human being and in the right country. Most good people know this.

'Now you have all attained such a birth on account of the good deeds that you must have done in a past life. Now you should put your mind to that religion which has been taught by the Omniscient One.

'And that religion is said to be two-fold in practice, for the monks and for the lay believers. You should put all your effort into religion, for it has been said by the wise:

There will always be unending misfortunes; there will

always be the cycle of passion and other bad feelings; there will always be the production of karma; and there will always be the cycle of births;
There will always be miseries and there will always be false and vain hopes; there will always be men pitifully complaining to other men;
There will always be poverty, there will always be disease, there will always be this terrible ocean of transmigratory existence with its many sufferings.
Just as long as this true religion spoken by the Jinas is not encountered by people. But as soon as people, even by chance, encounter this teaching, then:
Shaking off all sin they will reach the highest place which is filled with unending happiness and is devoid of all suffering.

At this there arose in Devadiṇṇa a desire to practice religion, and he said, 'I shall make arrangements for my family and then I shall obey your command by becoming a monk.'

The teacher said, 'Do not wait.' 'I shall be back.' With these words Devadiṇṇa returned home. He appointed his eldest son Dhaṇavaī, "The Rich", as head of the family. And as festivities were celebrated in the Jain temples, as hosts of monks and nuns were given pure alms, as fellow Jains were honored and feted, as wealth was distributed to the poor and the needy, what more can I say, as everything that was supposed to happen was carried out to perfection, Devadiṇṇa and his wives were ordained by the teacher. He gave them this instruction:

'Hear this! There are people who drink the drink of immortality, the nectar of the Gods. They are the people who have become monks and nuns and are filled with a happiness that nothing can sully.

'And now you all have taken this Blessed Ordination. You have obtained what there is to be obtained in this ocean of births.

'But I warn you that as long as you live you must be careful and exert yourselves, for it is said:

> Those without good fortune, those lowest of men, do not master the religious life. But those who do are the best among men.

And when Devadiṇṇa said, 'We desire further instruction,' the teacher handed the women over to the nun Sīlamaṇī. They all took upon themselves two sets of vows. They lived a perfect life as ascetics for many years. At the end of their appointed lifespan they all fasted to death and became gods in the twelfth heaven. When they fall from there they will be reborn in Mahāvideha where they will achieve their ultimate liberation.

And so I say,

The fact that although he had fallen into distress, the lord of the ocean Suṭṭhia was pleased with him, and the fact that he was able to return to his parents, all of this is the result of his giving away wealth.

The fact that he obtained those women to enjoy sensual pleasure with, women who had conquered the women of the Gods with their charm and their beauty, all of this is the result of his giving away wealth.

The fact that he got so many gorgeous silk clothes, fine, beautiful, of every different colour, all of this is the result of his giving away wealth.

The fact that he got so many glowing jewels, wish-granting jewels, cats-eyes, diamonds and more, all of this is the result of his giving away wealth.

The fact that he got heap upon heap of valuables, jewels, pearls, coral, gold and other such things, all of this is the result of his giving away wealth.

The fact that he enjoyed so many pleasures that delighted his ears, his sense of smell, his taste, touch and eyes; the fact that he got unparalleled glory, all of this is the result of his giving away wealth.

Considering all of these fruits that come about in this very life from the act of giving away wealth, give all you can with all your might!

(from the *Mūlaśuddhiprakaraṇa* of Pradyumnasūri, p. 169)

31

VICE AND VIRTUE

The account of the transmigrating soul that has been reborn in animal bodies is completed. Now follows an account of the soul in its human births.

The transmigrating soul said: 'Then my lady Agṛhītasaṃketā, "Ignorant of the Truth", was given a magic pill to send me to my next rebirth and off I went. Now in this city that we call Life as a Human Being there is a small area called Bharata. Its most famous town is known as Jayasthala, "Place of Victory". There reigned King Padma, endowed with every virtue necessary to rule. His chief queen was named Nandā; she was like the Goddess Rati, wife of the God of Love, whom her husband indeed resembled in his fine looks. I entered her womb and because that was the way things were to be, I lived there in her womb for the required time. I emerged from her womb along with Puṇyodaya, "Rise of Merit". When Queen Nandā saw me, she felt a false sense of ownership over me and thought to herself, 'I have a son.' A young servant, Pramodakumbha, "Vessel of Joy", informed the king of my birth. The king, too, conceived the notion, 'My son has been born.' The king was so delighted that shivers of joy ran through his entire body. He gave a reward to the servant, who had given him the news. He commanded that a great celebration be held in honor of my birth. And so great gifts were given; prisoners were released from prison; the guardian deities of the city were worshipped; the markets and city gates were decorated; the main thoroughfares were adorned; drums were struck to mark the happy occasion, and the townspeople decked out in their finery hastened to the palace. They were welcomed there and the proper ceremonies were carried out. A chorus of drums resounded. Auspicious songs were sung. The women danced, along with the men who guarded the harem, the hunchbacks, dwarfs, and the rest of the king's retinue. Thus a great celebration took place at my birth. When the festivities were over a month later, my name "Transmigrating Soul" was set aside in favor of a new name, Nandivardhana. Even I wrongly came to think of myself as belonging to my mother and father; I now thought of myself as their son. I grew to be three years old, constantly bringing joy to my mother and father, and tended by five nursemaids, who saw to my every need.

'Now, ever since I had left the realm of Insentient Beings I had been accompanied by a two-fold retinue, that is, I had internal and external companions. Among my internal companions was a nursemaid, a brahmin lady named Avivekatā, "Lack of Discrimination". On the very day that I was born she had also given birth to a son, who was named Vaiśvānara, "Fire". He had always been with me, but in a subtle state; now he was with me in a more concrete and solid form. Here is what I mean. He had two clumsy looking large feet, Hostility and Belligerence. Jealousy and Thievery made up his two calves that were fat, rough and stumpy looking. Hatred and Discontent were his hideous thighs. Vicious Backbiting constituted his hips, which were deformed, one side being unnaturally higher than the other, while an uncanny Ability to Ferret Out the Weaknesses of Another made up his ugly, fat and pendulous belly. His chest, Remorse, was rough and lumpy, while he sported short and stubby arms, Envy and Spite. He strutted about with Brutality as his long and crooked neck, displaying Vulgar Speech and the like as his teeth which, though few in number, were sharp like fangs and unconcealed by any lips. He had nothing but gaping holes for ears that made him look totally ludicrous; they were Fiendishness and Resentment. He was quite a charmer with his flat nose, Evil Nature, barely distinguishable from the rest of his face. He made something of a stir with his round eyes that were red like cut open guñja berries; they were Brutality and Ruthlessness. Barbarous Conduct was his enormous triangular-shaped head. He was true to his namesake, with his red hair, Tormenting Others, that resembled a mass of flames. This is what the brahmin boy Vaiśvānara looked like.

'I grew quite fond of him, since I had known him for such a long time. I considered him to be my friend and had no clue that he was actually my worst enemy. I got the idea that being with him was good for me; after all, he was the son of Lack of Discrimination and an intimate associate of mine. Realizing how I felt, he thought to himself, "Aha! The prince likes me. I'll go to him." And so he did. He embraced me and openly showed his affection for me. We grew closer and closer and began to be the best of friends. Wherever I went, in the house or outside, he never left my side even for a moment. Rise of Merit, dwelling in my mind, became angry at my friendship with Vaiśvānara and thought, "My goodness. This Vaiśvānara is my sworn enemy. But that doesn't stop this foolish Nandivardhana from casting me aside, although I care deeply for him, and becoming friends with that one, who is really his worst enemy and whose very body is made up of all the vices. Or perhaps there is nothing unusual in the behavior of the prince. People who are deluded do not realize the true nature of their wicked companions. They do not understand what terrible things can happen to them from hanging around with the wrong crowd. They do not listen to the good person who would put an end to their association with the wrong friends. They give up their decent friends for the sake of their bad ones. They go astray under the influence of such harmful company. They never give up their bad friends because someone tells them to; they have to get into trouble first, like a blind man who rushes headlong into a wall. Clearly the prince Nandivardhana is deluded and that is why he hangs around with the likes of Vaiśvānara. What use would it be for me to try to stop him? The lady Fate will eventually bring us together. Besides, I became his friend because he impressed me when he was in his birth as an elephant and he cultivated such an attitude of supreme equanimity despite the pain he was suffering. That is why it would not be right for me to abandon Prince Nandivardhana completely, even though I am good and mad at him for keeping such bad company." Rise of Merit considered all these things and did not leave my side. He stayed with me, although he chose to remain in hiding.

'I have told you about my internal companions. I also had many external friends from the time I was born. As I grew up I played all sorts of games with them. When we played, even the older children, who were also of noble birth and were physically quite strong, trembled in fear of me when they realized that Vaiśvānara had got his clutches into me. They would come and bow down to me and try to curry favor with me. They would do whatever I commanded. None of them would dare to ignore anything that I said. What more do I have to tell you? They were even terrified if they saw a picture of me! But really the cause of my superior position among the other children was actually Rise of Merit, that was in hiding near me. Because I was deluded, this is what I thought, "These boys, even though they're bigger than I am, treat me like this because of my good friend Vaiśvānara. His presence makes me powerful. He makes me tough. He increases my might and gives me strength. He makes my mind firm. He makes me resolute and steadfast so that I won't give up. He makes me a real hero. What more do I have to say? I owe all my manliness to him." Thoughts like this made me even fonder of Vaiśvānara.

'I turned eight years old. King Padma decided, "It is time for the prince to learn the various traditional arts." The propitious day for me to start was determined. The best of teachers was summoned. The teacher was properly honored. Everything that needed to be done was done. With great deference my father handed me over to the teacher. My brothers, the other princes, had already been entrusted to the care of the teacher. Along with them I began to learn the arts. In a very short time I mastered them all, for nothing was lacking in my education and I was an eager student. The teacher was also a good teacher for me, and as a prince I hadn't a care in the world to distract me. Fate was kind; Rise of Merit was at my side and much of my bad karma that might have prevented me from learning had already been destroyed. And so I soon mastered the arts with a joyful heart.

'My best friend Vaiśvānara was always by my side. He was constantly putting his arms around me, sometimes for no reason at all. And when he put his arms around me I forgot what my elders had taught me. I didn't care about my family's good name. I wasn't afraid of making my father suffer. I didn't realize what the true state of affairs was. I wasn't even aware of my own inner suffering. I had no idea that if I was going to behave like that, I shouldn't bother cultivating the arts. I thought that there was no friend as dear to me as Vaiśvānara and so I did whatever he told me.

Sweating, my eyes bright red and my brows furrowed in anger, I fought with the other children and hit them where it hurt. I lied and I wouldn't tolerate it when any of them said anything, even something neutral. I would beat them with whatever I could find nearby, pieces of wood, whatever. When they saw me in Vaiśvānara's clutches like this, they were struck with fear. They would say what they thought I wanted to hear and would do things to try to appease me; they would try to win me over by throwing themselves at my feet. What more do I have to say? Those courageous princes would begin to act differently even when they caught wind of my presence, like poisonous snakes robbed of their power by some magic spell.

'Those princes were all terrified and trembled in fear. They were like prisoners, though, and obedient to the wishes of their parents, they continued to study with me, although they were clearly miserable. They never told the teacher what was going on; they were convinced I would kill them all. But since we were always together, the teacher was aware of everything I was doing. The only thing was that he was also afraid of me, since he had seen what I was capable of doing and so he didn't dare to chastise me openly. If he would even so much as hint at my wrong doing, I would scream at him and beat him up. And so he came to behave towards me just as the other princes did. In my great delusion I thought to myself, "Look at what power my best friend has! Look at the great things he does for me! He's so clever and he's so devoted to me. See how firm his affection for me is; he puts his arms around me and makes me so powerful that no one dares to disobey my commands! He never leaves my side. He is truly my best friend, my second self, my everything, my life, my law. Without him a person is impotent, no better than a straw man." When I thought things like this my affection for Vaiśvānara grew even deeper.

'One day when we were alone and sharing our innermost

secrets with each other, I told him, "I won't beat about the bush. I entrust you with my life. Take it and do with it what you will." When I said this, Vaiśvānara thought, "My efforts have been successful; now he is entirely in my control. By saying what he has said he has shown me how devoted he is to me. And such devoted friends listen to you. They accept your words without question. They obey them in their hearts and with their actions. Now is my chance." So Vaiśvānara thought to himself; but to me he said, "Prince! I do not doubt you for a minute. That the prince says these words to me, even though I know full well what is in his heart, is evidence of the great favor he bestows upon me. The munificence of the prince causes him in his great joy to utter these words, though they do not need to be spoken. But let me come to my point. I must make the prince immortal; it is my duty to my sovereign." I asked him, "How can you do that?" He replied, "I know some alchemy." I told him, "Best friend! Then go ahead!" He now replied, "As the prince commands." He then prepared some pills called Cruel Thoughts and gave them to me when we were alone. He told me, "Prince! Here are some pills that I made for you with my special skills. They fill a man with courage and allow him to accomplish whatever he wishes; they also grant him long life. Take them."

'At that very moment someone in another room said in a soft voice, "There is no doubt. He will end up in the place you have chosen for him." I did not hear these words, but Vaiśvānara did and he thought to himself, "I shall succeed. He will go to hell when he takes these pills. Once he gets there he will have a long life, right there in hell. What else could those words mean? Hell is exactly the place I have chosen for him." The thought of all this brought joy to his heart. I said to him, "What can I not accomplish with you as my best friend and at my service?" When he heard these words he was doubly pleased and handed over the pills to me. I took them from him. He told me, "Prince!

You must do me one more favour. When I give you the sign, you must not hesitate; you must swallow one of the pills." I replied, "You need not ask. I have already handed over my life to you, my best friend." Vaiśvānara said, "Great indeed is your favor. The prince does me great honor."

'Now my father had appointed one of his favorite and most trustworthy young servants to watch over me, saying, "Listen here, Vidura! I said to the prince, 'You must devote yourself wholeheartedly to the mastery of the arts. Do not come to see me. I will come to you.' But I have been so busy with managing my kingdom that I have not yet had the chance to go and see the prince. You must give me a daily report on how the prince is doing." Vidura replied, "As my lord commands." And when Vidura was carrying out the duty with which he had been entrusted, he saw exactly how I was tormenting the other princes and even the teacher. For a while he hesitated to tell my father, not wanting to cause him pain, but when he saw how things had gotten totally out of control he did tell him. My father thought to himself, "Now it is true that Vidura would never lie to me, but the prince has never behaved like this before. I don't understand what has happened." He was disturbed by this thought, "If the prince torments the teacher too, then what is the use of his mastering the arts." He then decided, "It is time for me to ask the teacher what is going on. Once I know what the prince is doing I can figure out some way to stop him." And so he sent Vidura to summon the teacher.

'My father respectfully rose to greet the teacher. He offered him a seat, honored him and then when the teacher had given him leave to sit too, my father said, "Noble Buddhisamudra, Ocean of Wisdom, are the princes learning the arts?" He replied, "Indeed my lord, by your grace, they learn well." My father then asked, "Has Prince Nandivardhana also mastered the arts?" The teacher answered, "My lord, Prince Nandivardhana has indeed mastered the arts. He is accomplished in all the arts. For example, he has mastered all the scripts; he can teach mathematics. He might have invented the science of grammar himself. He knows astrology and has mastered the art of prognostication with all its branches. He even explained to the others the science of versification. He is skilled in dancing and has mastered the art of singing. The art of taming elephants is under his control, as a woman is under the control of her lover. Archery is like a devoted friend to him and medicine is like his familiar companion. Alchemy stands ready to do his bidding, while such things as the skill at interpreting auspicious and inauspicious marks on a person, the ability to cut fine designs on the leaves of plants and a ready knowledge of what to buy and what to sell wait upon him like faithful serving maids. What more need I say? There is no art that has not reached its pinnacle, having found the prince to practice it."

'At that my father's eyes were brimming with tears of joy. He said, "Noble One, is it any wonder that such should be the case, when you are the prince's teacher? Fortunate indeed is the prince to have a teacher like you." Buddhisamudra responded, "My lord, do not say such things. I am insignificant. It is all due to your greatness that the prince has succeeded so well." My father replied, "Noble One! You flatter me. It is on account of you that the prince has become the vessel in which are contained all of the arts, and I am so filled with joy." Buddhisamudra now said, "If that is so, then there is something I must tell you, for it is said that those who are entrusted with a task by their sovereigns should never deceive them. My lord must decide if I have spoken rightly or wrongly and must pardon me for what I say. It is indeed rare, my lord, for words to be both true and pleasing at the same time." My father said, "Speak, noble man. What need have you to ask for clemency when you speak the truth?" Buddhisamudra said, "In that case, I will speak. When you rejoiced that the prince has become the vessel in which are contained all of the arts, well, there is no question that such is the case if you consider the prince's natural ability. But all of the prince's many accomplishments are marred by a single imperfection, as the moon is stained by a dark spot on its surface, as a red lotus is flawed by having thorns, as wealth is tarnished by stinginess, as a woman is blemished by a lack of modesty, as men are sullied by cowardice and as religious practice is defiled if it causes pain to others. Your son's flaw is his friendship with Vaiśvānara; tranquility is essential to proficiency in all of the arts, but this Vaiśvānara, your son's dangerously evil companion, is always with him and he employs all of his powers to destroy the prince's peace of mind. The prince is totally deluded and he thinks that Vaiśvānara, who in reality is his worst enemy, is his best friend. The natural flow of the nectar of tranquility, which is the very essence of knowledge, has been obstructed in the prince by his evil friend. And so all of his many virtues are now useless."

'When my father heard this it was as if he had been struck by a bolt of lightning. He was overpowered by great sorrow. My father said to the trusted Vidura, "Sir! There is no more need to fan me with palm fronds that feel as cool as a spray of sandalwood essence. It is not a physical fire that burns me; it is a mental fire. Go and summon the prince so that I can rid myself of this unbearable inner fire that rages within me, by putting an end to his consorting with evil friends."

'Vidura put down the palm frond and prostrated himself before the king, saying, "As the king commands. But given the enormity of the task, the king must not be angry with me if I speak beyond my station." My father replied, "There can be no cause for anger towards one who speaks out to help another. Kind sir, say what you will." Vidura spoke, "Lord, in that case I will speak. I have known the prince for a long time and I know that Vaiśvānara is his very dear friend No one will be able to separate them. The prince thinks that Vaiśvānara is actually good for him. He cannot bear to be without him even for an instant. When Vaiśvānara is not there the prince becomes anxious and agitated. He thinks he is totally worthless, as worthless as a blade of grass, without Vaiśvānara. I am convinced that if anyone says anything to the prince about giving up Vaiśvānara, the prince will become extremely upset; he might even kill himself or do something else drastic and disastrous. And so I believe that the king must not say anything to the prince about this." Buddhisamudra concurred, adding, "Lord, everything that Vidura has said is true. I too have been trying to keep the prince from consorting with his evil friend. I kept thinking that if only the prince could be made to separate from his friend he would come to his senses and be himself once more. But I also thought that the bond of affection that binds them is so strong that the prince might come to some harm if he is forced to give up his friend. And so I had come to the conclusion that it was not possible to prevent the prince from being friends with Vaiśvānara." My father then said, "Noble sir, then what can we do?" Buddhisamudra replied, "Lord! I have heard that a sage who knows the past, present and future, has come. His name is Jinamatajña, "Knower of the Doctrine of the Jinas". He can foretell the future and is expert at reading omens. It is possible that he might know what can be done." My father said, "Good idea, gentleman, good idea. Summon him at once." Vidura replied, "As my lord commands."

'Vidura then went out and soon came back with that sage, who was skilled in reading omens. My father was delighted when he saw the sage. He offered him a seat and honored him with all the appropriate ceremony and then proceeded to tell him what was going on. The sage went into a state of yogic trance in which he saw the entire situation. Then he told my father, "Great king! There is no other way. There is only one solution and it is not going to be easy." My father said, "Tell me what it is, O noble man!" Jinamatajña said, "Listen, O Great King!

'There is a city called Perfection of the Mind. It is a place devoid of misfortune; it is the abode of every good virtue. It is the cause of every kind of happiness and prosperity, but it is a place that is not easily reached by those of little merit.

'"The fortunate people who live in this city are never harassed by the thieves, passion and its cohorts.

'"There hunger and thirst never afflict a man; and so the wise say that it is a place that is devoid of misfortune.

'"Through its power men acquire knowledge and other desirable qualities; skill in the arts is not possible anywhere else.

'"The people who live there have all the virtues, like nobility of character, dignity, steadfastness and courage, and so it is said to be the abode of every good virtue.

'"The people who live there go from one happy experience to another, each more intense than the one before it.

'"Nothing ever attacks this city and so it is said to be the cause of every kind of happiness and prosperity.

'"And because it is devoid of all misfortune and adorned by every positive quality, the cause of happiness and prosperity, meritorious beings joyfully seek out that city, Perfection of the Mind, which is difficult for those of little merit to reach.

'"In that city reigns King Śubhapariṇāma, Auspicious Leanings. He promotes the welfare of all living beings.He is alert to punish the wicked and on guard to protect the good citizens; he is endowed with both wealth to dispense and the might with which to punish.

'"Since he is capable of putting an end to all worry, mere contact with him causes great joy.

'"He sets people on the right path, and that is why valiant men say that he promotes the welfare of all living beings.

'"The king is never idle, always engaged in destroying passion, hatred, great delusion, anger, greed, intoxication, confusion, lust, jealousy, sadness, despondency and other things that cause people to suffer, and that constantly torment people, forcing them to commit evil deeds.

'"Knowledge, withdrawal from worldly desires, contentment, renunciation and gentleness, things like these that bring joy to everyone, are what are called here "the good citizens". The king is always on guard to protect them, uninterested in any other duties.

'"His treasury is filled with these jewels: the good virtues, wisdom, steadfastness, mindfulness, desire to pursue the religious path, and freedom from desires.

'"His method of punishment is his fourfold army, in which the chariots, elephants, horses and foot soldiers are the components of leading a virtuous life.

'"The king, intent upon punishing the wicked, constantly vigilant in protecting the good, is thus said to be endowed with both wealth to dispense and the might with which to punish.

'"The chief queen of this king Auspicious Leanings is named Niṣprakampatā, Fortitude. She wins the beauty contest because of her physical allure. She has conquered all the three worlds, heaven, earth and the netherworld, with her skill in the various arts, and she puts to shame even Rati, wife of the God of Love, with her charms. In her faithfulness to her husband she surpasses even Arundhatī, wife of the sage Vasiṣṭha, known far and wide for her chastity.

'"If one were to take all of the most beautiful women in the three worlds, goddesses in heaven, mortal women on earth and demon women in the underworld, and carefully deck them out with jewels so that they might tempt the sages to break their vows of chastity, Queen Fortitude would be in another camp altogether. For the minds of the sages are attached to her and to no other woman. And so it is said that she wins the beauty contest because of her physical allure.

'"All of the gods, including Rudra, Indra, Viṣu, and Candra, skilled in the arts, and others who are famous in the three worlds for their skill, all of them without exception have been conquered by greed and lust and the other mental enemies.

'"That is why it is said that they do not really have any great skill. But this queen has some wondrous skill, beyond words, for she effortlessly conquers all these mental enemies. Thus it is said that with her skill she has conquered the three worlds.

'"The amorous charms of the Goddess Rati bring delight only to her husband Kāma, the God of Love; sages know nothing at all of them. But this lady's charms, which include steadfast practice of the monastic vows, stir the minds of the sages. And so it is said that with her charms she puts to shame the charms of Rati.

'"Let me tell you now in what way she is faithful to her husband. She infuses her own life into her husband when he is in danger and renews his strength. That is why it is said that she is faithful to her husband. But Arundhatī was not able to save her husband and so it is said that she has been surpassed by Queen Fortitude, who was even more devoted to her husband.

'"Need I say more? In every endeavor she ensures her husband of success. Queen Fortitude is the most vital person in his kingdom.

'"This royal couple, Auspicious Leanings and Fortitude, have a daughter named Kṣānti, Forbearance, who is the epitome of all that is beautiful, the birthplace of everything that is marvellous, the jewel box of a heap of jewels, namely virtuous qualities. By her unusual beauty she even succeeds in captivating the minds of the sages.

'"She is a constant source of joy when worshipped; just thinking about her puts an end to all sins.

'"The man upon whom that lady with lovely eyes playfully gazes is praised by the wise, who call him a noble soul.

'"The man whom she embraces, I think, will become a ruler over all men, a mighty Emperor of the world.

'"And so it is said that there is no women more desirable than she in the world; for these reasons wise men declare that she is the epitome of all that is beautiful.

'"All of the most excellent states of mind, right meditation, omniscience, the powers that come from the cultivation of yogic states, tranquility and the like, all of these things that are a constant source of wonder and are endless in number, spanning past, present and future, arise through her favour in those living beings who worship her. For this reason she is said to be the birthplace of everything that is marvellous.

'"Listen to me now as I explain why I have said that she is like a jewel box. There are many virtues in this world that are considered to be valuable like jewels:

'"For example, generosity, good conduct, practice of austerities, knowledge, a good family, handsome form and courage, truthfulness, purity, honesty, absence of greed, heroism, wealth and the like.

'"All of these rest in Forbearance, which is their support. That is why the wise say that she is a jewel box.

'"These virtues do not shine without Forbearance, which is their foundation.

'"Here is another way of saying all of this:

Forbearance alone is the great act of charity; forbearance is great austerity.

Forbearance is the highest knowledge; forbearance is the greatest restraint.

Forbearance is perfect conduct; forbearance is the most noble of family lineages.

Forbearance is the greatest heroism; forbearance is the greatest act of courage.

Forbearance is contentment; forbearance is control of the sense organs.

Forbearance is the highest purity; forbearance is the highest compassion.

Forbearance is great greatest physical beauty; forbearance is great power.

Forbearance is great riches; forbearance is said to be steadfastedness.

Forbearance is the Absolute that some call Brahma; forbearance is truth.

Forbearance is the highest release; forbearance is the source of all accomplishments.

Forbearance and nothing else in this world is worthy of worship; forbearance is the most propitious and auspicious of all things.

Forbearance is the best of all medicines that puts an end to all diseases.

Forbearance and nothing else is the four-fold vast army that destroys all enemies.

What more need I say? Everything depends on Forbearance.

'"That is why it is said that this woman captivates the minds of the sages. What thinking man would not turn his mind to a woman like this?

'"Moreover:

'"When this charming lady takes hold of a man's mind, that fortunate man becomes just like her.

'"And so what man who hears these words and yearns for virtue would not give his heart to this woman, who can give him all that he desires?

'"Now since this is the case, this woman, who is lovely in every way, possessed as she is of the highest virtues, stands diametrically opposed to Vaiśvānara.

'"I believe that Vaiśvānara would flee in abject terror at the mere sight of her.

'"He is the sum total of all vice and that woman is the

abode of all virtue; that wicked man is fire incarnate; she is cool like snow.

'"The two could never exist in the same place, for they are polar opposites and that is why I say:

'"If the prince were to marry this woman, he would give up his association with his wicked friend."

'At this point Vidura thought, "Basically, this is what Jinamatajña, who can read omens, is saying: from Fortitude united with Auspicious Leanings in the state of Perfection of the Mind is born Forbearance. She alone is capable of putting an end to Prince Nandivardhana's harmful association with his evil friend Vaiśvānara there is no other way to put an end to their friendship. Everything Jinamatajña has said is correct. But what is surprising in that? No one who knows the doctrine of the Jina, no one who is a Jinamatajña would ever say anything that is not true."

'Now when my father heard what the sage had said, he glanced over at his minister Matidhana, "Rich in Wisdom", who was right next to him, waiting for his order. My father said, "Noble Matidhana, did you hear what he said?" Matidhana replied, "My lord, I heard." My father said, "In that case you will understand why I am so concerned that all of the prince's virtues, though they might well be the envy of many a gentleman, have been reduced to naught, sullied by his association with a bad friend. You must go at once and dispatch our most noble courtiers, skilled in words, to Perfection of the Mind. Let them take with them gifts, such things as cannot be found there, and instruct them to speak with clever and flattering words so as to bring about this marriage without delay. They are to ask Auspicious Leanings for the hand of his daughter Forbearance on behalf of the prince." Matidhana replied, "As my lord commands." And with those words he proceeded to leave. Jinamatajña said, "Great king! This is not necessary. The city cannot be reached in this way." My father asked, "Noble One, explain that to me." Jinamatajña said, "Great King! In this world there are two kinds of everything, of cities, kings, wives, sons, friends, of everything. What I mean is that there are internal and external objects. It is only with respect to the external objects that the actions of people like you, for example going, informing, and so on, can apply. These actions have no relevance to internal objects. Now this city, the king, his wife and their daughter, are all internal objects. It is useless to send your counsellors there." My father asked, "Noble one, in that case, who has power there?" Jinamatajña said, "The one who is the inner king." My father then asked, "And who is that?" Jinamatajña replied, 'Great king! The king there is Ripening of Karma. In fact it is Ripening of Karma that gave the city to Auspicious Leanings as his fiefdom. That is why Auspicious Leanings is dependent on Ripening of Karma.

'My father asked, "Noble One, is Ripening of Karma amenable to a petition from the likes of me?" Jinamatajña answered, "O King, he is not. He does what he wishes and does not wait for a petition from another person. He is not swayed by words of flattery. He is not won over by another's pleas; he does not even feel pity when he sees a person in distress. When he acts the only ones he consults or considers are these: the sister of his minister, who is named Lokasthiti, "The Arrangement of the World"; his wife Kālapariṇati, "Force of Time" and his courtier, Svabhāva, "Inherent Nature". He does listen to Prince Nandivardhana's secret wife Fate, who has been with him throughout all of his many births. What would he have to fear from Nandivardhana's own prowess as he goes about doing what he must do? This is how the great king Ripening of Karma carries out his affairs; he shows his deference only to counsellors like these that also belong to the inner realm; he pays no attention to anyone from the exterior world, no matter how they may shout and scream. He does exactly what he wants. That is why I told you that you should not bother to plead your cause with him. When he decides to, he will cause Auspicious Leanings to give his daughter Forbearance to the prince."

'My father then said, "In that case, Noble One, I am dead. For I cannot be sure that he will do that. And so long as that wicked friend remains by the side of the prince, the prince is worthless, and my life too is of no use." Jinamatajña replied, "Great King! Do not despair. What can anyone do in a case like this? For it is said:

A man who fails to act properly when there is something that his actions can actually accomplish becomes the object of censure. But when there is nothing that his actions can accomplish a person is not blamed for not acting. Moreover, a person who sets out to do something impossible, without any consideration for what can and cannot be done, becomes ludicrous in his own eyes and in the eyes of others in the know. Since this is the case, you should stop worrying and abandon yourself to Fate.

'I can tell you something more to help you find peace of mind. Men like you should never feel despondent and without help in this world."

'My father said, "Noble One, you have spoken well. I am comforted by these last words that you have spoken. Now tell me what that other advice is that will help me find peace of mind." Jinamatajña said, "Great King! The prince has a secret friend called Puṇyodaya, "Rise of Merit". As long as Rise of Merit is with the prince, then whatever trouble Vaiśvānara may cause the prince by being the kind of evil friend that leads him astray, will actually turn out to be for the prince's good." When he heard this my father was somewhat reassured.

'In the meantime the sound of a conch could be heard along with the beating of the drum that marked the time, signalling that the sun had reached the midpoint of the sky. The bard whose duty it was to announce the time recited this verse:

> The sun has reached the middle of the heavens, as if to proclaim to all and sundry this truth: one becomes greater in splendour not through partisan anger, but by assuming a position in the middle.

'My father said, "My goodness. It is noon already.' Thinking that it was time for him to break up the gathering, he dismissed the members of the court. He honored the teacher of the arts and the monk who could read the omens and dismissed them both with a show of great respect. A parent's love for a child is the cause of great mental confusion; that is why my father summoned Vidura, although he knew well from what the monk had told him that there was nothing that could be done for me. My father said to Vidura, "You must see what the prince really feels. See if you think that he can be separated from his evil friend or not." Vidura said, "As my lord commands." At that my father got up to go. He performed all the duties that were required of him.

'The very next day Vidura came to see me. He bowed down to me and then sat down near me. I asked him, "Sir, why did you not come yesterday?" Vidura thought to himself, "The king has instructed me, "See what the prince feels". I think I will tell him a story that I heard from some monks that illustrates all that is wrong with associating with bad people. From his reaction I will be able to know what is in the prince's mind."

Embedded in the longer story that Vidura told was this Tale of the Couple, related by the lady Ordinary to her son Average

'There is a city named Tathāvidha, "Just So". King Rṛju, "The Straight", reigned there. His chief queen was named Praguṇā, "Upright". They had a son Mugdha, "Naïve", who was as handsome as the God of Love. He had a wife, who was like Rati, the wife of the God of Love; her name was

Akuṭilā, "Not Tricky'. Mugdha and Akuṭilā, deeply in love, passed their time enjoying the pleasures of the senses. One spring morning Prince Mugdha rose early. From his room on the top storey of his palace he could see the palace garden with its rows of flowering trees, all laden with different kinds of beautiful blossoms. He suddenly felt like going out and amusing himself in the garden, and so he said to his wife, "Queen! The garden looks extremely beautiful and alluring today. Get up. Let's go to the garden and pick flowers. We can bring some of that beauty back here." And so they took golden baskets studded with jewels and went to the palace garden. They began to gather flowers. Mugdha said, "Let's have a contest and see who can fill their gold basket first. You go in one direction and I will go in another." Akuṭilā agreed. The two of them went off to gather flowers in different groves of trees and were soon out of each other's range of sight. Now it just so happened that a demi-god couple also came to the garden; this was "Kālajña, Knower of what to do at the right moment", and his wife Vicakṣaṇā, "Clever". As they were flying in the sky they saw the human couple. Now because the workings of karma are impossible to fathom; because the human couple was so handsome; because Love makes a person act rashly; because the season of spring inflames the passions; because the garden was so alluring; because demi-gods like to have fun; because the sense organs are extremely flighty; because the desire for pleasures of the senses is difficult to restrain; because the mind is wild and unsteady; and simply because Fate had determined that this was to be, for all these various reasons, Kālajña fell madly in love with Akuṭilā and Vicakṣaṇā fell madly in love with Mugdha. Kālajña thought that he could trick her and so he said to Vicakṣaṇa, 'My lady, you go on ahead. I will just gather some flowers here in this garden of the city of Rājagṛha for us to use in our worship.' But Vicakṣaṇā didn't budge; she stayed right where she was, not making a sound, for her heart had been stolen by Mugdha. Kālajña went to where Akuṭilā was gathering flowers and descended from the sky. Vicakṣaṇā could no longer see him. He thought to himself, "Hm. I wonder why this couple are so far apart from each other." He used his supernatural knowledge and came to know the reason why they were not together. Thinking, "This is a good stratagem," he used his divine powers to turn himself into a magical duplicate of Mugdha. He made himself a gold basket and even filled it with flowers. He walked over to Akuṭilā and excitedly told her, "My beloved, I beat you. I beat you." For a minute Akuṭilā was upset at having been defeated in the contest; she thought to herself, "How is it that my husband has just popped up like this?" Kālajña said, "Beloved, do not be unhappy at such a small thing. But now our flower gathering is finished. Let's go over to that plantain bower, which is truly an ornament to enhance the beauty of this garden." She agreed. They went to the bower and made themselves a bed of flower petals.

In the meantime Vicakṣaṇā thought to herself, 'Kālajña is gone. Before he comes back and while this lady is still somewhere off in the distance, let me descend from the sky and honour that young man, who looks like the God of Love, though now he is without his beloved wife Rati. I shall reap the pleasures of being alive.' She too used her supernatural knowledge and came to understand why the couple was not together. She turned herself into Akuṭilā's look-alike and made herself a gold basket filled with flowers and went over to Mugdha. She said, 'Noble One, I have beaten you. I have won!' Startled, Mugdha looked at her and said, 'Beloved! I accept my defeat. What shall we do now?' Vicakṣaṇā said, 'Whatever I say.' Mugdha said, 'And what might that be?' Vicakṣaṇā said, 'Let us go to the bower of creepers and enjoy from there the splendour of this excellent garden.' He agreed. And so Mugdha and Vicakṣaṇā went to the very same plantain bower where Akuṭilā and Kālajña were. They saw the two of them. Both couples looked at each other in astonishment. They could not see a speck of difference between each other. Mugdha thought, 'I have become two through the grace showered on me by the Blessed Goddesses of the Forest. My wife has become doubled, too. This is a great cause for rejoicing. I must tell my father. I will tell the others what I think and then we can all go together to see my father.' Mugdha told them, 'Let's go,' and so all four of them went together to the assembly of King Ṛju.

The king and queen and all the members of the court were astonished when they saw the four of them. The king asked Mugdha, 'What is all this?' He replied, 'It is the grace of the Goddesses of the Forest.' Ṛju said, 'What do you mean?' And so Mugdha told him all that had happened. Ṛju thought to himself, 'How lucky I am. See how the gods look on me with favour!' In his great joy he declared that a festival, though out of season, be celebrated in the city. He ordered great gifts to be distributed and commanded that the city gods be worshipped. In the midst of his court the king then proclaimed:

'From one son I now have two and from one daughter-in-law I now have two. O good men, eat and drink your fill, sing and play music and dance!'

Even Queen Praguṇā, obeying these words of the king, had drums beat so that everywhere you turned you were deafened by their joyous sounds. She began to dance with her arms raised high. Akuṭilā was delighted, as she thought, 'I have become two.' All of the women of the harem danced. The city was joyful. With much crush and commotion the great festivities began.

Kālajña, who loved to have fun, was delighted. But he did wonder, 'Who is this second woman?' He used his supernatural knowledge. He realized, 'Oh no, it can't be, it is my own wife Vicakṣaṇā!' Then he got mad. He thought, 'I'll kill that evil man. She is immortal, so I can't kill her too. But I will make her so miserable that she will never go near another man again.' When he had made up his mind that this is what he would do, his Fate ordained it to be otherwise. Fate made him think, 'That was wrong of me. I must not torment Vicakṣaṇā. After all, I was no better. I did exactly the same wrong deed that she did. And I should not kill Mugdha. If I do kill him, then Akuṭilā will find out and she won't want anything to do with me; Vicakṣaṇā will be even more disgusted with me. Maybe I should just grab Akuṭilā and before anyone sees me make off with my own wife, I should just get out of here. That's not a good idea either. If I dash away like that Akuṭilā is sure to realize that something is wrong and that might make her stop wanting me. There's no point in my going without her. I guess I just have to give up this jealousy and bide my time and see what happens.'

Vicakṣanā thought, 'My goodness! That's my husband Kālajña, who now looks like this other one. How could it be anyone else?' She became ashamed of herself, thinking, 'How can I be with another man when my husband is right here?' She also became jealous at the thought that her husband had another woman. Her feelings of propriety made it difficult to stay, but she knew too that she could accomplish nothing by going; she found no pleasure in staying there and yet did not see that she had any real choice. And so she too bowed to Fate and stayed there, biding her time, waiting to see what would happen.

One day a monk named Prabodhaka, "The Awakener', possessed of countless jewels in the form of special knowledge and the like, surrounded by a host of his disciples, stopped in the garden Mohavilaya, "Abode of Delusion'. The gardener informed the king of the monk's arrival. The king and all the townspeople went out to pay their respects to the monk. The gods had made a golden lotus for the monk. The king saw the monk sitting there, expounding the Jain doctrine. The king bowed down at the monk's feet, his crown touching the earth. He then bowed down to all the other monks. The chief monk and the other monks all welcomed the king with words of blessing that were like a sharp axe capable of striking down the forest of trees that were karma. The king sat down on the ground. Kālajña and the others also bowed down respectfully to the monks and then sat down in their proper places.

The monk began to expound the doctrine. He showed them the worthlessness of worldly existence; he described to them the causes of binding karma; he spoke harshly about the prison house of transmigratory existence; he praised the path of Release; he told them of the possibility of great happiness and peace; he told them that desire for the objects of the senses was the cause of wandering from birth to birth, and that it was a stubborn obstacle to happiness and peace.

When Kālajña and Vicakṣaṇā heard the words of the Blessed One that were like the divine drink of immortality, the net of delusion that had entrapped them was torn asunder; right faith was born in them; the fire of remorse at their wrongdoings blazed up in them, capable of burning up the fuel of their karma. At that moment there emerged from both of their bodies a hideous woman, whose own body was made up of red and black atoms; she was horrifying to behold; her very form was a cause of terror to those who know right from wrong, truth from falsehood. She was unable to endure the power of that Blessed monk. She emerged from them and stood far away from them all, her back to the group.

Vicakṣaṇā and Kālajña wept; it was as if their hearts had melted in the fire of their great remorse, and they fell at the feet of the Blessed One. Kālajña said, 'Blessed One! I am the lowest of the low. I deceived my own wife and slept with the wife of another man. I conceived terrible hatred for the innocent Mugdha. I made the king and his queen wrongly believe that they had another son. I also cheated myself by keeping myself from the true religious doctrine. Having been so evil, how can I now cleanse myself of all these sins?' Vicakṣaṇā then said, 'And how can I? For I was also very wicked and I did everything that he has done. But what need is there for me to confess before you; you have supernatural knowledge and can see everything right before your very own eyes.'

The Blessed One told them, 'Good people, do not despair. None of this was your fault. You are by nature absolutely pure.' They asked, 'Then whose fault was it?' The Blessed One replied, 'It is the fault of that woman who has come out of your bodies.' They said, 'Blessed One, who is she?' The Blessed One said, 'Good people, she is called Bhogatṛṣṇā, 'Desire for Sensory Pleasures."' Vicakṣaṇā and Kālajña said, 'Blessed One, how is she the cause of sins like the ones we committed?' The Blessed One said, 'Good people, listen:

Just as the night always produces darkness, so does Desire for Sensory Pleasures always give rise to the host of flaws, passion and the like.
The thoughts of those, in whose body that wicked one resides, turn at once to wrong deeds.
As a fire can never get enough of grass and wood, as the ocean is never satiated, even by torrents of water poured into it, so this one is never satisfied, no matter how many pleasures she enjoys.
The fool who seeks to quiet her with the enjoyments of the objects of the senses, sound and the like, resembles a man who would grasp the reflection of the moon in water.
The worst of men in their delusion take her as their beloved. They are doomed to wander endlessly in this terrifying ocean of transmigration.
But those best of men who realize that she is no good, chase her out of their bodies and lock the door of their minds.
Such men are free from afflictions; their sins are all gone.
Having purified themselves, they go to the Highest Place.
Those good men who are without her are praised in the three worlds; but those who are subject to her control are scorned by the good.

By her very nature she gives an ocean of suffering to those lowest of men, who out of delusion obey her commands. But for those best of men who oppose her she naturally brings pleasure after pleasure.

A man despises Final Release and values the cycle of rebirths just as long as this wicked Desire for Sensory Pleasures is in his mind.

But once they get rid of her through the power of their meritorious deeds, they see that this cycle of rebirths is as worthless as dust.

As long as this Desire for Sensory Pleasures is in a man, the fool imagines a woman's body, which is heap of stinking impurities, to be as beautiful as a jasmine blossom, a lotus or the moon, for he compares her face to the moon or a lotus, and her teeth to a jasmine flower.

But without the Desire for Sensory Pleasures a man would not even dream of a woman's body.

The fact that some men must serve others, though both master and slave are equally men; the fact that some must do the work that others would not touch, this is all the result of Desire for Sensory Pleasures.

Those great ones who no longer harbour Desire for Sensory Pleasures in their bodies are the true kings. Even though they may not be wealthy, those steadfast men are superior even to Śakra, king of the Gods.

It is said even in the religious texts of other groups that her body is made up of atoms of rajas mixed with tamas, the lower two of the three constituents of matter.

'This wicked one is the source of your sins. That is why I have said that everything was her fault alone, and not yours. In truth you two are both by nature absolutely pure.

She is the cause of all your sins.

She cannot stand to be near me and so she has withdrawn and stands apart. She is waiting for you to leave me.'

Vicakṣaṇā and Kālajña asked, 'When, O Blessed One, will we be entirely free of her?' The Blessed One replied,

'Good people! You will not be able to get rid of her entirely in this birth. But you do now have Right Faith, which is like a hammer to smash her. You must strengthen that Right Faith again and again by contact with good teachers. You must not do anything to appease this Desire for Sensory Pleasures. You must be on the guard for any changes in your thoughts that she has caused. You must chase away any such thoughts by contemplating their opposites. In this way she will become weaker and weaker with every moment and eventually, although she will still be with you, she will not be able to cause you any harm."

When they heard this Vicakṣaṇā and Kālajña said, 'You have shown us great favour,' and they fell at the feet of the Blessed One. Now when King Ṛju, Queen Praguṇā, Mugdha, Akuṭilā and the others saw what was taking place and when they heard the words of the Blessed One, they also felt remorse; they also conceived a pure desire to practice only good deeds. Ṛju and Praguṇā both thought, 'What a silly fuss we made, deluded by the idea that we had another son and another daughter-in-law! We actually encouraged our son and daughter-in-law in their improper conduct.' Mugdha thought, 'I have brought dishonor on my family by sleeping with the wife of another man.' Akuṭilā thought, 'In truth I have been unfaithful to my husband.' And all four of them alike thought, 'We must confess to the Blessed One. He is the only one who can tell us how we may counteract these sins.'

At that moment there emerged from the bodies of all four of them a child made of white atoms, who was white in color and radiant; he was a source of delight to the eyes and a source of pleasure to the minds of those who saw him. He was shouting, 'I have saved you, I have saved you!' With joy he gazed on the face of the Blessed One; he stood right there in front of the entire assembly. But then a second child came out of them in exactly the same way; this child was black in color and hideous in appearance; he terrified them all. A third child came out of this one, looking exactly like him, but even more hideous in nature. It began to grow larger and larger. The white child struck it on the head with his fist and made it stop growing and revert back to its original state. Both the black children then withdrew from the vicinity of the Blessed One.

The Blessed One then said, 'Do not despair that you have committed wrong doings. For it was not your fault. You are by nature absolutely pure.' They said, 'Then whose fault was it, Blessed One?' The Blessed One said, 'It was the fault of this black child who came out of your bodies right after the white one emerged.' They said, 'Blessed One, who is that child?' The Blessed One said, 'He is called Ignorance.' They said, 'And who is that second black child that came out of Ignorance, the one that the white child struck on the head and stopped from growing?' The Blessed One answered, 'His name is Sin.' They said, 'What is the name of the white child?' The Blessed One said, 'He is called Righteousness.' At that they said, 'What is the nature of this Ignorance and how does sin come from it? And how did Righteousness stop Sin from growing? We want to hear all about this.' The Blessed One said, 'In that case, then isten to me.

First of all, this Ignorance that emerged from your
bodies is the cause of all your sins.
When Ignorance is in their bodies, creatures cannot
tell the difference between right and wrong; they do
not distinguish between a woman they may approach
and one who is off limits to them.
They do not know what they may eat and what it is
wrong to eat; they do not know what they should
drink and what they should not drink. Like blind men
they take to the wrong road.
In their Ignorance they commit wrong deeds, and with
nothing to sustain them on their journey from birth
to birth, they wander in pain and misery.

Ignorance is the source of passion and the other flaws; even Desire for Sensory Pleasures depends on Ignorance to do her work.
Without Ignorance, Desire for Sensory Pleasures cannot act; even if she does get a start, she is suddenly stopped in her tracks.
The soul is by nature all-knowing and all-seeing, absolutely pure. But sullied by Ignorance it is no different from an insentient stone.
Ignorance, like a highway robber, sets up a road block on the right path and robs a person of all the wealth he may get in this world, and of the pleasures of Final Release.
It is Ignorance and nothing else that is said to be the most terrifying of hells, for its nature is abject darkness.
Ignorance is poverty; Ignorance is a man's worst enemy.
Ignorance is disease; it is even said to be old age.
Ignorance is every imaginable disaster; Ignorance is death.
In the absence of Ignorance the terrifying ocean of rebirth can no longer harm those who dwell in it.
Ignorance is the cause of all our distress; it is the cause of all our wayward behavior and whatever else is undesirable.
For people only commit evil deeds when Ignorance, which conceals knowledge, is in their minds.
But those fortunate ones in whose mind Ignorance no longer exists, are pure inside; they do only good deeds.
Having been worthy of honor in this world, those men of purified minds, freed from all taint of sin, eventually attain the Highest Place.
And all four of you had the same Ignorance. That is why I have said that what you did was not your fault. It is the fault of your Ignorance.
The second child, called Sin, is always the product of

Ignorance. That is why this second child here too came out of the first one.

The wise say that Sin is the cause of all suffering; it suddenly propels a person into an ocean of terror.

Sin is said to be the source of all the many defilements, and so a wise man should never undertake anything that is the cause of Sin.

A person must give up violence, lying, stealing, immoderate sexual behavior, and attachment to possessions; a person must never doubt the truth of the Jain doctrine; one must renounce anger, pride, deceitfulness and greed. These are the causes of Sin.

And so a wise man must studiously avoid all of these things; then there will be no Sin and from that Sin, no suffering.

Now your Sin, too, came from your Ignorance, for Ignorance is what leads a person to commit acts of violence, lie, steal, fornicate and covet.

Now listen to me as I carefully explain how Sin, increasing, was thwarted by Righteousness.

Righteousness by its very nature leads a person to have noble aspirations, and that is why it can stop people from committing more and more sins.

Now in your case you all have the same degree of Righteousness; your ever-increasing Sin, born of your Ignorance, was conquered by your Righteousness.

That is why your Righteousness in the form of a child with a smiling face joyfully proclaimed again and again, "I have saved you! I have saved you!"

Fortunate indeed are those in whose minds there is Righteousness. Even if they do commit sins out of Ignorance, they are sill only minor sinners.

As soon as they come to know the pure path, they shake off their karma and exert themselves along the path to Liberation.

Fortunate indeed are those who have purified their

minds by means of Righteousness; they perform many pure deeds and reach the final shore of the cycle of rebirths.
So should you now, all good people, shake off your Ignorance and Sin and pursue the religious life to perfection.
For wise men say that the religious life is the only thing worth holding on to in this cycle of rebirths; union with a loved one is impermanent and prone to grief and jealousy.
Youth is impermanent and is the abode of despicable conduct.
All forms of wealth are impermanent and arise from the bitterest struggles.
Life is impermanent and the cause of so many different conditions.
There is birth and then there is death, again and again; there is even birth in low and miserable states, time after time. There is no happiness in this.
Everything in this cycle of rebirths is by nature unappealing. And so I ask you, should a person who possesses the ability to discriminate have any attachment to anything here, except to the religious life, which is praised in this world, which is without stain and which is eternal, which is the means to accomplish the highest goal, and has been practiced by steadfast people of impeccable conduct?'

Hearing these blessed words which were like the drink of immortality, all of them turned their minds away from worldly life. The king said, 'I will do all that the Blessed One has instructed.' Praguṇā said, 'Great King! Why do you tarry?' Mugdha then said, 'Father, my mother is right. It must be done.' His wife, her lotus-like eyes wide with joy, agreed completely with her husband, but in her great modesty she did not say a word. Then all four of them fell at the feet of the Blessed One. King Ṛju said, 'Blessed One! We will do what you have said.' The Blessed One said, 'Such a course of action is worthy of people like you who are destined to attain Liberation.' Then the king asked the Blessed One when the propitious day would be. The Blessed One said, 'Today is the perfect occasion.' And so the king right then and there gave out great gifts and caused the gods to be worshipped. He placed his own son named Śubhācāra, "Pure Conduct" on the throne and brought great joy to all the townspeople. And then all four of them, having done what was to be done in order to renounce the world, surrendered themselves to this monk as their master and were ordained. At that the two black children fled and the white child in a flash reentered their bodies. Kālajña and his wife then thought, 'See how fortunate these people are. Their lives are complete; on account of their meritorious karma they have been able to be ordained as Jain ascetics.

'I believe that they have finally crossed this ocean of rebirth, the end of which is difficult to reach; their renunciation, like some magic jewel that brings a person safely across the sea, brings them across this ocean of rebirth.

'But we are gods and so are deprived of this opportunity, which is open only to human beings. Nonetheless, we too have obtained that most excellent right faith in the Jain Doctrine, which destroys wrong belief, and which is only obtained with difficulty after hundreds and thousands of births.

'We are not without some good fortune, then; a poor man, after all, does not get a sack full of jewels all at once.'

And so the two of them bowed down at the feet of the Blessed One, who gave them some instructions. That divine couple then returned home.

Desire for Sensory Pleasures went back into their bodies as they were leaving; only this time, because of the great power of their pure faith, it would cause them no harm.

(from the *Upamitibhavaprapañcakathā* of Siddharṣi, Ch.3)

THE STORY OF PENGUIN CLASSICS

Before 1946 ...'Classics' are mainly the domain of academics and students, without readable editions for everyone else. This all changes when a little-known classicist, E. V. Rieu, presents Penguin founder Allen Lane with the translation of Homer's *Odyssey* that he has been working on and reading to his wife Nelly in his spare time.

1946 *The Odyssey* becomes the first Penguin Classic published, and promptly sells three million copies. Suddenly, classic books are no longer for the privileged few.

1950s Rieu, now series editor, turns to professional writers for the best modern, readable translations, including Dorothy L. Sayers's *Inferno* and Robert Graves's *The Twelve Caesars*, which revives the salacious original.

1960s The Classics are given the distinctive black jackets that have remained a constant throughout the series's various looks. Rieu retires in 1964, hailing the Penguin Classics list as 'the greatest educative force of the 20th century'.

1970s A new generation of translators arrives to swell the Penguin Classics ranks, and the list grows to encompass more philosophy, religion, science, history and politics.

1980s The Penguin American Library joins the Classics stable, with titles such as *The Last of the Mohicans* safeguarded. Penguin Classics now offers the most comprehensive library of world literature available.

1990s The launch of Penguin Audiobooks brings the classics to a listening audience for the first time, and in 1999 the launch of the Penguin Classics website takes them online to a larger global readership than ever before.

The 21st Century Penguin Classics are rejacketed for the first time in nearly twenty years. This world famous series now consists of more than 1300 titles, making the widest range of the best books ever written available to millions – and constantly redefining the meaning of what makes a 'classic'.

The Odyssey continues ...